Study Guide to *Selected Poems* and additional poems by Sylvia Plath

by Ray Moore

Egg Rock Lighthouse, Nahant Bay, Massachusetts, USA 1898. US Coast Guard Photograph. Public domain. (Source: Wikimedia Commons)

Acknowledgements

Thanks to the ever helpful library staff at the Leesburg Campus of the Lake Sumter State College.

Special thanks to my wife Barbara for putting the text into the correct formats for publication. Any errors which remain are my own. As always, I am indebted to the work of many critics. Where I am conscious of having taken an idea or a phrase from a particular author, I cite the source in the text: failure to do so is an omission which I will immediately correct if it is drawn to my attention. Where I have selectively quoted from the writings of others in the course of my own argument, I have done so in the sincere belief that this constitutes fair use.

I believe that all Sylvia Plath quotations used in the book fall under the definition of fair use. Once again, if I am in error on any quotation, I will immediately remove it if it is drawn to my attention. The images used are in the public domain from Wikimedia Commons.

Copyright 2017 Ray Moore

Contents

Preface to the Second Edition 1
Introduction 3
Sylvia Plath: Biographical Fact File 5
Approaching Plath's Poems 7
The Development of Plath's Poetry 11
Exactly Why is Plath's Poetry So Difficult? 14
Recurring Themes 15
Recurring Images 16
Guide to the Selected Poems of Sylvia Plath 17
    How to Use this Study Guide: 17
    MISS DRAKE PROCEEDS TO SUPPER 18
    SPINSTER 21
    MAUDLIN 23
    RESOLVE 25
    NIGHT SHIFT 26
    FULL FATHOM FIVE 28
    SUICIDE OFF EGG ROCK 31
    THE HERMIT AT OUTERMOST HOUSE 33
    MEDALLION 34
    THE MANOR GARDEN 36
    THE COLOSSUS 38
    THE STONES 40
    THE BURNT-OUT SPA 43
    YOU'RE 45
    FACE LIFT 47
    MORNING SONG 49
    TULIPS 52
    INSOMNIAC 57
    WUTHERING HEIGHTS 60

BLACKBERRYING 64

FINISTERRE 67

THE MOON AND THE YEW TREE 70

MIRROR 75

THE BABYSITTERS 77

LITTLE FUGUE 80

AN APPEARANCE 83

CROSSING THE WATER 85

AMONG THE NARCISSI 87

ELM 88

POPPIES IN JULY 91

A BIRTHDAY PRESENT 94

THE BEE MEETING 100

DADDY 105

MEDUSA 113

LESBOS 120

FEVER 103° 127

CUT 130

BY CANDLELIGHT 133

LADY LAZARUS 137

ARIEL 143

POPPIES IN OCTOBER 146

NICK AND THE CANDLESTICK 148

LETTER IN NOVEMBER 151

DEATH & Co. 154

MARY'S SONG 156

WINTER TREES 159

SHEEP IN FOG 161

THE MUNICH MANNEQUINS 164

WORDS 168

BALLOONS	171
EDGE	173
Works Cited	177
Guide to Further Reading	177
Guide to Further Watching	178
A Sample Essay: Sylvia Plath's Sense of Place	179
Literary terms	181
Appendix 1: How I Used the Study Guide Questions	186
Appendix 2: An Alternative Approach to Daddy	188
To the Reader	192

* The poems in this Study Guide are those included in the Faber and Faber edition of *Selected Poems*. To these I have added six poems which seem to me to be important in a consideration of Plath's poetic development:

"The Colossus", "Blackberrying", "Medusa", "Fever 103°", "Lady Lazarus" and "Balloons".

Preface to the Second Edition

I get worried when someone says that they really love a poem even though they do not 'understand' it, or when I am told that poems are open to individual, subjective interpretation (as though one interpretation is as valid as another so long as each is held sincerely) because that is obviously not true. Interpretation must be firmly based *in* the text, and our reading of the text should aim to understand fully the meaning of the words put down on the page by the author. While researching a different book, I came across the following statement which expresses a basic principle I have always followed both in my teaching and writing:

> [A] book's meaning is [not] whatever the reader declares it to be. There are not as many meanings as there are resourceful readers ... There are logical curbs upon the person who suggests that meaning is private or social, or that there are multiple meanings, or that meaning, in any case, is only subjective. (Paul Holmer)

Of course, each reader brings different experiences to a text, and no two readers will *experience* a text in exactly the same way. What fascinates one reader will bore another; a sentence that totally eludes one reader, will be crystal clear to another. However, we owe it to the author to understand what the words she wrote actually *mean* – which is another way of saying that these poems are Plath's *before* they are ours. Of course, no two readers will see *exactly* the same meaning in a poem or react in *exactly* the same ways, nor should they, but some interpretations *are* better than others, and some interpretations *are* simply based on misreading and misunderstanding or, worse still, on the reader's imposition onto the text of his/her own preconceptions, values, emotions and/or ideology.

Sylvia Plath offers a particular challenge in this respect since some (though by no means all) of her poems are difficult, obscure, contradictory, and/or deliberately ambiguous. Bassnett is undoubtedly correct in writing that "There is no simple, definitive reading of Sylvia Plath's poetry or her life" (*An Introduction* 30), but I do *not* accept her conclusion that "there are as many versions of a text as there are readers reading it" (*Ibid*. 31). Interpretation is a question of balance. What I aim to do here is to offer a structure which will enable the reader to understand, on the basis of the text, what Plath *wrote*. Whether what a writer *says* is what she/he consciously *intended to say* is ultimately a fruitless and irrelevant question (termed the 'intentional fallacy'), and for this reason I try my best to avoid either using Plath's life to explain the meaning of the poems or the poems to explain the meaning of Plath's life.

A Study Guide

A Study Guide is an *aid* to the close reading of a text; it must *never* be a substitute for reading and reflecting on the text. Plath's poems deserve to be read *reflectively*, and my aim in this guide is to facilitate such reading. In producing this Revised Second Edition, I have substantially expanded the introductory material, and made my commentary on each poem much more detailed. However, I have not reduced the number of questions and they still have *no* answers provided. This is a deliberate choice. I am writing for readers who want to come to *their own conclusions* about the poems and not simply to be *told* what to think about them. Even 'suggested' answers would limit the exploration of the text by readers themselves which is the primary aim. In my classroom, I found that students frequently came up with answers that I had not even considered, and, not infrequently, that they expressed their ideas better than I could have done. The point of this guide is to facilitate a *guided* exploration of the text, not to close exploration down by providing 'ready-made answers.' (Teachers do not need their own set of answers in order effectively to evaluate the responses of their students.)

The First Edition was based on the poems included in the Faber *Selected Poems*. To these I have added a small number of other poems that I think should have been in that volume. In the course of writing this book, I have become increasingly aware that these poems, and this study guide, can only serve as an introduction to Plath's writing.

Spoiler alert!

If you are reading the book for the first time, you may wish to go straight to "Commentary and Study Questions" and come back to the introductory sections later.

Introduction

Background

Sylvia Plath (1932-1963) always wanted to be a professional writer, and she was from childhood fiercely competitive about it: as an adult she craved recognition as the greatest woman poet of her generation. Writing was also a psychological necessity to Plath: Axlerod explains that through writing (and increasingly this meant through her poems) she undertook a "quest to achieve satisfaction and authority in the symbolic order of language" (13). He terms this her "project of textual self-creation" (21). Plath wrote as a child, as a student of Smith College, and as a student at Newman College, Cambridge. Her work was occasionally published in newspapers and magazines, she won several prestigious prizes, but she also experienced the inevitable succession of rejection slips which is the fate of most would-be authors. The poems, short stories and longer fiction on which her reputation rests were produced in an astonishingly short period (1960-1963), her life being cut tragically short by suicide.

In the aftermath of her death, Plath was "seen as a relatively minor though gifted poet" (Bassnett *An Introduction* 1), but as her works reached a wider audience and new works were published posthumously both her popularity and her critical standing soared. It is not an exaggeration to say that Plath has become something of a cult figure, particularly to feminists for whom she seems to capture the essence of "women struggling for self-realization while endeavoring to conform to social expectations" (*Ibid.*).

Why Read this Text

Kendall calls Plath, "a writer who has attracted more attention, and from a broader readership, than any other post-war [i.e., World War II] English-language poet" (Preface). At the same time, her poems (particularly those she wrote in the last few months of her life) have been widely criticized. As Rose puts it, "execrated and idolized, Plath hovers between the furthest poles of positive and negative appraisal" (quoted by Wagner-Martin in Gill Ed. *Companion* 61). Thus, not everyone who reads Plath instantly becomes a convert (see, for example, Bloom's dismissive Introduction in *Views* 1-5), but those who do tend to become passionate, particularly about her poems. Feminists, in particular, find that Plath gives voice to feelings, fears and frustrations with which they can identify, but appreciation of Plath's poems (even on these grounds) is by no means restricted to the members of one sex.

Issues with these Poems

The critic David Holbrook offered the following warning about the poetry of Sylvia Plath: "these works may offer falsifications of forms of moral inversion which are absurd, or even deranged, and may even do harm to the sensitive and responsive young person" (*Sylvia Plath: Poetry and Existence*, 1976). I certainly would not go that far, but Plath does deal with sensitive, troubling, dark themes, so some of her poems (by no means all) demand of the reader a high level of maturity, experience and judgment.

The same requirement is demanded by her poems *as* poetry, because the writing is demanding and the meaning often (again, not always) opaque, ambiguous and even contradictory. Some readers find the experience of reading such poetry liberating and exhilarating, but others simply find it frustrating.

Sylvia Plath: Biographical Fact File

Born: October 27th, 1932, in Boston, Massachusetts, U.S.A.

Father: Otto Emil Plath (who had emigrated to America from Grabowa, Poland, at the age of 15 years), Professor of Entomology at Boston University.

Mother: Aurelia Schober, a first-generation American of Austrian descent who worked as a teacher and a secretary, but after her marriage became a full-time homemaker in line with her husband's views.

Raised: Winthrop, Massachusetts, a town on the Atlantic coast. Plath's early years were dominated by her love of the sea and the beautiful coast.

Death of father: Otto Plath died after a long illness in November 1940 when Plath was only nine years old. Ted Hughes (later her husband) writes that she "worshipped her father." When she was first told of his death, she said immediately, "I'll never speak to God again." On the day of her father's death, Plath wrote out a note and made her mother sign it. The note read, "I promise never to marry again." Strangely, she also insisted on going to school and behaving as if nothing had happened.

Education: Plath was an outstanding student who developed a love of literature. In September 1950, she entered prestigious Smith College as an English major. She studied hard and began writing short stories, two of which were printed. As her family was not financially well off, Plath depended on scholarships throughout her university education and was never entirely free of financial anxiety. She won a one-month placement as a guest editor of the magazine *Mademoiselle*.

First suicide attempt: In the summer of 1953, following several weeks of intense depression, Plath swallowed a large number of sleeping pills before hiding in the cellar of the family house. She was discovered there three days later by her younger brother, Warren, in a coma and very ill but alive. Plath was admitted to hospital and subsequently underwent electro-convulsive therapy. By the mid-winter of the same year she was able to return to Smith from which in 1955 she graduated *summa cum laude*.

Post-graduate Education: Between 1955 and 1957, Plath studied on a Fulbright scholarship at Newnham College, Cambridge, and continued to develop her own creative writing.

Marriage: February 25th, 1956, Plath met, and almost immediately fell in love with, Ted Hughes, also a student at Cambridge and already a poet with a growing reputation. On June 16th, they were married secretly because Plath feared the loss of her Fulbright scholarship if she was no longer single. The marriage seems to have been very happy on both sides – undoubtedly Plath was very much in love. The couple travelled extensively and spent the years 1957-1959 living in the US.

Children: One thing that Plath really wanted out of marriage was to have children – lots of children. Something about giving birth seemed to validate

Plath's view of herself as a woman. On April 1st, 1960, Plath gave birth to Frieda Rebecca in London, but in January 1961, she suffered a miscarriage and shortly afterwards had an appendectomy. In January 1962, a son, Nicholas Farrar, was born.

Separation: The marriage became strained, partly because Hughes' reputation outstripped Plath's and partly because of the conflicting demands of being both mother and professional writer. Hughes began an affair with Assia Wevill, a married woman. Plath confirmed her suspicions of Hughes' infidelity in July 1962, and there was talk of a legal separation. This happened in the October: Hughes left the cottage in Tawton, Devon, but Plath stayed on with her children until December when she moved with them to London. This was a period of intense poetic creativity when Plath wrote some of her greatest poems.

Death: February 11th, 1963, Sylvia Plath was found unconscious with her head in the gas oven. She had left a note in which she gave her doctor's telephone number and asked anyone finding her to call him. The baby-sitter was expected at 9 a.m. and she came on time, but she was unable to get into Plath's flat for some time. Plath was pronounced dead on arrival at University College Hospital.

Published work: Plath's first book of poems, *The Colossus*, was published on October 31st, 1960, and her novel *The Bell Jar* just before her death (under the pseudonym Victoria Lucas). Though having one book of poems published, Plath was making a reputation for herself as a poet. Most of her poetry was published after her death. *Ariel*, a collection of her later poems (including "Daddy") was put together by Ted Hughes and published on March 11th, 1965. Other books of poetry and short stories have followed as well as editions of her *Journal* (Hughes burned the final entries to spare the children) and *Letters Home*.

Approaching Plath's Poems

Critics have tended to approach the explication, the analysis and (even) the evaluation of Plath's poems by looking at them through one or more of the following perspectives:

Biography: Plath's relationships with both her father and her mother were complex and problematic, and her marriage to Ted Hughes hardly less so. There is no doubt that Plath's relationship with these three strong personalities had a great impact on Plath's tortured psychological development and that this is reflected in her writing. In point of fact, however, almost all of her poetry has its origin in autobiography, so that Magill is certainly correct in stating, "Few poets demand that we know as much about their lives as Sylvia Plath does. Her intensely personal poetry was often rooted in everyday experiences, the knowledge of which can often open obscure references on cryptic images to fuller meaning for the reader" (*Critical Survey of Poetry* English Language Series, Volume 5). Taken to its extreme, however, this approach has led many critics either to use the poems to illuminate Plath's biography or Plath's biography to reveal the 'meaning' of the poems.

Psychoanalysis: Plath suffered mental illness, severe depression, and suicidal tendencies throughout her life. Whatever their origin, and whatever label we choose to put on her disorder (psychosis, neurosis, bipolar, schizophrenia, etc.), her massive mood swings and terrible fascination with death are evident in her poems. This being so, many critics have used psychological theory (particularly Freudian and Jungian) as a mechanism for interpreting the poems and others have used the poems in an attempt to 'diagnose' Plath's mental illness. Appearing as it did in 1965, three years after her death, *Ariel* was treated by many critics and readers as a long suicide note, and the poems in it were interpreted as such instead of being read on their merits as poems.

Feminism: Plath is seen by many as a proto-feminist who was destroyed by a still male-dominated society and literary culture which did not allow her to be herself or to express herself as men were encouraged to do. Nelson writes, "Feminist critics ... regarded Plath's rage and madness as a protest against inauthenticity, in this case the masks of femininity that stifled female creativity and self-expression" (Gill Ed. *Companion* 32). Plath certainly struggled to fulfill the roles of wife and mother with that of professional writer; personally, she was torn between her maternal role and her role as an artist in ways that men (generally speaking) are not. This conflict also finds expression in the poems.

Mythology: Plath's poems are full of mythological references. (She did, after all, study at Smith and Cambridge and had a Masters Degree in English.) Robert Graves's book *The White Goddess* is often cited as having had a significant influence on her understanding of the female in mythology. Certainly, Plath found in various mythologies a way of talking about the issues, conflicts and fears that dominated her thinking.

Political engagement: Plath was writing in the immediate aftermath of World War II during the Cold War – a time of great political tension. The degree to which her poetry is informed by her knowledge of the political and social events of her time is frequently overlooked, though some critics have seen her very much as a product of her time. She considered herself a political person and admitted to being preoccupied by certain issues of her time such as nuclear weapons and what President Eisenhower called the threatening growth of the "military industrial complex." Axelrod writes that Plath's critique of the society of her time, though "ideologically complex and uncertain" clearly "emanates from a position on the political left and the social margins, and it reflects a feminist awareness that was ahead of its time" (Gill Ed. *Companion* 74). Other critics have questioned the depth of Plath's understanding of and engagement in the political issues of her time.

No doubt each of these perspectives has the ability, like a lens, to reveal aspects of Plath's poetry that would otherwise be missed or remain obscure. However, pursued too far, each one of them can become preconceptions which, also like a lens, distort what they seem to clarify. This is particularly true of the biographical/psychoanalytical approach which seeks to discover the 'real Plath' as a key to unlocking the meaning of the poetry. This seems to me to be dangerously reductionist. Plath's poems are not brilliant because she was oppressed in turn by father, mother and husband, crushed by a male-dominated society, and driven finally to a tragic suicide; nor are her poems of questionable value because she was a manipulative, jealous, conniving, egocentric person – to take two extreme positions. The fact is that at this stage it is impossible to know the 'real Plath' (perhaps it always was), and Lane is correct to point out that "the list of projected Plaths might go on for pages: everyone, it seems, has his own version of the Sylvia Plath myth" (*New Views* ix). More generally, presenting the poems as the result of external factors impacting upon the author ignores Plath's power as an artist to imagine, to invent, and to go beyond her personal experience. Rosenblatt puts this very well, "[T]he importance of Plath's work lies precisely in her alteration and heightening of autobiographical experience. In fact, we can distinguish between her successes and failures on the basis of her objectification of [the] personal through image sequences and metaphoric development" (107).

In any case, none of these approaches explains why the poems of Sylvia Plath have found so wide an audience in the half century since her death. The answer to that question comes in two parts. First, in exploring her own personal demons, Plath touched on universal human concerns so that many readers (men as well as women) find themselves empathizing with her protagonists and the situations that the poems explore. Sensing this, Plath wrote in her 1956 Journal, "Be stoic when necessary & *write* – you have seen a lot, felt deeply & your problems are universal enough to be made meaningful." In this, she largely, if unevenly, succeeded. Second, Plath was a genius with words – though she had certainly not reached the full potential of her powers at the time of her death, her writing stands up *as* writing in a way that defies the passing of decades. [It is sobering to recall that, had she lived, Plath would, at the time I am writing this, have been 84 – not a particularly unlikely eventuality. What might she have achieved had she lived?]

In this study of the poems, I take great care to refer to the protagonist (often, though not always, the I-speaker of a monologue) as a persona (or speaker, or narrator), a fictional character created by the poet. We can *never* simply assume that the views expressed in the poems are those of Sylvia Plath despite the obvious similarities between the two. The enotes essay "Sylvia Plath Poetry: American Poems Analysis" puts it brilliantly:

> Her poetry overwhelms its readers with its thematic consistency, drafted into this battle by Plath to help her survive another day, to continue the war against a world that seemed always on the verge of undoing the little progress she had made. Her personae were created from her and by her, but they were also created for her, with a very specific intent: survival of the self as an integrated whole.

Plath made art from her own suffering; she did not simply share that suffering in what is termed 'confessional poetry.' (The term was coined by the critic M. L. Rosenthal to describe Robert Lowell's volume *Life Studies* [1959], and came to be used to describe poems in which the poet speaks in his/her own voice of their own feeling, failings, suffering, etc.) Uroff defines the nature of the persona in Plath's poems, "They are generalized figures not real-life people, types that Plath manipulates dramatically in order to reveal their limitations." I would certainly agree with the general statement that the quality of Plath's poems improves in relationship to the distance that she is able to establish between her protagonists and herself.

In the early poems, Plath describes her protagonists from the position of a third person observer while in her later poems she gives them their own voice. The basic intention, however, remains the same, which judgment Uroff supports by quoting Plath herself:

> I think my poems immediately come out of the sensuous and emotional experiences I have, but I must say I cannot sympathize with these

> cries from the heart that are informed by nothing except a needle or a knife, or whatever it is. I believe that one should be able to control and manipulate experiences, even the most terrifying, like madness, being tortured, this sort of experience, and one should be able to manipulate these experiences with an informed and intelligent mind.

In her *Journal* for December 1958, Plath wrote:
> Writing is a religious act; it is an ordering, a reforming, a relearning and reloving of people and the world as they are and as they might be. A shaping which does not pass away like a day of typing or a day of teaching. The writing lasts; it goes about on its own in the world.

That is why so many readers respond personally to issues and dilemmas that are inherent in the human condition, not limited to the experienced of a particular individual however tortured and talented.

The Development of Plath's Poetry

Kendall observes, "[Plath's] *Collected Poems* reveals that she wrote poems in groups, working obsessively through a particular theme or preoccupation before falling silent and awaiting the next surge of inspiration ... She is a poet constantly remaking herself, experimenting, casting off styles" (Preface). The result is that "[t]hroughout her career Plath demonstrated a striking ability to change styles and aesthetic attitudes with great rapidity. In fact, nothing better exemplifies the themes of transformation and inner change in her work than does her own remarkable transformation as a poet during her brief lifetime" (22).

Given this feature of her poetic development, it is helpful to divide Plath's poetry into stages. There is not universal agreement about how this should be done, but I am happy to follow Axelrod ("The Poetry of Sylvia Plath" in Gill Ed. *Companion* 73-89):

1950-1955: These early poems, written during her childhood and student years in America, are termed 'juvenilia' a term not intended to be dismissive but to describe them frankly as apprentice pieces in which Plath explored poetic forms and techniques. None of these poems is represented in the *Selected Poems*.

1956-1959: Many of these poems, written during the years when she was (apparently) happily married to Ted Hughes, appear in *The Colossus*. Some critics, and Plath herself (under the influence of Hughes' judgment) include these poems among Plath's juvenilia, but this is to underestimate their quality. Bassnett argues that the early poems of *Colossus* show "a very clear sense of structure, where rhyme, stanza, line length, and imagery are all carefully patterned in making a consistent whole ... these early poems are, in the most literal sense of the word, crafted. She uses the form of the poem to shape the experience she wants to convey ... she conceives of poetry as wordcraft, as a medium through which experience can be shaped and represented" (*An Introduction* 50-51). Hughes describes Plath as composing these works very slowly with her thesaurus by her side for constant reference. Bloom, more critically, records that when he first read *The Colossus* he found it, "too derivative, though accomplished enough" (*Views* 1).

1960-1962: This period coincided with the disintegration of her marriage and culminated in her separation from Hughes. It was a period of amazing poetic productivity, and it is these poems on which her reputation ultimately rests. They were eventually published in *Ariel* (following her death Hughes edited this volume removing some poems, adding others, and reordering those that remained) which soon eclipsed *The Colossus* as Plath's most popular collection. Plath herself commented on the essential difference between the poems of *The Colossus* and those of *Ariel*, "[M]y first book *The Colossus* – I can't read any of the poems aloud now, I didn't write them to be read aloud. In fact, they quite quietly bore me. Now these very recent ones – I've got to say them. I speak them to myself. Whatever lucidity they may have comes from the fact that I say them aloud." Hughes states that the *Ariel* poems were "written for the most part at great speed, as she might take dictation." Kendall agrees with this description commenting, "Hughes' chosen simile carries inescapable implications for the nature of Plath's poetic gift: he intimates that her rational, conscious mind in these later poems is subservient to some deeper dictating force ... the unstoppably mantic [i.e., relating to divination or prophecy] inspiration of Plath's mature work" (66). Bawer comments that "her new poems are colloquial, muscular, unafraid of repeating words or odd line lengths or the first person singular pronoun" (Bloom Ed. *Views* 16). These poems are also Plath's most controversial: not all critics see them as successful attempts to forge, out of her intensely personal experience, statements relevant to what Plath in her *Journal* called "the larger things, the bigger things such as Hiroshima and Dachau" (quoted in Gill Ed. *Companion* 85). Where some find the imagery innovative and (in a positive sense) audacious, others find it merely sensationalist and (frankly) in bad taste.

1963: The final, brief, tragic weeks of Plath's life produced poems of tremendous power – indeed, knowing what we now do of her imminent suicide, reading them is at times almost unbearable. Nevertheless, it is important to read the poems as poems. Kendall argues that if we do this then, "Paradoxically, the final crisis of her life coincided with a style and vision more detached than anything she had attempted in *Ariel* ... they lack *Ariel*'s relentless rhythmical energy, and dispense with the motor of rhyme: motion gives way to stasis, and the element of fatalism ..." (Bloom Ed. *Views* 149). Perloff, whilst acknowledging the "extraordinary *originality*" of the later poems, adds an important qualification, "Plath's limitation is that, having finally ceased to be Sivvy [the cheerful alter-ego she assumed for her mother's benefit], she had really only one subject: her own anguish and consequent longing for death" (Lane Ed. *New Views* 173). Whether Plath had written herself into a cul-de-sac or would have, having come through her personal crisis, have found new subjects and themes we can never know.

During her lifetime, Plath published only one collection of poems, *The Colossus and Other Poems* (1960), though many of these and later poems were published in magazines – very prestigious ones at that. *Ariel* was published posthumously in 1965 in an edition edited by Ted Hughes. This volume differed considerably from the manuscript version of *Ariel* that Plath completed in either November or December 1962 and left at her death. In Plath's version the first word of the collection was "love" and the last was "spring" – a deliberately affirmative choice which conveyed the poet's confidence that she

Selected Poems by Sylvia Plath

had come through the worst of her trials and was ready for rebirth, which is a central theme of the collection. This left a number of poems written before her move to London in December and, of course, the poems that she was to write in the last weeks of her life. These would be edited by Hughes in the collections *Crossing the Water* and *Winter Trees*, both published in 1971. Plath's *Collected Poems*, published in 1981, received the 1982 Pulitzer Prize for Poetry, the last of the many glittering prizes that Sylvia Plath won.

Exactly Why is Plath's Poetry So Difficult?

Despite its popularity, Plath's poetry has the reputation of being difficult. This is in a way surprising because her poems do not employ complex versification, or a plethora of rhetorical devices. There are exceptions, but generally she writes in short verses which have short lines and a simple, colloquial vocabulary – Plath uses more monosyllables than any poet I can think of. There are four main factors that contribute to the difficulty that readers encounter. First, Plath was an academic and an intellectual who, from her childhood, read widely and was always an outstanding student. Naturally, she incorporates her knowledge of history, mythology, poetry, psychoanalysis, etc. into her poems. With the exception of readers in universities, most of us cannot match the sheer depth and width of her learning and so inevitably miss some of her conscious, and unconscious, references. Second, Plath mined her own life-experiences in creating the characters and scenarios for her poems. Although knowing about her life does not explain the meaning of the poems, it can certainly shed light on allusions in particular lines. Third, is the way in which Plath uses imagery. Increasingly as her work matures, she expresses her meaning through images that are juxtaposed rather than connected, surreal rather than naturalistic, and never explained. The meaning of her similes, metaphors and symbols is as a result often ambiguous – sometimes deliberately so. The reader is rather in the position of a person completing a large jigsaw puzzle without a picture to work from. Finally, Plath's poems are frequently inconsistent, not only between poems but also within individual poems many of which seem to unsay the very thing that they affirm. The imagery in a poem will suddenly, and inexplicably reverse its implications; that which was reviled will suddenly and inexplicable be adored. Plath does not inhabit an either/or world. Her works capture the complexity of life, love, hate, etc. without attempting to rationalize or simplify reality.

I have read many attempts to capture Plath's greatness, but I cannot improve on Davison's assessment of the *Ariel* poems (except to say that I think it is true of almost all of her poems), "[I]f we take the internal evidence of the poems ... as our guide, she stood at the edge of the abyss of existence and looked. Steadily, courageously, with holy curiosity, to the very bottom" (Wagner Ed. *Essays* 39). Her poems are reports from the edge written in a distinctive voice that no other poet even approximates.

Selected Poems by Sylvia Plath

Recurring Themes

What concerns does Sylvia Plath explore in her poetry?

- **Relationships** (parent-child, husband-wife, friend-friend), and particularly the inadequacy, failure or coercive nature of relationships and the damage and pain caused by them;

- **Motherhood** – its obligations, demands, joys, fears, etc.;

- **The passage of time** – which Plath associates with entropy; that is, the decline from order and predictability through gradual decline into disorder which means the loss of past happiness;

- **The modern, male-generated stereotype of women** – as an expression of the male's fears of the female and as an image that confines, restricts and ultimately destroys women;

- **The search for a transcendent meaning to existence** – in conventional religion (particularly Christianity), paganism, mythology, and personal mysticism;

- **The external world as threatening and inimical to** life – both in the form of the modern urban environment and of natural landscape;

- **Life and death** – where Plath is at her most inconsistent, at one moment speaking for life, beauty, vitality and joy, and at the next self-negating and expressing the attractions of suicide;

- **Escape** – Plath has an occasional sense of glimpsing another and better form of life lurking just below the surface of reality, which leads her to perceive death not as an end but as a transformation to a superior form of existence;

- **Victimization** – whether as woman, daughter, wife, or individual, the poems explore the sense of being abused, tricked and abandoned;

- **Freedom** – ultimately from mortality, from growing old and from having to fulfill adult roles which are restrictive.

15

Recurring Images

Many images recur throughout the poems, though they develop and change their meaning:

- The journey – Plath's protagonists are often in movement, trying desperately to get somewhere better or to experience life in a more meaningful way;

- The male as a colossus that intimidates and dwarfs women;

- The sea as the primal source of life and a promise of survival beyond death;

- Pregnancy as an image for producing a poem and a story;

- Blood and the color red as emblematic of life;

- White and blue as emblematic of non-life;

- The harsh landscape as an image of all that threatens life;

- Reflections (for example, in a mirror or a lake) which sometimes reveal the physical reality and sometimes the imagined;

- The moon as pagan goddess;

- Fire as purification.

Guide to the Selected Poems of Sylvia Plath

How to Use this Study Guide:

The aim of this guide is to help you towards a fuller understanding and appreciation of the poems of Sylvia Plath. Her poems do not unfold their meaning to a superficial reading. She demands a lot of her readers, but the rewards are *usually* worth the effort. The poems are arranged in chronological order based on the recorded date of composition (not on the date of publication).

For each poem in the collection the guide provides a brief introduction, a number of questions, and a detailed interpretation. An author has no control over how his/her text is used, so I can't stop readers from jumping over the questions and going on to the interpretation, but I do urge you *not* to do so. The aim of this guide is to help readers to experience the poems for themselves, not simply to be told about them by someone who has done that. Some questions are carefully worded to draw your attention to important aspects of the poem which you need to understand. Other questions are very open-ended: they are not designed to lead you in any direction, but simply to elicit your ideas. It should always be clear to you which type of question you are being asked. Although they can be used in a variety of ways, the questions work best as an aid to small group discussion. Disagreement is to be encouraged!

My interpretation of each poem is based on the belief that "the only thing available for commentary and analysis is the text" (Rose 5). My readings are based on the assumption that the protagonist, who is often (though not always) the I-speaker, is a persona which is *never* to be simply equated with Sylvia Plath. For this reason, I have entirely avoided expressions such as "in this poem Plath says." I do *not* regard Plath as having written confessional poetry (if there really is such a thing); I regard her as having produced universal images and meanings from her personal experience; it is those images and meanings that are my concern, not the poet's biography.

What I have written represents my best understanding of each text at the present time. I make no claim to be definitive or comprehensive. I certainly have no illusions of infallibility.

Note: Plath recorded several poems for the BBC in the months before her death, and the recordings are available on YouTube as I have indicated in my introduction to relevant poems. If you search YouTube for "Sylvia Plath Reading Her Poetry" you will find selections from the Caedmon recording of Plath reading her poems (Parts 1 and 2). There is also on YouTube an audio (in three parts) called "Sylvia Plath Reads from *Ariel*."

MISS DRAKE PROCEEDS TO SUPPER

Rosenblatt writes that "Sylvia Plath's early work differs so greatly from her late poetry both in style and in substance that they would appear to have been written by two different poets … Only the general mood of depression and fear in this body of work anticipates the character of the late poetry" (47). This is certainly true of the style of the early poems, but I believe that most of the themes that she would explore in her mature poetry are inherent in her earlier work.

The poem was written in 1956, three years after Plath had been hospitalized in a psychiatric ward following her first mental breakdown and suicide attempt. Plath was drafting the poem on June 19 while on honeymoon in Paris with her husband of a few days, Ted Hughes. The term 'confessional poetry' is sometimes used to describe works which draw heavily on painful parts of the poet's experience. In the 1950s you just did not disclose that you had spent time in a mental hospital because of the stigma. (This explains the later publication of *The Bell Jar* under a pseudonym.) However, it is important to bear in mind the qualification that, rather than speaking in her own voice, Plath sought to control her own terrifying experiences through her poetry. In this poem, she creates a character through whom she is able to demonstrate the way in which the embattled mind attempts to cope.

The setting of this poem is a psychiatric hospital ward; the protagonist is, "The new woman in the ward." Little is said definitely about Miss Drake, but her careful dress, and the other elaborate rituals designed to preserve her own dignity and sense of self (she "proceeds" not 'walks' in "purple" the color of royalty), suggest an older woman of relatively high social class.

Structurally, the poem has two thirteen-line stanzas each of which is a single sentence.

1. Is this poem a satire of this middle aged woman's attempts to preserve her dignity or a tribute to her efforts to 'keep herself together' despite her frightening hallucinations? Give and briefly explain examples of humor in the description of Miss Drake's progress.
2. Five animals (or types of animals) are mentioned in the poem. What are they? Do you see any particular significance in the emphasis on animals?

The author conveys Miss Drake's fears and confusion whilst at the same time putting them into context at the end of each stanza. The rhythm of the first eight lines is slowed and deliberate, reflecting Miss Drake's controlled entrance: only she knows the "malice" of the table and chairs; only she knows the location of "her secret combinations of eggshells." The reader shares the protagonist's view of reality because no alternative view is presented. Notice how Miss Drake begins by being relatively confident – she may be new to *this* ward, but she is by no means a "novice" when it comes to negotiating her way

Selected Poems by Sylvia Plath

around a hospital environment:

> The ne*w w*oman in the *w*ard
> *W*ears purple, steps carefully

The long 'w' sounds and the heavy caesura (mid-line pause) in the second line of the above quotation slows the rhythm of these lines even more – one almost hears her footsteps. Yet she immediately feels threats ("malice") and appears to be going through her own ritual of stepping carefully (the equivalent of not stepping on the cracks in the sidewalk) in order to keep herself safe and to maintain her illusion of control.

After line nine, the press of words (uncluttered because of the absence of rhyme and punctuation) conveys how one observation is immediately followed by another, capturing Miss Drake's feeling of being overwhelmed and threatened by her new environment. The ground is perceived as dangerous. The "cabbage-roses" have "furred petals" like animals, and these animals quickly become predatory and threatening. The tension is build at the end of the first stanza by the alliteration of the hard 'd' sound, "To devour and drag her down." The final line, the answer to the riddle of exactly what it is that (objectively speaking) Miss Drake is experiencing, comes as a comic anti-climax. At least on the literal level there has been no threat at all – she has been seeing things in the floral pattern of the carpet. Yet Miss Drake's fear is very real (the reader has experienced it directly), if entirely subjective, paranoid and delusional.

The second stanza repeats the structure of the first. Now Miss Drake has one eye wide open for the perils that she anticipates, and she seems confident of her own ability to spot them "in the nick of time" and so save herself. She is walking on bare floorboards, but she perceives in them "perilous needles," sharp as brambles, that appear to be planning to attack her. Even the air through which she walks seems to be full of "bright shards / Of broken glass" (presumably light beams streaming in through the windows) which she must carefully negotiate. She no longer "steps" but "edges." Notice the harsh vowels and sharp monosyllables in phrases such as, "brambled plan," "ambushed air," "bright shards," "broken glass," and "jag and tooth." Finally, Miss Drake is able to make her way into the relatively unthreatening patients' dining room. The rhythm slows as though to reflect her triumph:

> Into the *s*till, *s*ultry weather
> Of the patients' dining room.

Notice the long vowel sounds and the calming sibilance of the 's' alliteration, as well as the heavy caesura in the first line of the quotation, which indicate a lowering of tension.

The true relationship between poet and persona is explained by Uroff:

> Miss Drake is superbly sensitive, wildly
> inventive in objectifying her fears, and skilled
> at controlling them. But there is also a vast

> distance between Miss Drake and the poet, a distance that may be measured by the techniques of parody, caricature, hyperbole that Plath employs in characterizing her ... She has been distanced from us by the poet who sees her as a grotesque reflection of herself, employing the manipulative strategies of the uninformed mind against an undefined terror, channeling what might have been creative energy into pointless rituals.

This ability of Plath's poems to create protagonists with whom the poet (and therefore the reader) sympathizes even while their limitations, and occasionally their absurdities are exposed, will be a recurring theme of our analysis.

Selected Poems by Sylvia Plath

SPINSTER

Search "brainpickings Sylvia Plath Reads 'Spinster' in a Rare BBC Recording."

On the surface, this is a sad little tale in which we can see Plath's reverence for love and life and her hatred of life-denying isolation. The protagonist is a young woman who, as Plath explains in her BBC introduction, "would prefer, if she had the choice, a picture or a painting of the sea rather than the sea itself, because she finds motion, untidiness, and chaos too upsetting" – a 'control freak' then. Plath adds, "This poem explores her tendency towards spinsterhood and shows the neat disease setting it." The poem records an epiphany: walking through the spring countryside with her lover, the girl experiences not the romantic stereotype of a perfect picture postcard world, but a world of disorder and chaos: "the birds irregular babel ... the leaves' litter." The source of the "intolerable" disturbance is immediately seen to be her lover whose "gestures unbalance the air." The walk is described as "ceremonious," and the man as her "suitor," because it is part of the formal ritual of courtship which will lead ultimately to marriage and to the loss of the girl's autonomy.

Stanzas 1 - 2

1. What emotion is it that the girl suddenly feels and why does she dislike it so violently?
2. Collect together the words and phrases which suggest lack of order in the world. Explain any that need explanation.

Stanza 3

3. What characteristics of winter appear attractive to the girl? How are they described?

Stanzas 4 - 5

4. Which words and phrases suggest how threatening the girl found the emotion released by her walk with her "latest suitor"?
5. What is so sad about the last line of the poem?

Spring, the season normally associated with love, is ruined for the girl, and she longs for winter which she associates with order in the simile, "Exact as a snowflake" – snowflakes being, of course, each unique and each symmetrical – but also cold and white and dead. The girl feels devalued by the chaos, her "five queenly wits" (touch, taste, sight, smell, hearing) reduced to "motley" (an incongruous mixture of clothing worn by the poor). Notice the use of the adjective "burgeoning" as a noun, and the violence of the verb "pitch" – together they stress the girl's feelings of helplessness in the face of a force (call it the expectations of a patriarchal society) that she feels helpless to resist. So

21

A Study Guide

the young woman retreats into her house where she can protect herself from every threat and danger, but at the cost also of cutting herself off from love. The young man with whom she walked was, indeed, her "latest" (i.e., last) lover.

Structurally, the poem has five stanzas each with six lines and each of which ends with a period. As a result, the stanzas each deal with a new topic in an order which reflects the young woman's obsession with order. The final stanza is the only one which uses end-rhyme (full and half) in an a a b c c b pattern. This also adds to the sense of finality which the words convey about the protagonist's choice of isolation.

A post on the site *Plagiarist Poetry* says, "I fully believe that the girl was hurt (cheated on, most likely) by her suitor ..." This is a perfectly natural explanation, but there is zero evidence for it in the poem. The girl perceives the man to be a threat to her sense of who she is simply because he *is* a man – a man who in marriage will erase her identity and usurp her control of her own life, not because he is vicious but because that is just the way society is. (Take time out to listen to the song "I am a Rock" by Paul Simon which explores similar themes.)

Is there, however, a subversive message in the poem? The protagonist is, after all, described as "this particular girl," a phrase which singles her out from the crowd of young women who accept the role of wife and mother that society restricts them to. The girl is said to have, "Observed her lover's gestures" and "judged petals," verbs which suggest her detachment from the man and her ability to evaluate the world rationally. So, a poem which appears to be "a lamentation of the anguishing lonesomeness of feeling unworthy of love," turns out to be *also* "a sort of subversive elegy – ... a celebration of the buoyant autonomy of being single" (brainpickings). The man is not described at all: he has no identity outside that of threatening male (the "latest" in a long line of such). Readers should prepare themselves for such double perspectives in Plath's poems.

MAUDLIN

Written in 1959, this is a very difficult poem which many critics simply ignore. The following reading is offered tentatively. The poem is written in two unrhymed stanzas each of four lines which have no set meter.

1. "Maudlin" means foolishly tearful or sentimental, which certainly describes the self-pitying mood of the poem's protagonist. The word is derived from the Middle English "Maudelen" a spelling of the name Mary Magdalene, the woman taken in adultery and saved from stoning by Christ, who is typically portrayed as a tearful penitent. This, in turn, brings to mind the Virgin Mary, who is (at least in Christian tradition) Mary Magdalene's opposite. What further light do these references shed on the poem?

The theme of the poem is child-birth, and it seems to be based on the experience that Plath had of observing a difficult birth by caesarian section that was performed at the Boston Lying-in Hospital. (The incident is also described in Plath's autobiographical novel *The Bell Jar*.) The birth described in stanza one is clearly agony for the woman who, all bloodied, curses the male baby she births. The baby is "the moon's man" because he is the result of the monthly menstrual cycle. The moon is here male (as in 'the man in the moon'). The baby emerges with its caul (the amniotic sac) intact, which is a rare event. This marks a contrast with the mother whose egg was cracked by a man's sperm – that's how women become pregnant.

"Mud-matressed" appears to refer to the woman's drying blood on the bed. The woman is "under the sign of the hag," a reference to the shop signs which indicated the trade of the proprietor (like pub signs in Britain today). The idea of woman as "hag" seems to be a very male stereotype of woman exhausted by childbearing and old before her time, and also perhaps of woman as whore. The mother is "sleep-talking" because she has been given an anesthetic to dull her pain.

The gibbet was a gallows, particularly one on which the dead body of a criminal was hung up as a deterrent to others: the woman wants this baby to hang and remain on view as a warning to other women not to allow a man to get them pregnant. In the phrase "Faggot-bearing jack," the word "Faggot" is often censored, but this involves a misinterpretation. This is the English spelling of the word 'fagot' which means "a bundle of sticks or twigs bound together as fuel." Inevitably, the reader recalls the faggots placed around the feet of witches ("the hag") being burned at the stake which is a metaphor for the burning pain that the baby has caused the woman in being born. Since "Faggot" also means 'penis', this directly blames the male for both the pain of intercourse and the pain of child birth. The boy-child to whom the woman has given birth will keep the cycle going by getting another woman pregnant.

A Study Guide

Why "Jack"? During the Middle Ages, the name was very common, and it became a slang word meaning "man" (as in the modern English colloquialism 'Jack the Lad'). It was frequently used in fairy tales and nursery rhymes, such as "Jack and Jill," "Jack and the Beanstalk," "Little Jack Horner" and "Jack Sprat." Plath's lines are a reference to the traditional English nursery rhyme "Jack Be Nimble" first collected in 1815. It exists in several variations of which this is the fullest:

>Jack be nimble,
>Jack be quick,
>Jack jump over
>The candlestick.
>Jack jumped high,
>Jack jumped low,
>Jack jumped over and burned his toe.

The brevity of the rhyme makes it difficult to be certain about its meaning. "Jack" seems to be a reference to Black Jack Smart, an English Caribbean pirate in the late 16th century who was notorious for his knack of escaping from the authorities. The improbable medieval sport of candle leaping (which developed when the much more dangerous sport of fire leaping was banned) used to be practiced at some English fairs. "Good luck was said to be signalled by clearing a candle without extinguishing the flame" (Wikipedia article). The reference stresses the ability of the man to escape the flame and the inability of the woman to do likewise. Here, of course, Jack carries the faggots that will consume the woman.

The price that the woman pays for the birth is "a pin-stitched skin" (it was a caesarian birth) while the male baby is born without feeling pain to inherit, by right, the superior position of men in the world, "He kings it." The poem warns women about the pain the mother suffers in childbirth as a result of the loss of her virginity – much better to remain a virgin spinster it appears to be saying. The "claret hogshead [large cask of deep red wine] to swig" is the blood that the mother has spilt during the baby's birth; in contrast the cutting and tying of the umbilical cord cause the baby no pain at all, "navel-knit to no groan." By mythical tradition, mermaids have no need of sex with men to reproduce (another reflection of the theme of self-sufficiency in Plath). In one theory, they excrete eggs which are fertilized by the male outside their body, but they give up this self-sufficiency in order to exchange a tail for two legs at the great cost of having to have sex with men.

Selected Poems by Sylvia Plath

RESOLVE

In late December 1956, England suffered from days of dense fog (actually 'smog', fog containing added pollutants from coal smoke) which seems to be the origin of this poem which was first published on March 9th, 1957. For the most part, it offers a simple but evocative description of an ordinary day in a misty, cold winter. The poem is free verse.

1. Much of the description is purely realistic and gives the impression of having been directly observed (e.g., "the one-eared cat / laps its gray paw," "a milk-film blurs / the empty bottles on the windowsill"). These are, however, details of the description which appear to have a symbolic dimension suggesting a religious significance to the poem. Can you locate these details?

2. Explain the significance of the title of the poem. ['Resolve' is a word with multiple meanings. Adapted from Merriam-Webster: to dissolve or melt; to cause something to break up or disintegrate; to cause resolution of (a pathological state); to come to an understanding of, to clarify; and to decide formally on a course of action (or resolution). How does the title play on the word's multiple meanings?]

'Ordinary' is actually the key point, for the speaker in the poem is a description of the boring domesticity into which she seems trapped by the surrounding fog. The "tarnish" of the polluted mist has fallen on everything and "no glory descends." Life appears mundane. The woman can do nothing but wait ("with hands unserviceable") until the milk man has made his delivery. There is something threatening in "bent bow of thorns" and "the cat [that] unsheathes its claws." As bad as her protected life is, it is perhaps preferable to the vaguely threatening world out there ("the world turns").

For this reason, the rebellion that is rising in the speaker will not burst out today. She pictures herself as a student facing "my twelve black-gowned examiners" who will decide, like a jury, on whether or not she fulfills the roles of wife and mother adequately. Neither will she, in more Romantic fashion, rail against the elements. At least, she will not do these things "today": the word seems to imply that the day will come when she *will* rebel.

A Study Guide

NIGHT SHIFT

In this poem, first published in *The Observer* June 14th, 1959, the speaker describes her initial shock at hearing the repeated beating in the night from a silver factory which is in full production – a shock not shared by her neighbors who are accustomed to it. She is eventually sure that it is not the sound of her own heart beating that she has imposed on the night but an external sound shaking the ground of the "stilled suburbs." In fact, whatever produces the "beating" is evidently not a living entity at all; this is a dead sound.

The poem is written in unrhymed four-line stanzas all of which end with a run-on line.

1. Explain what is meant by the line, "It took root at my coming."
2. Once she has discovered the cause, how does the speaker seem to feel about the noise?
3. Look carefully at the use of run-on lines and punctuation in the first three lines of stanza five. How does Plath manipulate rhythm to convey the movement of the hammers?
4. Which of Plath's other poems seem to you to embody a similar attitude to the effect on humanity of industrialization?

The poem is full of the threatening sounds emanating from the factory which are contrasted with the human sound of the speaker's heart beating. The onomatopoeia (words that actually sound like the sound they describe) suggests explosive, metallic sounds like shells exploding: "muted boom … clangor … drumming." The sound reverberates; it can be felt in the verbs: "Shook … pounding … thudding." It seems as though the area is under attack, "metal detonating," though the sound is so familiar that no one (except the speaker) notices it anymore.

The factory is personified as being "native" to the neighborhood and as "imposing" its clamorous noises on its inhabitants. The reference to Main Street suggests that the location is a town in America. The source of the noise is purely mechanical, "Hammers hoisted, wheels turning, / Stalled, let fall their vertical / Tonnage of metal and wood," yet the human cost is to be "Stunned in marrow" – literally shaken to the bone. Humanity has been reduced to the subservient role of serving the destructive force of the machine. Twice the poet repeats the phrase "Tending, without stop," to emphasize that the humans have lost their sense of identify and their independence to the machine.

In contrast to the men who serve the machine, the speaker struggles to construct and sustain a self against the "Indefatigable fact" of a crushing environment. It is a losing battle, as can be seen in the fact that the first person only breaks through once: "It took root at my coming." This indicates that the speaker is the only one who is bothered by the sound, everyone else has got use to it. What the explosive noise represents is not specified: it could be capitalism and industrialization, or it could be a more personal reference to the teaching at Smith that Plath was doing at the time.

FULL FATHOM FIVE

Until the age of nine, Plath spent her childhood summers vacationing on the North Atlantic coast with her father, mother and brother. Then Otto Plath died, and following his death Plath's mother relocated the family inland, so that Plath was cut off from both coast and father. She developed a life-long love of the Nauset coast and the sea, which became inextricably linked in her mind with her father. In an unsent letter, dated December 28th, 1953, Plath wrote about an early attempt at suicide, "Well, I tried drowning, but that didn't work; somehow the urge to life, mere physical life, is damn strong, and I felt that I could swim forever straight out into the sea and sun and never be able to swallow more than a gulp or two of water and swim on. The body is amazingly stubborn when it comes to sacrificing itself to the annihilating directions of the mind." (Quoted by Lowe at the start of his essay "'Full Fathom Five': The Dead Father in Sylvia Plath's Seascapes.")

The poem was first published (together with "Lorelei" and "The Hermit at Outermost House") in *Audience*, Spring 1959. The poem is written in three-line stanzas with no rhyme scheme and no uniform number of syllables in the lines that would become Plath's most characteristic form, though the second line is generally longer than the first and third lines. It has been suggested that this creates both a visual and aural image of waves lapping on the shore. [What do you think?]

1. It is clear that the "old man" seldom surfaces, but what does the description make clear about those times when he does so?
2. The first four stanzas end in run-on lines but the fifth is end-stopped. Why is this? What is the effect on the meaning?
3. What dangers are involved for the speaker in the surfacing of the father?
4. Look closely at the final stanza. Does it indicate that the speaker has chosen a course of action?

The title of this poem is taken from the opening lines of Ariel's Song from Shakespeare's *The Tempest:*

> Full fathom five thy father lies
> Of his bones are coral made.
> Those are pearls that were his eyes:
> Nothing of him that doth fade,
> But doth suffer a sea-change
> Into something rich and strange. (1.2)

The song is about Ferdinand, who has lost his father Alonso in a shipwreck and spends the play looking for him on the shore. Five fathoms is about thirty feet, so neither Ferdinand's father nor the speaker's is a long way away, but a pun on the word "fathom" (meaning 'understand') suggests the speaker's inability to fully fathom her father either in life or death. The theme of the poem is the

Selected Poems by Sylvia Plath

speaker's ambivalent feelings about her dead father who is transformed into a god, a Poseidon/Neptune-like figure, too large to be grasped. The sea is equated with death, and the speaker considers herself exiled from his kingdom as she walks on its borders. Water has become the living embodiment of the dead father and drowning holds out the tantalizing prospect of the rediscovery of happiness. Rosenblatt writes, "[D]eath is seen as both the enemy of everything that the self loves and the ultimate escape from the life of pain ... The father becomes the central object of conflict, for he is the focus of widely divergent opinions" (67). Such ambivalence is typical of Plath's poetry.

The physical reemergence of the father from the sea is a metaphor for the memory of the speaker's father flooding back into her mind since he is indelibly associated for her with the Massachusetts coast. The description has the surreal quality of a dream. The speaker apostrophizes (i.e., directly addresses) the father-figure, but her attitude toward him is ambiguous: she reveres her father and is in awe of his vastness, but she also senses the threat and danger that he poses to her. He is associated with white (his beard and the sea foam) and with cold (the water and the "ice-mountains / Of the north"), both of which suggest death. The father's long white hair is immediately perceived as a "dragnet" with which he could pull his daughter into his domain for in the "wrinkled skeins" of his hair is caught the "Unimaginable" myth of her own birth (since he is her father.) His hard rock ("ice mountains") is a threat to the speaker's navigation: she must steer clear of the rocks lest they sink her boat. She knows that the dangers represented by the father "are many." As she looks at the incoming tide, the image of the father that she thought she detected there vanishes ("your form suffers / Some strange injury") in the flux of the waves like morning mist on the sea.

Yet for all the perceived threat, there is a reality to the vision of the father which points to a kind of immortality. Against the "muddy rumors" of his burial, which the speaker only half-believes, is the reality of the "reappearance," of the timeless image of the father, whose wrinkled face sheds off time as it does rainwater "in runnels," just as the rain beats to no effect on the "unbeaten channels / Of the ocean." Thus, the speaker concludes, the idea of the immortal father makes "away with the ground- / Work of the earth and the sky's ridgepole" – that is, it destroys every assumption that has previously appeared to give life meaning. The sky has fallen for the speaker as a tent collapses without a ridgepole.

Below the waist (and therefore presumably below the sea) the father takes his root amongst bones, for he *is* death. Yet he is also "Inscrutable" which alerts the reader to a pun on the phrase "Full fathom five": the father/God is too large, too great to be fully fathomed (i.e., fully understood). He defies understanding and rationality. Though he and his watery life are dangerous, the speaker feels like an exile breathing the "thick air" of life without him. She wants to "breathe water" in order to join him. In the end, the protagonist's sense of admiration and love for him permeates this poem, overcoming the sense of threat that she also acknowledges. O'Hare argues that "nothing in 'Full Fathom Five' justifies the sudden death wish of its last stanza" (Lane *New Views* 83), but it seems rather that *everything* in the poem does so.

Selected Poems by Sylvia Plath

SUICIDE OFF EGG ROCK

Written February-March 1959. [Ochre is a yellow/orange color which in Plath always seems to have negative connotations. A comber is a long, curling wave. You can find photographs of Egg Rock on the Internet.]

The incident draws on Plath's nervous breakdown during the summer of 1953 during which she visited Egg Rock. She would later use the situation and much of the language of the poem in Chapter 13 of *The Bell Jar* where the protagonist, Esther, plans to kill herself by drowning. Plath distances herself from the suicide described in the poem by using the past tense, by making the gender of the protagonist male, and by speaking in the third person. In her *Journal*, Plath identified the poem's greatest quality as "forthrightness."

1. The opening sentence describes what was behind and what was in front of the man as he stood on the edge of the water contemplating suicide. How is this setting made to seem unattractive?
2. In the remainder of stanza one, how does the text point out the contrast between the man and the other people on the sand?
3. Stanza 2 describes the man standing on the beach at the edge of the water contemplating suicide. How does the stanza make it clear that the man regards both his life and the alternative of death as horrific?
4. In the final four lines, Egg Rock seems to be given an importance which suggests a symbolic meaning. Can you suggest what it might symbolize?
5. The man finally walks into the water to die. Is this decision/action presented in the poem as positive or negative and how do you know?

The third person narrative describes a suicide against the ugly industrial background of factories and gas tanks and the unattractive description of people spending their leisure time at the beach: the "landscape of imperfections." The hotdogs on the public grills which "split and drizzled" are set against a background of "Gas tanks, factory stacks." The protagonist is an outsider looking on: both the worlds of leisure and of work are equally indifferent to him. Notice, however, that the natural world also appears antagonistic: the spindrift is violently "wind-ripped from the crest of the wave" and the scorching sun "struck the water like a damnation," so that the protagonist sees the grills and factories through the rippling lens of heat rising from the "ochreous salt flats."

In a description which (consciously or not, I do not know) recalls Camus' description of Meursault on the beach outside Algiers just before he shoots the Arab (*The Stranger* Chapter 6), the protagonist appears vulnerable with no place to hide from the attacking sun. The heat causes Plath's protagonist to become conscious of the beating of his heart, "And his blood beating the old tattoo / I am I am I am." Though the alliteration of the hard 'b' sound conveys the power of the life force, there is nothing life-affirming in this rhythm. The

31

persona appears to be alienated from his own body as well as from his surroundings. (Compare the attitude of Hamlet, who signs his letter to Ophelia, "*Thine evermore, most dear lady, / whilst this machine is to him, /* Hamlet" [*Hamlet* 2.2].) The ambivalence of the poem is captured in two opposing interpretations of the description of the beating heart: Rosenblatt calls it evidence of a life that is "unendurably meaningless and repetitious" (66) while Kendall sees it as an "assertion, almost celebration of selfhood at the moment of annihilation" (13). (Note the contrast with the later poem "Tulips" where the protagonist's growing awareness of the beating of her heart confirms in her the will to live.)

The third-person narrator turns her attention to what is happening on the beach: human activity is no more attractive. The children are not laughing but "squealing" as they play in the waves and "A mongrel [was] working his legs to a gallop" in order to put to flight a flock of gulls, a description which makes the action appear unnatural and labored. The dog, "Hustled a gull flock to flap off the sandspit," complements the antagonism of the sun and the wind. Life in this world has become meaningless, glittering "like blank paper." It offers the protagonist, "No pit of shadow to crawl into." The sea is the only viable alternative, but it means death.

The protagonist feels alienated from his body because it seems determined to go on living. It is a "machine to breathe and beat forever." In addition to this, the man obviously feels that the sea is his natural element and that he is at the moment a stranger stranded on the shore, "His body beached with the sea's garbage." He identifies (perhaps even *becomes*) the dead skate through whose eyehole a fly enters the brain. He feels that every achievement of his life has been wiped out, "The words in his book wormed off the pages."

Return to the sea seems to offer the only cool alternative to "the sun's corrosive / Ray." As he wades deeper and deeper, the surf seems to wipe away his horrible memories so that he finds peace. The color blue is a contrast with the sun-colored beach and the "creaming" waters appear nourishing. Yet there is a level of ambiguity in the ending of the poem, for Egg Rock would appear to symbolize birth rather than death. The world is more beautiful at the moment the man leaves it than he conceived it to be. Surely a suicide off Egg Rock is an oxymoron?

Selected Poems by Sylvia Plath

THE HERMIT AT OUTERMOST HOUSE

This poem was published in the *Times Literary Supplement* in 1959.

The Outermost House: A Year of Life on the Great Beach of Cape Cod (1928) is a book by naturalist Henry Beston which chronicles his year spent living on the dunes of Cape Cod. Beston's small beach cottage served as the setting for the book and so became known as 'The Outermost House'. Beston called it "Fo'castle" because its ten windows and commanding position on top of a dune overlooking the open Atlantic Ocean gave him the feeling of being aboard a ship (Built in June 1925, the cottage was moved several times and finally washed into the sea in February 1978.) Sylvia Plath and Ted Hughes stayed there. (Adapted from a variety of sources, including Wikipedia and "The Outermost House, Henry Beston's Cape Cod" by Don Wilding.)

1. How does stanza one establish the hermit's indestructibility?
2. At what is the hermit on his doorstep laughing?
3. The last three stanzas of the poem try to establish in what lay the hermit's superiority to the "Hard gods." The clue seems to lie in the symbolic significance of "a certain meaning green." What connotations does the color green have?

The hermit of the title is Henry Beston, portrayed in the poem as a figure of heroic struggle – a representative of masculine values of survival against the harsh natural elements. The poem opens with the alliteration of harsh, short consonants:

>*S*ky and *s*ea, *h*orizon-*h*inged
>Tablets of *b*lank *b*lue, *c*ouldn't,
>*C*lapped shut, flatten this man out.

The sounds convey the power of the destructive forces ranged against this single man. The anthropomorphized (i.e.,, presented as having human form and feelings) Gods of nature ("Stone-Head, Claw-Foot") look upon him as being as indestructible as are they. He has endured exactly what they have endured: the heat of summer and the cold of winter, but he has done so with laughter.

The difference is that the hermit, unlike the gods, was creative, "he thumbed out something else." This is a reference to the earliest and most primitive form of pottery (the thumb pot), but it was not inert pottery that he created "no stony, horny pot, / But a certain meaning green." This is an ambiguous image: I take it to refer to Beston's literary work and more generally to the faith in the life-force that it represented. The word "green" is repeated three times in the last four lines where it is placed in contrast with the hardness of nature, "Rock-face, crab-claw." Green is associated with the freedom to fly, "Gulls mulled in the greenest light." It is the man's creativity that gives life meaning.

A Study Guide

MEDALLION

This poem was first published in *Critical Quarterly Poetry Supplement*, no. 1. 1960. It is written in unrhymed three-line stanzas and describes the speaker's memory of finding a dead snake. You might read "Snake" by D. H. Lawrence with which it has been compared, and also "Pike" by Ted Hughes.

1. How was the snake killed?
2. What parts of the description suggest the beauty of the snake?
3. How does the speaker bring home the fact of the snake's death?
4. What do you make of the image, "Knifelike he was chaste enough, / Pure death's-metal..."

The speaker recalls finding a dead snake, though in stanza 1 it is not clear that the snake *is* dead. The poem is full of precisely observed detail. The snake lies by a distinctive "gate with star and moon" hard to see because its color blends into the "peeled orange wood" on which it lies. The snake's death is absolute, though the body is "pliable still": it lies completely unmoving, "Inert as a shoelace," a simile that compares it to something that never had life; the jaw is "Unhinged" and the "grin crooked" descriptions which tend to personify the dead snake. A metaphor describes the snake's tongue as "a rose-colored arrow." On the literal level this simply describes the snake's forked tongue, but the arrow might also be seen as a sign to all living things that death is ultimately in the future.

The narrator does not explain why she picks up the snake and it hangs it over her hand. The dead snake's eye is "vermillion" (red or reddish-orange) and, as the light catches reflects on it, "Ignited with a glassed flame." The speaker likens the effect to garnets that she found when she "split a rock one time" because they burned with the same fiery color. In contrast, the snake's back is dust covered and yellowed, "The way sun ruins a trout." 'Ocher' is an orangish or reddish yellow color which always seems to have negative connotations in Plath's poems. The speaker's use of the word "Bust" is striking. One immediately suspects a misprint for the word 'dust' since that is the word the reader expects in this context. "Bust" is a colloquial synonym for 'death' (we later learn that the snake's back has been broken with a brick), so the change in the snake's color under the influence of the sun (like that of the trout) is part of the early stages of decomposition following death by which both are ruined.

At this point the reader realizes that images of life and of death are alternatively being used to describe the snake. Thus, the speaker next notes that the snake's belly, having been protected from the sun, retains the color it had in life. In a metaphor, she compares the scales of the snake to a knight's chainmail under which life still seems to be present. The "fire ... smoldering there" implies life and the "old jewels" she sees in "each opaque belly-scale" are glowing like the embers of a dying fire. The speaker compares the effect to the vibrant colors of a sunset seen through milk glass. ("Milk glass is an opaque or translucent, milk white or colored glass, blown or pressed into a wide variety of shapes. First made in Venice in the 16th century …" [Wikipedia article].)

The maggots that "coil / Thin as pins" are a clear sign of decomposition. Ironically, the snake was killed in the process of "digesting a mouse" – that is, death came to the snake as it was in the process of completing a kill. In life, the snake was a "pure" killing machine, with all the efficiency and lack of emotion of a knife.

The title of the poem suggests that the snake is a thing of beauty and value. In death, it is somehow "perfected," it's "grin" frozen and captured. Such perfection is, however, an illusion.

THE MANOR GARDEN

This was the initial poem in *The Colossus*, Plath's first published collection of poems. It was written in the late autumn of 1959 at Yaddo, an artists' community located on a 400-acre estate in Saratoga Springs, New York, where Plath stayed for several months with husband Ted Hughes. Plath was pregnant with her first child, and these two facts may be of great help in understanding this poem in which Plath constantly juxtaposes life and death. Mazzaro explains, "[The poem] opposes the harvest of nature to the growing foetus within the speaker. As the outer world comes to represent death, the child moves 'through the era of fishes,' reliving in its development the history of evolution" (Lane Ed. *New Views* 228). This marks the appearance in Plath's poems of a new theme: from this point on, her speakers will frequently express their concerns for the safety and survival of their children threatened both by the psychological darkness that afflicts each speaker and by an external world that seems destructive to life.

Kendall comments, "Criticism rarely portrays Plath as a nature poet, but landscapes occur regularly throughout her work, and become increasingly frequent during these intervening years [i.e.,, 1960-1961]. Her exploration of the relationship between the individual and the natural world is fundamental to the development of her mature voice … [I]t becomes increasingly difficult to separate Plath's landscape poems into a discrete category. As the natural world is internalised [*sic*] by her personas, so images from nature become more pervasive" (31, 35).

1. What season is described in stanza one? How do you know?
2. Who is the "You" addressed in stanzas one, two and three?
3. What do you make of the final stanza? Can you find any suggestion of hope in the last two lines?

The speaker is in an ornate garden. However, the summer is over: the fountains have been drained, the roses have passed blooming, and a cold, obscuring mist lies over the lake. Death seems to have control over both the world of man and the world of nature. The end-stopped first line suggests finality. The mist appears to be "dragging" the lake in search of a dead body. Notice the perfect balance of the second line, "Incense of death. Your day approaches": the world is dying, but the child is approaching its birth. The smell of death is in the air, and the word 'incense' suggests that the speaker does not find it unattractive, yet she breaks off to address the child growing in her womb whose birth is getting closer. In the garden, only the pears represent fruition, for they are still ripening; they "fatten like little buddhas," a shape with which the pregnant speaker associates herself.

The second stanza is addressed to the unborn child which, in growing from conception, recapitulates evolution. "[T]he era of fishes" is the Devonian period when life began to make the transition from sea to land. At a very early stage of its development the human fetus has gills, like a fish. Slowly, the fetus develops "Head, toe and finger." The last line of the stanza returns to describing the manor house, which has seen several centuries of history as is evident in its "broken flutings, / These crowns of acanthus." Flutings are vertical grooves forming a surface decoration for example on grooves running on a column shaft or a pilaster. Acanthus Crown Moulding, consisting of elegant carved acanthus leaves, is found at the junction walls and ceiling or Corinthian column capitals. Time has left its mark in the "broken flutings," and the crow (a carrion bird that feeds on the flesh of the dead) spreads its wings over the manor house. Crows have, for centuries, symbolized death. If the speaker associates herself with the manor house (which may have been transformed in her mind into a classical Greek ruin), then she seems to be saying that she has also been damaged by time, yet out of her damaged body and psyche will come new life.

On the final line of stanza three, the speaker again turns to address her unborn child. The first two items on the baby's inheritance are positive: "white heather" suggests purity, good luck, and has protective powers; and "a bee's wing" suggests delicacy, sweetness and flight. The stanza break gives the next line added force. The baby will also inherit "Two suicides, the family wolves, / Hours of blankness." A history of suicide in the family, of antagonism within the family, and of depression is a difficult inheritance. To this is added, "Some hard stars / Already yellow the heavens," which refers to the baby's horoscope which foretells inevitable suffering. (Compare Romeo and Juliet who are described in the Prologue as "A pair of star-cross'd lovers.")

The speaker turns back to describing her environment. The spider is an example of the determination of nature; a determination that the speaker will follow in giving birth to her baby. Surely the worms are the gifts that the birds bring – that's what birds feed their young on. If so, then the final message of the poem is ambiguous: life and death coincide, which is why it will be "a difficult borning." Nevertheless, the child *will* be born. The word "borning" is unusual; one expects 'birthing'. "[B]orning," however, suggests both 'morning' and 'dawning' two very positive words.

A Study Guide

THE COLOSSUS

Written in October 1959, Plath described the poem in her *Journal* as embodying "the old father-worship subject. But different. Weirder." At this time, Plath had been experimenting with a Ouija board. The name of the entity whom she identified as her father's spirit was "kolossus." The Colossus is also the Colossus of Rhodes, that huge statue astride the entrance to Rhodes harbor that was destroyed by an earthquake in 225 BC and never rebuilt. The greatness and order of the classical world is beyond the speaker's power to recapture. You might like to read the sonnet "Ozymandias" in Percy Bysshe Shelley which deals with a similar theme.

The poem is written in six unrhymed five-line stanzas.

1. In stanza one, to whom is the persona speaking? Describe the setting.
2. What elements of comedy do you find in stanzas one and two?
3. Where does the speaker identify the colossus with her father? In what sense has she been trying to put together the father for "Thirty years now"?
4. Apart from trying to reconstruct the colossus, what is the persona described as doing?
5. With particular reference to the final stanza, assess the impact that the fallen colossus has had on the speaker.

At the start of the poem, imagine a vast fallen statue with grass growing up between the shattered stones and a variety of farm animals grazing on the grass. Now conjure up the absurdly comic picture of a person (let's say a young woman), "Scaling little ladders with glue pots and pails of Lysol" trying to clean off the stones and put them together again. Relish the further comedy of the colossus thinking itself "an oracle, / Mouthpiece of the dead, or of some god or other," when the only sounds that appear to come from its mouth are the brays, grunts and cackles of the animals that inhabit its ruins. Add the self-mocking description of the speaker as "an ant in mourning" and the massive disproportion in scale between the persona and the "immense skull-plates" of the ruined face.

The *Oresteia* is a Greek tragedy in three plays by Aeschylus. The story begins with Agamemnon returning from his great victory over Troy only to be murdered by his faithless wife Clytemnestra, who will in turn be murdered by Orestes, son of Agamemnon and Clytemnestra. Thus, "A blue sky out of the Oresteia" is an oxymoron: the speaker's point is to contrast the greatness of the fall of the colossus, something that would take "more than a lightening-stroke," with the current, rather idyllic, setting. There is more comedy in the image of the speaker opening up her lunch and picnicking amid the "fluted bones and acanthine hair," or curling up on the ear of the statue at night to go to sleep.

The last stanza of the poem is, however, more somber. As the sun rises amid the ruins, the speaker admits that her hours "are married to shadow." She no longer listens for the sound of boats scraping against the landing, because she has given up on life.

Gill writes that the speaker "struggles with the task of restoring the shattered features of a colossal statue" adding that the poem "has been read variously in terms of mythology, autobiography, history and female creativity" (Gill Ed. *Companion* 93). The result is a multiplicity of interpretations. (What one sees depends very much of where one is observing from.)

Axelrod interprets the poem as a symbolic comment on the (very marginalized) position of women in Western literary culture. He sums up the theme of the poem as being that " if the colossus of poetry is inherently male, a woman can choose to devote herself to it as a copier and a restorer (like Hawthorne's Hilda), or she can have no existence in art at all ... Plath imagines accepting the terms of that choice; evokes the depression that such a choice would certainly bring to a woman who once dreamed of being a "Kid Colossus" or "small god" herself ... ; and translates that depression into a doom that makes the choice seem not a choice but a necessity" (49). However, Axelrod goes on to argue that, paradoxically, Plath finds her assertive female voice in her criticism of the monolith of the patriarchal literary tradition, "The poem demonstrates its author's creativity while lamenting the incapacity of its invented speaker, the author's textual double ... [Plath] approached her poetic strength by exploring the margins of her weakness ..." (51).

A Study Guide

THE STONES

A recording of Plath reading this poem is on YouTube.

This is the final poem of the seven-part "Poem for a Birthday" which marked a huge development from the style of poetry Plath had written to this point. The American publishers of *The Colossus* found the entire sequence too reminiscent of Theodore Roethke and included only the final two parts "Witch-Burning" and "The Stones." Ted Hughes wrote that Plath later "dismissed everything prior to 'The Stones' as Juvenilia, produced in the days before she became herself" (quoted in Kendall 24).

The poem is easier to follow than some of Plath's other poems because the images appear less random, indeed some critics have found them to be explained in too much detail. Kroll makes this distinction:

> Many of the images in the earlier poems crowded one another, making conflicting claims; in "The Stones", the imagery, even when grotesque, is unitary and coherent, reflecting the coherence of the speaker, who has understood and ordered her experience.
> (Quoted in Rose 41)

The situation in the poem draws on Plath's experience of electro-shock therapy following her attempted suicide in 1953. The first line is a reference to the story "The City Were Men Are Mended" from Paul Radkin's *African Folktales and African Sculpture* (1953).

1. Which words, phrases and images suggest to you the speaker's feeling of helplessness as a patient?
2. Which words, phrases and images suggest to you the speaker's feeling that as a patient she is the victim of violence?
3. How optimistic do you find the final line of the poem? Some critics have found it to be a weak ending. Do you agree?

The speaker of this monologue is a patient in hospital (the "city" of the first line), but her attitude to the healing process which she is undergoing is deeply ambiguous. She feels like a sacrificial victim. In terms of Radkin's tale, she is the ugly daughter of the evil mother who has crushed her bones into stone. The girl has come to the city for physical transformation and rebirth. Unfortunately, in the folk tale, the girl is not reborn as a beautiful girl but as an even more ugly and misshaped baby.

The anvil metaphor conveys the speaker's feeling of helplessness: she is like hot metal being reshaped by the blacksmith. She feels herself cut off from the sky since she was brought into the hospital. The metaphor, "The flat blue sky-circle / Flew off like the hat of a doll," suggests how easily she has been separated from the world of nature – the "light" out of which she has fallen

Selected Poems by Sylvia Plath

(perhaps as the rebel angels fell out of heaven in Book One of Milton's *Paradise Lost* or as Icarus did in the Greek myth). In contrast to the world from which she came, two metaphors are used to describe the hospital: it is "The stomach of indifference, the wordless cupboard." These images capture the impersonality of the institution where she is a body ('Joe Patient') to be manipulated and healed, not a person with whom the doctors and nurses will interact on a personal level. The protagonist feels as though she has been ground down by a mortar in a huge pestle into an inert, inorganic pebble.

Lines 9-15 appear to describe the process of diagnosis by which the "people of the city" determined the source of the pains in her stomach having given her drugs to numb the pain:

> They hunted the stones, taciturn and separate,
> The mouth-hole crying their locations.

These lines describe the process of examinations with the persona telling the doctors where her pain was. The speaker imagines herself as having reentered the fetal state: the "food tubes" are like the umbilical cord, and she feels "drunk" because the sedatives she has been given mean that she is barely conscious. The ambiguity of her situation is captured in the line, "I suck at the paps of darkness." The act of sucking suggests an instinctive, and strong, will to live, but the ingestion of darkness seems ominous. She conceives of herself as an old, weathered stone being cleaned ("Sponges kiss my lichens away") so that the "jewelmaster" (the surgeon/stone mason/gem cutter) may begin cutting the stone, prying the eye open again. The word "pry" tells the reader that all of this is happening without the patient's consent, without her support.

Stanza eight describes the protagonist regaining consciousness. It is a painful experience, "the after-hell: I see the light." This would seem positive: the speaker has come through hell and back to the light, but as she regains her hearing she knows herself still to be the "old worrier" – nothing has fundamentally changed. A sip of water softens the hard flint of her lips, but the daylight to which she awakens is still the same. The metaphor of "grafters" is rich and complex. To "graft" is implant a shoot or bud into a growing plant. This suggests that being treated still makes the speaker feel like an inanimate object (a plant rather than a human being). In a medical context, to "graft" means to implant tissue surgically into a body to replace damaged tissue (a skin graft, for example). In this case, the 'damaged tissue' is psychological in nature: the "grafters" are preparing the electrodes for the ECT that the protagonist is to receive. Ironically (since they are treating her suicidal depression) they are "cheerful" which suggests at the least a lack of empathy. She returns to the image of herself as heated metal being hammered back into shape, but the word "delicate" is out of place since the "current agitates the wires / Volt upon volt." The reader understands that the current does not agitate the wires, it sends the protagonist's body into convulsions and it is *this* that agitates the wires. The procedure complete, she says, metaphorically, "Catgut stitches my fissures." The "fissures" are not physical, but the idea of physical healing returns us to the idea that she is there to be mended.

The hospital becomes a factory as the speaker reports that "A workman walks by carrying a pink torso." What is missing from this description is humanity: it is as though the man (presumably a doctor) is carrying part of a manikin; "hearts" are simply "spare parts," as though the speaker were describing a garage. She no longer feels (or smells) human: her legs and arms are like new tires on a car, "My swaddled legs and arms smell sweet as rubber." The next few lines are hyperbole – a fantasy of the all-powerful "city" able to cure every ill ("heads, or any limb ... hooks for hands ... eyes for others").

The speakers conflicted feelings about what has happened to her are brilliantly conveyed in the next four lines. "Love" is incongruously personified as an unattractive "bald nurse" and even more ominously as a "curse." The poem ends on an image of qualified hope for a future in which the protagonist is remade. She is the "vase, reconstructed" that contains "The elusive rose" which symbolizes the protagonist's vulnerable self. She is a finger bowl shaped by others, yet she is "a bowl for shadows" which represents her depression. Gill adds the interesting suggestion the "ten fingers" also symbolize "the writing self which seeks desperately to make something of this profound trauma (*"The Colossus* and *Crossing the Water"* in Gill Ed, *Companion* 101). This opens up an entirely new perspective: perhaps the city where men are mended represents poetry through which Plath sought to cure her own psychological wounds, in which case she (as writer) would be her own nurse and doctor. The two interpretations are not mutually exclusive.

The final two lines are similarly ambivalent about the process through which she has passed:

> My mendings itch. There is nothing to do.
> I shall be good as new.

The idea that the speaker is mending is positive, but she seems strangely detached from the healing process: it is still something that is being done *to* her. Critics have often commented on the weakness of the final line. If it is supposed to represent the views of the speaker then it seems terribly trite. I suggest, however, that it is more likely to represent the naïve optimism of the city where people are mended. In this interpretation, the protagonist remains consistently skeptical about the healing transformation through which she has been put.

Selected Poems by Sylvia Plath

THE BURNT-OUT SPA

In the fall of 1959, Sylvia Plath and Ted Hughes stayed for eleven weeks at a writers' retreat called Yaddo in Saratoga Springs, New York. In her *Journal* Plath records, "I wrote a good poem this week on our walk Sunday to the burnt-out spa." The spa in question was the Saratoga Sulphur and Mud Baths at Eureka Park, which advertised itself as, "Recommended and recognized by the medical profession as the most effective remedy known in the treatment of arthritis, lumbago, sciatica, and rheumatic disorders." It opened in 1928 and burnt to the ground on October 28th, 1958 (*Sylvia Plath Info Blog* by Peter K. Steinberg).

The poem has eight unrhymed four-line stanzas with a single-line stanza at the start and the end. The vocabulary is a little strained in places giving evidence that Plath had not yet cast aside her thesaurus.

1. The first five stanzas are an extended personification of the destroyed building as a dead man/beast. Trace the stages of the development of this image.
2. Explain the meaning of the paradox, "The small dell eats what ate it once."
3. Why do you think that the speaker is so firm in rejecting the idea that the woman she sees reflected in the stream "is not I"? Who are "the durable ones"?
4. Why do you think that the speaker concludes, "The stream that hustles us / Neither nourished nor heals"?

Plath seemed to be fascinated by ruins that gave evidence of former occupation – see, for example "Colossus" and "Wuthering Heights". The poem describes a building destroyed by fire and abandoned in contrast to the stream which flows past unchanged. The theme of mortality is introduced in the first line: the ruins of the buildings symbolize the very temporary nature of human achievement: the heat of the fire has melted the metal parts of the construction and blackened the surface of the burnt wooden structures. ("Karakul" is a type of wool clothing.) The vegetation of summers and falls has covered most of the "carcass" of the building, so that the speaker cannot estimate how long it has been since it was destroyed.

This huge beast, so apparently strong and invulnerable, is now overcome by "little weeds" and "crickets." Now, "The small dell eats what ate it once," meaning that nature is reclaiming this work of man. The speaker feels like "a doctor or / Archæologist" investigating the now defunct parts of a dead body or a dead civilization. In contrast, the spring (which was, of course, the reason the spa was built in the first place) still flows "clear as it ever did": it has survived the burning. The speaker's reference to "the ichor of the spring" is, however, ambiguous. In Greek mythology, Ichor is the ethereal golden fluid that flows in the veins of the gods, but in modern pathology it is a foul-smelling, blood-tinged watery discharge from a wound or ulcer. The former meaning is

43

consistent with the poem's presentation of the stream as a contrast with the spa: eternity contrasted with mortality. The latter meaning suggests that the stream is the still-bleeding wound of the great beast. The ambiguity is unresolved.

As she leans over the "Balustrade of a sag-backed bridge," the stream shows the speaker her own reflected image "one / Blue and improbable person." The woman's face is surrounded by cattails (tall marsh plants) – an idealized image of the speaker with which she cannot identify, "It is not I, it is not I." As Rosenblatt explains, "The narcissistic image below the water lives in a world of peace and harmony that the real self can never reach" (80). Time and mortality have nothing to do with this mystical place beneath the water. In the real world, "The stream that hustles us / Neither nourishes nor heals." For the speaker, the stream represents time hustling her toward the end of her life without offering any consolation.

Selected Poems by Sylvia Plath

YOU'RE

Written in January or February 1960, during Plath's first pregnancy, this poem is a string of loving, humorous, absurd descriptions of an unborn child which convey the sense of wonder and amazement the narrator feels at what is happening inside her body. The speaker also describes her hopes for her baby's life. It is written in two unrhymed nine-line stanzas.

1. What is being described in the first two and a half lines?
2. How does the unborn baby give a "thumbs-down on the Dodo's mode"?
3. What other images are used to describe the unborn baby? Which is your favorite and why?

The string of images begins with the description of the fetus as a tumbling clown. In its early stages, the fetus has gills, recapturing the entire span of evolution in its own development. The very existence of the baby is, "A common-sense / Thumbs-down on the dodo's mode." The dodo is, of course, the flightless bird native to the island of Mauritius which became extinct in the mid-seventeenth century. The fetus is a living embodiment of the life-force – the very opposite of the idea of extinction. The images, quite naturally, have roundness as a common element: coiled like a spool, round as a turnip.

The nine months that the baby would take to develop is described in "from the Fourth of July to All Fools' Day" (April 1). The protagonist addresses the fetus as "high-riser, my little loaf," a humorous reference to the colloquial English expression "having a bun in the oven" meaning to be pregnant. Her use of the phrase also conveys the speaker's high hopes for the child's future. The fetus is "our travelled prawn," a reference to the appearance of a fetus in the early stages of its development and to all the places to which the unborn child has already travelled inside the mother. Similar comparisons are made: "bud … sprat …eels … Mexican bean." The image of the expected child as "Bent-backed Atlas," however, again conveys the strength of the life in the fetus since Atlas was the God who held up the skies/heavens (not the globe – a common misconception). There is also a paradox in the description of the fetus as, "Vague as fog and looked for like mail. / Farther off than Australia." The speaker waits for the delivery of the baby as someone anxiously looks for the postman delivering the mail, and yet the fetus is still "vague" and distant – no ultrasound images in those days! There follow a number of comparisons of the fetus with nature:

> Snug as a bud and at home
> Like a sprat in a pickle jug.
> A creel of eels, all ripples.
> Jumpy as a Mexican bean.

So often in Plath's poetry nature seems to be inimical to life, but here the fetus takes its place amongst small, rounded life forms.

45

The conclusion of the poem is uncharacteristically positive: the baby represents a completely new start. The speaker takes delight in her baby being, "Right, like a well-done sum." There is a sense of personal achievement in that statement. The baby will have its own identity, and will be free to write its own story' starting with "a clean slate." The speaker's excitement and pride are evident. One has to almost strain to find any undercutting of the poems sheer joy. Perhaps it is evident in the alienation between mother and baby implied in "Farther off than Australia," or perhaps in the image of the "sprat in a pickle jug" which describes the small fish picked in a glass jar in a way that recalls fetuses preserved in formaldehyde.

FACE LIFT

Plath's friend Dido Merwin had a cosmetic operation that inspired this poem in which Plath explores the theme of rebirth. Dyne comments that "Plath regarded [her friend's face life] as a pathetic effort to remain sexually attractive to her husband, the act itself a concession of defeat" (88).

The first three lines describe the speaker meeting her friend after the plastic surgery with the good news that the operation has restored her young face. In fact, so pleased is the older friend with what has been achieved that she dramatically whips off her concealing silk scarf to reveal her face still swathed in bandages (like a mummy, the speaker thinks) and assure her friend, "I'm all right."

The poem is written in four unrhymed stanzas with varying line lengths.

1. How is the voice of the poem different in the first three lines as compared with the rest of the poem?
2. Why is the image of "mummy-cloths" particularly well chosen given the themes of the poem?
3. How is the friend's first experience of anesthetic made to appear unattractive?
4. How is the friend's more recent experience of anesthetic made to appear pleasant?
5. Explain the image in the line, "Tapped like a cask, the years draining into my pillow."
6. Why is the poodle "dead"?
7. How does the friend now regard the older self which she has cast off? (Examine particularly the section, "Now she's done for ... her thin hair.")
8. In what sense is the friend "mother to myself"? Do you share the friend's unqualified self-satisfaction?

In her earlier poems (e.g. "Spinster"), Plath writes of her protagonists in the third person, but increasingly she gives them first person speech (e.g. "The Colossus"). This poem is something of a hybrid since it begins with one speaker but quickly transitions to the words of the speaker's friend. On line four, the "I" changes to the older friend who recounts her experiences of recent surgery. She begins with a horrendous experience at age nine when the anesthetic was probably nitrous oxide (laughing gas). The memory of the sweet banana taste lingers, as does the rubber mask being placed on her face, the immediate desire to vomit, and the god-like voices of the surgeons as she went under. As she awoke, her mother's face "swam up" into her vision and she was sick into a basin, "O I was sick." (Anyone who went to a dentist before they started using novocain (procaine hydrochloride), will know exactly how the she felt!)

47

Decades later, the second speaker assures her friend that "They've changed all that." The process of being taken to the operating theater and put to sleep is described as relaxing and human. She feels like Cleopatra – a classical image of female beauty. The surgeon is not a "Jove" but a "kind man" to whom she can relate and who conducts her through the transition into unconsciousness which has none of the negative aspects of her childhood experience.

Post-operation the speaker still feels special, like wine or whiskey maturing in a cask. The difference is that during this process, she is getting younger: the years drain away; the old skin "peels away easy as paper" leaving new skin; "I grow backward. I'm twenty." Going through this process of regaining a new physical body, she remembers feels herself to be twenty again, living with her first husband, stroking a poodle that is long dead. All of this is achieved without anyone knowing, "Even my best friend thinks I'm in the country."

Evidently, the aging process transformed the speaker into another person entirely, one whom she does not recognize or accept as herself, but now the transformation is complete: the "dewlapped lady" whom she was, is dead ("done for"). The lined face that she had watched develop year by year in her mirror so that it looked like a wrinkled "Old sock-face, sagged on a darning egg," has been trapped by the doctors and put away "in some laboratory jar." The speaker feels no affection for her former self: she totally dissociates herself from the old woman, "Nodding and rocking and fingering her thin hair." She *is* someone else.

The speaker has achieved the impossible: she has become "Mother to myself." If the reader finds this an unsettling image (because the idea of the woman as both creator of life and created seems paradoxical), it does not do so to the second speaker who is delighted. Exactly like the mother of the fetus in "You're," she regards herself as a clean slate (or in her case a freshly wiped blackboard), ready to begin life again, her gauze bandages like the swaddling clothes of a new baby. The split between the former and the new self is complete and absolute.

The original speaker does not reappear, so the last word is left with the older friend. Nevertheless, the poem raises questions about whether identity *is* only skin deep. The friend "dissociates herself from her body in order to control it" (Dyne 89). This is the first appearance in Plath's poetry of the reincarnation image that would be so common in her later poems. To what extent is it possible, or even desirable, to recreate oneself? That is a question with which Plath would grapple in her poetry for the rest of her too-short life.

Selected Poems by Sylvia Plath

MORNING SONG

Plath wrote this poem in February 1961 after she had given birth to her daughter, Frieda. Throughout the poem, the speaker addresses her child. The result is a delightfully simple poem describing, and celebrating, a woman gradually forming an emotional bond with her newborn baby. The birth of a child not only brings a new being into the world, it also changes the being of the mother who now has new responsibilities, obligations and priorities. This lyric is structured in six three-line stanzas (tercets) with no formal rhyme scheme.

1. In what ways is the image in the opening line appropriate to describe the origin of a baby's life?
2. What does the speaker mean by "your nakedness / shadows our safety"?
3. Try to explain the image in stanza 3.
4. How appropriate are the animal images in stanza 5?
5. What is the effect of the image on the last line of the poem?

Most commentators seem to agree that "mother love is strangely absent in the beginning of the poem"; that the mother begins by expressing "a strange alienation" from her child; that "One striking surreal image that somehow supports the 'thingness' of the baby is that of its cry as 'bald'"; and that the watch simile, which compares the animate child to an inanimate, mechanical object establishes "the great distance between the act of love and the fact of the baby" ("Morning Song by Sylvia Plath: Critical Analysis"). It may be so, but this is not quite how I read the opening stanza. It is important to remember that line one, though it is addressed to the child, refers not to a child but to the moment of conception, which is an act of "Love" – significantly the first word of the poem. The simile of the "fat gold watch" is certainly mechanical, but this aspect of the image refers, I think, not to the fetus but to the timeline of pregnancy: from the moment of conception, the clock of birth was ticking, and the act of love will be separated from the birth by nine months. The roundness of the "fat" watch (Plath has in mind a pocket watch presumably on a chain which would be the umbilical cord), its value, its color, and its purity all seem appropriate to show how the speaker values the pregnancy. The simile does, however, recognize the independent being of the fetus: from the moment of conception (winding the watch), the fetus is, in some sense, itself, a part neither of its mother nor father.

The next two lines fast forward to the moment of birth (which seems to have occurred at home rather than in a hospital, which was pretty common at that time). The speaker certainly emphasizes the independent existence of the newborn baby whose cry assertively, as though by right, takes its place "among the elements." Again, some might feel that this does not reflect maternal bonding, that the mother is more of a detached observer at the event. That is

49

not, however, how the lines strike me: to me they suggest loving respect for the independent being to whom she has given birth: it takes its rightful place as an integral part of the world.

Stanza two continues the description of the reaction of those present at the birth (presumably both parents and a midwife). Their voices give added significance to the arrival of the baby who is compared to a "New statue. / In a drafty museum." The child takes its place in the world, but the world "drafty" suggests threats to its "nakedness." Instinctively, the baby needs its parents for protection ("Shadows our safety"), and their former "safety" is now threatened to some extent by their obligation to look after this delicate, vulnerable being. The parents' lives will never be the same. As this realization sinks in, the mother and father "stand round blankly as walls." They are the walls that keep the baby safe (by preventing the ceiling from falling in), but for the moment they seem to be in shock. Here the reader *does* sense that the new mother finds it difficult to bond with this life which she has produced: she is an observer of the baby to which she feels no emotional attachment. Lane comments, "This wary disenfranchisement echoes through the extended comparison of the very slow third stanza, leaving the mother to watch, in the mirror of her infant, the diminishment of her own vitality for the increase of its" (Lane Ed. 134). This feeling continues in the hours after delivery. The speaker asserts that she does not feel herself to be the baby's mother any more "Than the cloud that distills a mirror to reflect its own slow / Effacement at the wind's hand." This is a complex simile: the cloud produces raindrops to reflect its own obliteration by the wind. On the one hand, this image establishes the baby as part of the natural world, something phenomenal (in every sense of the world). On the other hand, the idea of the "Effacement" of the cloud in the act of producing rain conveys the speaker's fear that in giving birth she will lose her sense of her own identity because she will have some new form (no longer simply 'wife', but 'wife and mother') imposed upon her.

During the first night of the baby's life, the speaker listens to her child's delicate breathing. (Contrary to some commentators, I assume that the mother is at home because you do not get to wear a "Victorian nightgown" in hospital and that she is in the same room as the baby.) The breathing she describes in a metaphor, "your moth-breath / Flickers among the flat pink roses." Some may see this as a visual image (in which case it is an example of synaesthesia, that is, an image in which a thing, here breathing, is described in terms of a sense other than the obvious one, here visually rather than by sound). Personally, I think that you can hear moths flying, particularly if they are doing so near flowers (I take the roses to be in a jar, the gift of a proud husband). Either way, the comparison suggests at once the delicacy and vulnerability of this new life which seems to prompt maternal feeling for the speaker wakes to listen. What she hears is "A far sea [that] moves in my ear." This is another elemental image that associates the baby with vast natural forces which exist quite independent of the mother.

However, it takes only the baby's first cry for the mother to react instinctively and to get up to breastfeed. She stumbles, which is inelegant, and feels "cow-heavy" with milk, which describes part of how her being has physically and emotionally changed. She still seems uncomfortable in her new role; however, she perceives the baby's mouth as "clean as a cat's" as it in turn instinctively opens to suck. The baby is no longer a "statue"; it is animate.

Dawn coming through the window pane, "Whitens and swallows its dull stars," indicating that the world is suddenly less threatening. This is a new beginning to life *for the speaker*. The humanization of the baby is complete as it sings its morning song using its "handful of notes." This is very different from the "bald cry" at birth which was primal and impersonal; the word "song" suggests the structure and order of poetry. This is the beginning of language: the baby is no longer a cat; it is human. Its "clear vowels rise like balloons," a simile which reflects the speaker's newly discovered joy in motherhood, her high hopes for her baby, and for her relationship with her baby. Middlebrook concludes, "By the end of the poem ... the child begins to acquire language ... For the mother, the infant has ascended from mere animate existence into human being she can recognize – whom she can love. Now she becomes a mother" (Gill Ed. *Companion* 162). The balloons are a celebration.

… A Study Guide

TULIPS

A recording of Plath reading this poem is on YouTube.

Dated 18th March, 1961, this is a poem based on Plath's experiences as a patient after being recently hospitalized. In January, she had suffered a miscarriage and shortly afterwards had been readmitted for an appendectomy. Following Ted Hughes, most critics take this poem to mark a radical change in Plath's poetry, the beginning of her mature phase. Hughes writes, "She wrote this poem without her usual studies over the Thesaurus, and at top speed, as one might write an urgent letter. From then on, all her poems were written in this way" (quoted in Lane Ed. *New Views* 129).

The situation is that the protagonist has been wheeled into surgery, given anesthetic, and returned unconscious to her bed in the ward where she slowly regains consciousness. She has given herself up to the doctors; her fate is entirely in their hands. In this world of whiteness and motionlessness, the red tulips sent by her husband are an intrusion, symbols of the life of activity that exists outside. Like the photographs of her husband and children, the flowers disturb the speaker because they are trying to pull her back to her 'normal' life, away from the peace of the hospital. Dickie writes, "'Tulips' is not a cheerful poem, but it does move from cold to warmth, from numbness to love, from empty whiteness to vivid redness, in a process manipulated by the associative imagination. The speaker herself seems surprised by her own gifts and ends the poem on a tentative note, moving toward the far-away country of health." Rosenblatt argues even more strongly that the poem illustrates the full cycle of ritual transformation that Plath envisaged by describing "entry into darkness, ritual death, and rebirth" (27). He explains, "On the one hand, Plath seeks her own death because life appears unbearable, guilt-ridden, and worthless; on the other hand, she seeks death because it gives her new life by releasing the reservoir of love that will refresh the self" (29). As always, I would dispute that the speaker should be identified as "Plath."

The poem is written in nine seven-line stanzas each of which is made separate by end-stopping on the final line so that each forms a unit.

Stanzas 1 - 3

1. Although the speaker seems to be enjoying the "peacefulness" which she has learned in hospital, certain words, phrases and images draw the reader's attention to the inherent dangers of such an existence. Make a list of these and add comments as necessary.
2. What two kinds of "baggage" does the speaker reject in stanza 3?

Selected Poems by Sylvia Plath

Stanzas 4 - 6

3. What images are used in stanza 4 to describe the process by which the speaker has been stripped of all of the different aspects of her life? What is the significance of the image of drowning which is used?

4. Once again, in stanza 5, an approving description by the speaker is actually given rather ominous overtones by the poet. Where?

5. Why are the tulips like a "baby"? Why does the speaker think of them as like an "*awful* baby"?

6. Explain, "Their redness talks to my wound, it corresponds."

7. The last three lines of stanza 6 return to the image of drowning. Comment on this in the light of the previous drowning image.

Stanzas 7 - 9

8. In stanza 7, the tulips finally force the speaker to review the state into which she has fallen under the influence of the hospital. What change of attitude is clear?

9. By the end of the poem, what effect have the tulips had upon the speaker?

In the first stanza, the speaker of this monologue expresses how much she appreciates the calm world of the hospital. She has entered an alternative state of consciousness such as might result through meditation:

> I am learning peacefulness, lying by myself
> quietly
> As the light lies on these white walls, this bed,
> these hands.
> … I have nothing to do with explosions.

These lines are entirely positive: the speaker is at one with her environment, at one with the light that streams through the windows. The problem is that this peace has been brought at the price of relinquishing her very identity so that she is "nobody." She is now entirely defined by her role as a passive patient who has "given … [her] body to surgeons" to do with as they see fit. She has relinquished agency (self-determination) in a place which suggests not life and health but death. The whiteness of everything carries connotations of bloodlessness (an implicit contrast with the tulips which bring color – though we do not as yet know *what* color). The imagery of winter also suggests death: everything is "snowed-in" and thus cut off from the outside world, the world from which the speaker has come, where she does have an identity and relationships – a life. The tulips remind her of all that she has given up, and this disturbs her.

The protagonist is fresh out of surgery. Her head has been arranged in a position on the pillow that she never attempts to change; she views the ward as a camera would, static and receptive, "Stupid pupil, it has to take everything

53

in." One gets the impression that, if she could, the speaker would simply close her eyes again and cut herself off entirely from the world outside her mind. The renunciation of her own identity leads the speaker to depersonalize others. The nurses in their uniforms are all alike, indistinguishable members of a flock of gulls flying inland. Since one is indistinguishable from another, "it is impossible to tell how many there are." The nurses make no demands on her, so "they are no trouble."

    The third stanza contrasts the dehumanizing effect of the hospital with the human demands placed upon the reluctant protagonist by the outside world. The nurses treat her like an inanimate object, a pebble. They have no more human relationship with her than water has with the pebbles over which it "must run," but the effect is "smoothing" as is that of the painkillers administered by "bright needles" that bring sleep. All of this the speaker finds liberating: she is free of the "baggage" of her life – the literal baggage of her "overnight case" and the psychological baggage of her husband and child who smile at her, and by doing so claim an emotional connection with her. [Merriam-Webster defines 'baggage' as meaning "intangible things (as feelings, circumstances, or beliefs) that get in the way" as in "emotional baggage."] The speaker uses a simile which often occurs in Plath's poems, "Their smiles catch onto my skin, little smiling hooks." The hooks are not only painful, unlike the hypodermic needles, but they also seek to drag the protagonist back into the psychologically demanding real world unlike the anesthetics which allow her to slip away from it.

    The fourth stanza is an extended metaphor in which the speaker compares herself to "a thirty-year-old cargo boat" slowly slipping under the water. There is a play on words in the line, "They have swabbed me clear of my loving associations." Doctors use a small piece of absorbent material for cleansing the surface of a wound, while sailors swab the decks of a ship. At the moment she was rolled into surgery ("Scared and bare on the green plastic-pillowed trolley"), the speaker 'saw' her life recede from her in all of its material triviality as she went under the anesthetic ("the water went over my head"). Coming into the hospital is, for the protagonist, like taking vows as a nun: it means leaving behind family and "loving associations." Nuns also take a vow of chastity, and this is what the speaker refers to when she says, "I have never been so pure." (Compare the opening line of "The Munich Mannequins", "Perfection is terrible, it cannot have children.") Self-contained and self-sufficient, she feels that she has recaptured her identity, her true sense of self.

    The next stanza has an interesting change of verb tense. The speaker says, "I only wanted / To lie." It seems that the tulips have already been successful in disrupting the freedom and peace of the hospital ward which appears already to be a kind of paradise lost which she describes as a kind of Zen state:

        How free it is, you have no idea how free –

Selected Poems by Sylvia Plath

> The peacefulness is so big it dazes you,
> And it asks nothing, a name tag, a few trinkets.

The verb "dazes" is the only negative note implying that the state the persona so loves is an illusion. The closing image is deeply ambiguous:

> It is what the dead close on, finally; I imagine them
> Shutting their mouths on it, like a Communion tablet.

The speaker is beginning to see the ultimate cost of the withdrawal from life which she has found so seductively attractive. While the "Communion tablet" is seen by believers as a guarantee of eternal life, taking the "tablet" of freedom is evidently a way to eternal death (or at the very least to a form of death-in-life).

In contrast with the dead state of the "white" hospital and the near-death state of the protagonist, the tulips are annoyingly alive: their "too red" color suggests blood; they "breathe"; they have "sudden tongues" and "talk to my wound," which presumably means that they encourage healing. The red of the tulips "corresponds" with her wound, a playful pun since the word means both 'communicates with' and 'marches, shows a similarity with.' In the second sense, the speaker is suggesting that a form of sympathetic magic is going on by which the life-force of the flowers is transferring to herself. (The concept of sympathetic magic comes up in several Plath poems.) In an ambiguous simile, the speaker describes "their white swaddlings [the paper in which the tulips are wrapped], like an awful baby." Thus, the tulips represent rebirth, but it is an unwanted, disturbing rebirth, a constantly crying baby demanding attention. Ironically (given that the speaker has just described herself as a "thirty-year-old cargo boat" sinking), now it is the tulips that weigh her down – literally bringing her back down to earth. She uses the metaphor of "A dozen red lead sinkers round my neck," a reference to the lead weights that fishermen use to keep their line and hook submerged. It is the new self, the self created through drowning, that is in danger of being hooked and hauled back to the surface by the tulips.

The speaker complains that whereas previously no one watched her, now the tulips watch her. Under their influence, however, the protagonist now watches herself in the reflection of the window, and what she sees is shocking, "I see myself, flat, ridiculous, a cut-paper shadow." This marks a moment of epiphany: the speaker understands that she has reduced herself to a two-dimensional paper cut-out of a person who has no identity ("no face"). Notice the tense of her statement "I have wanted to efface myself" (technically the present perfect tense which indicates that an action has recently been completed), for she no longer wants that. Having been woken to life by the tulips, the protagonist sees them as rivals in living, "The vivid tulips eat my oxygen." It is the most life-affirming statement in the poem so far.

The penultimate stanza speaks of the atmosphere of the hospital that was described at the start of the poem as a thing of the past: the tulips have shattered it with their "loud noise." The protagonist no longer sees herself as a stone being smoothed by flowing waters but as "a sunken rust-red engine" being stirred back to life by the "snags and eddies" of the river water. Finally, she abandons metaphor, to explain in simple terms the impact that the tulips have had on her:

> They concentrate my attention, that was happy
> Playing and resting without committing itself.

Notice the unequivocal past tense.

The final stanza pays tribute to the power of the tulips which have warmed even the walls of the ward – though what is actually happening is that the protagonist's medication is wearing off. The similes of the tulips as "like dangerous animals / ... opening like the mouth of some great African cat" are comic hyperbole. The images point to the tulips as killers, but what they have killed was the withdrawal from life that threatened the protagonist:

> And I am aware of my heart: it opens and closes
> Its bowl of red blooms out of sheer love of me.

These lines capture the moment of self-awareness as the speaker becomes conscious of the beating of her own heart. The opening of the heart muscle is like the blooming of the tulips: both her heart and the tulips love her – and, for the first time, she seems to consider herself worthy of that love. The "I" who narrates the poem has *become* the tulips and the tulips have *become* her heart; there *is* only the red of living organisms. The poem closes on an image of the submerged protagonist resurfacing:

> The water I taste is warm and salt, like the sea,
> And comes from a country far away as health.

Far from having drowned, the protagonist reemerges from the sea. She is still far from well, but she has resumed the journey to health; she has reengaged with the world. Yet those last two lines are deeply ambiguous since not only is health still so far away, but she associates it with the sea. It seems that at least part of her consciousness would echo the lines of John Keats:

> Darkling I listen; and, for many a time
> I have been half in love with easeful Death,
> Call'd him soft names in many a musèd rhyme,
> To take into the air my quiet breath;
> Now more than ever seems it rich to die,
> To cease upon the midnight with no pain,
> ("Ode to a Nightingale" lines 51-56).

Selected Poems by Sylvia Plath

INSOMNIAC

The poem is written in the omniscient third person and is about a man, two techniques that separate the poet from the protagonist. It is written in five unrhymed stanzas each of seven lines. Each stanza ends in a period which means that each forms a separate unit.

1. What image is used in the first four lines of stanza one to describe the night sky?
2. What image is used in the last two lines of stanza one to describe sleeplessness?
3. In stanza 2 the poem describes the waking thoughts of the insomniac. What is their nature and what images are used to describe them?
4. What does the poem mean by describing the experience which the sleeping pills used to give the insomniac as, "A life baptized in no-like for a while"?
5. The final stanza contains two extended images of the man's suffering. What do you think they mean?

The narrator describes the sky as "only a sort of carbon paper / Blueblack, with the much-poked periods of stars / Letting in the light." (Carbon paper was inked on one side and was used for making copies when typing. The period key, being sharp, could penetrate the carbon paper, leaving a tiny circular hole.) This metaphor implies that the night is simply a time when the protagonist experiences copies of what has happened in his past. The light peeping out from behind the sky is "bonewhite ... like death," a simile that suggests that the man's restlessness is so unbearable that he longs for the ultimate relief, the slumber of death, which is, after all, the ultimate reality. The "eyes" of the stars appear to watch his suffering like voyeurs, while the moon's "rictus" is a fake, mocking grin. The man's insomnia is a "desert pillow" and his sleeplessness a "Stretching of fine, irritating sand in all directions." There is no physical position in which he can get comfortable. The imagery of the desert suggests not only discomfort but also barrenness. There is also a pun on 'deserted', for the insomniac is alone in his interminable hours of unbearable torment.

Lying awake, the man is helpless as painful memories run through his mind like a "granular" film running raspingly through a projector. It is not that the man is consciously thinking; it is that he is at the mercy of his memories as they recur, "Over and over." Nor is there anything particularly terrible or unusual in these memories: the dull days of childhood ("mizzling" means drizzling, fine steady rain); the wet dreams of his teens; physically looking up at his parents, who appeared as inhuman "faces on tall stalks, alternately stern and tearful"; and crying in the "buggy" rose garden. Since roses are associated with romance, this detail may suggest a failed love affair, but frankly it could be anything that shows the corruption beneath a façade of beauty. His brow is made "bumpy as a sack of rocks" by his teenage acne (most readers will

57

identify with this) and also by the number of memories cramming into his head. The image of rocks suggests that they weight him down. The memories that "jostle each other" to get into his consciousness are compared in a simile to "obsolete film stars," an image that suggests the man's mind is a tumult of memories competing for recognition – memories that should have been forgotten like old movie stars. No meaning emerges, no understanding of the problems of the man's earlier life: things that should have been forgotten simply keep him awake night after night.

We learn that the man used to find relief in pills: 'uppers' once "lit the tedium of the protracted evening," while sleeping pills brought him, "A life baptized in no-life for a while." The oxymoron here points to the unnatural and self-defeating nature of the pills. The natural function of sleep, the narrator implies, is a *real* baptism – a washing away of the troubles and worries of the day so that the sleeper wakes purified and new ready to begin life again. The pills he took offered a temporary respite, but no more. The influence that the "sugary" pills had is compared in a metaphor to that of the planets in a person's horoscope, the alignment of which is supposed to influence one's future. The "sweet" pills had the effect of returning him to the infant state so that he experienced the "drugged waking of a forgetful baby," another image which suggest the unnatural and self-defeating nature of the pills. Now, however, even this respite is not available to the man because he has become immune to the drugs which "are worn-out and silly, like classical gods."

The insomniac's head is described as "a little interior of grey mirrors" a metaphor which calls to mind a hall of mirrors at a fun fair – mirrors which distort images sometimes grotesquely. It seems that this man experiences life only as a series of visual images which are reflected in his mind until they finally drain "like water out the hole at the far end" without him having gained any sense of meaning or "significance" from them. The reflecting mirrors are "grey" suggesting that the man's life is tedious and depressing. Because he cannot sleep, he cannot shut out the images: it is as though his eyes are always open, for the images come even when they are closed. Thus, he appears to live in "a lidless room" with nowhere to hide. It is as though his eyelids are forced open by the continuous flickering of the memory-movies projected onto his mind.

One would think that the coming of morning might bring the insomniac some relief, for the internal agony of his mind has been exacerbated by the howling of cats outside in the yard. The outside world is, however, a harsh place ("granite") and day only makes his condition worse. The growing daylight of dawn is "his white disease" for his life is simply repetitious trivia. The city comes alive with birdsong, but for the man, "The city is a map of cheerful twitters now." This description involves an oxymoron because the song of the birds is both cheerful and meaningless ("twitters"). Nor does it appear that the other people in the world fare better than the insomniac, for they go unthinkingly to work in regimented rows. They are, however, the very opposite of the insomniac, whose brain is over-stuffed with images, for they take in nothing: their eyes are "blank." Sleep has washed out *everything* from their brains so they are ready to start the day anew as they are every day, but because of this they do not learn; they do not develop; their lives are meaningless. Plath's vision of urban life in the final stanza owes a great deal to the early poetry of T. S. Eliot in *The Love Song of J. Alfred Prufrock* [1917] and *The Waste Land* [1922]. Compare:

> Unreal City,
> Under the brown fog of a winter dawn,
> A crowd flowed over London Bridge, so many,
> I had not thought death had undone so many.
> Sighs, short and infrequent, were exhaled,
> And each man fixed his eyes before his feet.
> (*The Waste Land* lines 60-65)

Perhaps the insomniac symbolizes the tortured artist, set apart from others because he perceives life more deeply and lives a prisoner to his own thoughts.

WUTHERING HEIGHTS

The title of this poem suggests that the speaker is walking on the bleak and cold Yorkshire Moors up to the ruined farmhouse which was the setting for Emily Bronte's novel *Wuthering Heights*. (In reality, the house is called Top Withens, and on the morning in late October when I visited it I think I was colder than at any other time in my life!) Plath visited the location with her husband Ted Hughes who also wrote a poem with the same title. The two poems are, however, very different and you might find it interesting to compare and contrast them. As Britzolakis explains, in Plath's poem, "The natural world appears to the speaker as an actively hostile force threatening her with extinction; all of its elements seek to reduce her to their common denominator …" (Bloom Ed. *Views* 118).

Wuthering Heights is written in five nine-line stanzas which have no rhyme or fixed meter.

Stanza one:

1. The simile "ring me like faggots" compares the speaker to a witch being burned for heresy. (Compare "Faggot-bearing jack" from the poem "Maudlin".) This immediately tells us a lot about how she is feeling about herself. Make a list of words and phrases which come to mind to describe her feelings.
2. Actually, Plath was not alone when she visited Wuthering Heights – she was with her husband Ted Hughes. How does that information add to the impression you have of the speaker? [This does *not* imply that Plath and the speaker are the same.]
3. This stanza describes an experience which everyone who has walked in hilly country will recall. What happens to the seemingly firm lines of the horizon as you walk on? How is this described in the poem? Comment particularly on the simile "dissolve / Like a series of promises."
4. The one positive in the entire stanza is the hope that "Touched by a match, they [the faggots] might warm me," and that the lighted faggots might 'pin' the constantly-moving horizon. Lighting the faggots would, of course, be a human action. It would prove that the speaker was not alone in the world. On the other hand, …?

Stanza two:

5. The speaker stresses how out of place she is in this environment. The enemy of life is the cold wind. Which lines imply that the wind is deliberately attacking the speaker? Why is this?

Selected Poems by Sylvia Plath

Stanza three:

6. The speaker is intimidated by the sheep because (unlike her) they are at home in this environment. When the sheep look at her directly, she writes, "It is like being mailed into space, / A thin, silly message." What is she feeling? Why

7. The sheep are said to "stand about in grandmotherly disguise, / All wig curls and yellow teeth." This is a reference to the disguise used by the wolf in *Little Red Riding Hood*. What does the reference to this fairy tale add to the picture you are building of the speaker's psychological condition?

Stanza four:

8. The speaker comes to an abandoned and ruined building. What is left and what is not left of the farmhouse? Why does the speaker find what she sees so threatening?

9. The end of the stanza perhaps contains a reference to the novel *Wuthering Heights* in which the spirit of Cathy cries out to be readmitted to the house. Now, however, the only sound of the wind is "a few odd syllables, / It rehearses them moaningly: / Black stone, black stone." What connotations do the last four words carry for you?

Stanza five:

10. What comparison is suggested by the metaphor, "The grass is beating its head distractedly"?

11. The poem ends with a paradox, "Now, in valleys narrow / And black as purses, the house lights / Gleam like small change." The only light (and by implication warmth) lies where? But the light turns out to be only "small change." What does this add to your understanding of what the speaker feels about herself in relation to society?

  The opening image conveys the speaker's feeling of entrapment. The perception of landscape is entirely egocentric: the speaker describes the horizons as ringing her and eluding her like false promises. The metaphor of being ringed by unevenly piled "faggots" recalls images of witches being burned at the stake in the Middle Ages. There may also be an oblique reference to the wedding ring that Plath wears, the symbol of a relationship which hems her in and seeks to define and limit her. (Again, this is not to say that Plath *is* the persona, only that the poet uses elements of her own feelings in constructing that persona.) The references to color, "orange ... a soldier color [red]," suggest that the sun is going down imparting its color to the horizons. The essence of the speaker's problem seems to be that, though she feels trapped, she cannot come to terms with that which traps her. If the faggots were set on fire, "Touched by a match, they might warm me." I take this to mean that in confrontation, she would rebel and come to life. The horizons are, however,

61

less solid as the observer walks, for the line of each rise vanishes as she approaches it to be replaced by a further horizon behind (a phenomenon which any reader who has hiked in hilly country will recognize). The speaker feels let down, cheated, as though "a series of promises" made to her have been broken.

The second stanza appears to escape egocentricity by turning its attention to a precise description of life in these high moors where no animal or vegetable life exists "higher than the grasstops / Or the hearts of sheep," where there are no trees, and where the prevailing wind bends "Everything in one direction." (Anyone who has been on high moors above the tree line will recognize the accuracy of this observation.) By the fifth line, however, the speaker personalizes her description. She has a paranoid sense that the wind is hostile to *her*, is trying to rob *her* of life ("funnel my heat away"). On the literal level, the speaker may be aware of the possible onset of hypothermia, but symbolically she seems to think that the whole of nature is conspiring against her. If she stoops down to examine the heather, she feels that she may never rise again so that her bones will "whiten … among them."

In stanza three, the speaker turns her attention to the sheep which are closely observed and accurately described with some humor. Their fleeces are "dirty wool-clouds," and with their "wig curls and yellow teeth" they seem to be disguised as grandmothers. The difference between the speaker and the sheep is that the latter are at home in this environment because they lack critical consciousness. Thus, the "black slots of their pupils" take in every image (including that of the speaker) without actually processing it. The effect, she says "is like being mailed into space, / A thin, silly message." The blackness behind the sheep's eyes is infinite, and it robs her of any feeling of significance. They have no language, only "hard, marbly baas" – another indication of meaninglessness.

Stanza four describes a ruined farmhouse (perhaps the very one that Emily Brontë had in mind when she wrote her novel). Evidently, the vast expanses of primal nature are more powerful than all the achievements of society Very little is left of the people who once inhabited the ruined building: the doorsteps, hollowed by generations of passing feet, now lead from grass to grass, for nature has reclaimed the habitation, and the lintels and sills of doors and windows are "unhinged." Only the air, "Remembers a few odd syllables" spoken by the vanished people and repeats them in a form of lamentation, "Black stone, black stone." The stone will always outlive man who has little lasting effect on the landscape: his ultimate memorial will be a headstone in a graveyard. The water (either in the wheel ruts or perhaps from a stream) runs "Limpid," that is, 'crystal clear.' The speaker imagines it running through her hands "the solitudes / That flee through my fingers." Once again, the simile implies that the speaker can grasp no sense from her existence, make no meaning of it.

In the final stanza, the speaker is more confident and more assertive. The sky leaning on her describes the gathering darkness, an oppressive nature determined to crush her because she is "the one upright / Among the horizontals." The grass appears to be "beating its head distractedly" as though insane – terrified by the on-coming darkness. The new-found confidence of the speaker is shown by the fact that the first person occurs only on the first line of the stanza ("me"); the rest of the stanza describes the scene around her without the egocentric reference to self found throughout the rest of the poem. For the first time, an alternative to the hard life of the moors is acknowledged as the speaker sees the lights going on in the valleys below her, which represents the social world. There is no indication at all that she will go to these valleys and join in this life for though its gleaming lights are an attractive alternative to the oppressive, terrifying darkness, they only amount to "small change" (i.e., a handful of gleaming coins). There may be an oblique reference in the description of dark valleys and purses to a woman's sexual organs: the world of people is also the world of love and sex and procreation. The life of conventional society appears, however, to offer nothing of real value; better to stand in opposition to the crushing forces of nature. She chooses the solitude of the artist. Kendall captures the essence of the poem when he writes, "Plath's location of human consciousness as an intruder amidst a brutally indifferent nature … is exactly the measure of her achievement. Plath's personas are courageous pioneers, confronting landscapes … attempting to assimilate these resistant environments" (42).

Schwartz and Bollas point out that this vision of the world is a characteristic of Plath's poetry from this point on, "[The] landscape we experience in *Ariel* is almost without exception terrifying and so loaded with psychotic content as to obliterate the possibility of a supportive structure of external reality. Plath created in her poetry a world in which she could no longer find the possibility of survival" (Lane Ed. *New Views* 181).

BLACKBERRYING

Written October 1961, after Plath and Hughes returned to England from America, the poem was not published until the posthumous collection of poems *Crossing the Water* (1971). A letter to her mother (November 1961) confirms that this poem is based on "the day we all went blackberrying together down the land that sloped to the sea." The obvious difference is that the protagonist is alone. Axelrod offers the following helpful overview of the poem, "[A] walk in the country becomes an occasion for the speaker's numbed encounter with the void … The speaker's interior pain becomes evident through her paranoid relations with a natural scene that is aggressive and ugly in almost every detail … The sea towards which she wanders is not beautiful, comforting or transcendent but 'heaving', making an incomprehensible noise. This uncanny world of sights and sounds becomes a specular [i.e., having the reflective properties of a mirror] image of the subject's own loneliness … anger … and despair …" (Gill Ed. *Companion* 80-81).

In this poem, Plath abandons traditional stanza form and rhyme scheme. Her free verse gives the impression of conversation. The three nine-line stanzas use repeated end words, widely separated rhymes, half (or slant) rhymes and internal rhymes. Each stanza ends in a period making it a separate unit.

1. Draw and annotate a sketch map of the setting of the poem on which you chart the speaker's movements.
2. What does the speaker mean by the "blood sisterhood" that she feels she shares with the blackberries?
3. What references to death do you find in the second stanza?
4. What does the sea symbolize in the poem? How do you know?

The speaker is alone in a country lane picking blackberries which she places in a milk bottle. The tone is joyous: she revels in being alone with nothing but the blackberries. These she personifies: they "squander" their "blue-red juices" (symbolic blood) on her fingers as she picks them. The alliteration of the 'b' sound in lines that suggest the closeness of picker and fruit is playful, "*B*lackberries / *B*ig as the *b*all of my thumb." She seems pleased, even honored, by their friendship saying, "I had not asked for such a blood sisterhood; they must love me." A sign of their supposed love is how they "accommodate themselves" to the shape of the milk bottle into which the speaker puts them: she relishes the experience of harvesting the blackberries. The only discordant note is "a sea / Somewhere at the end of it, heaving." The sea (the use of the indefinite article 'a' rather than the definite article 'the' suggests that the speaker has no relationship with this sea) is obviously not visible to the protagonist, though she can hear the waves rhythmically crashing against the shore. The word "heaving" is vaguely threatening; it implies strength. The word also involves a personification of the sea which is in opposition to that of the blackberries: what the blackberries have in common with the speaker is that they are alive, each having "blue-red juices." The sea is "Somewhere at the end of it." On the literal level "it" refers to the lane down which the protagonist is walking toward the sea; on the symbolic level, however, the lane represents life and the sea represents the death that awaits everyone at the end of their life.

If anything, the second stanza is more obviously positive than the first. The only sound is that of the "choughs" (members of the crow family with glossy blue-black plumage) flying in "cacophonous flocks." The birds are "wheeling" in the wind, full of life and "protesting, protesting" (presumably that they will live). From this display of confidence and mastery, the speaker concludes triumphantly "I do not think the sea will appear at all." Symbolically, this means that today she will not have to encounter death – she can remain in the realm of the joyously living. She sees herself as at one with the plants and birds which exude life, "The high, green meadows are glowing, as if lit from within." Nothing, it seems, can put out that inner light. However, ominous details have already crept into the description of the birds. Their black feathers suggest death, and the metaphor, "Bits of burnt paper wheeling in a blown sky" that they are already dead and being tossed helplessly in the wind like paper. It appears that, in her enthusiasm, the speaker has missed the full implication of her own observations.

Such evasion is no longer possible when the protagonist encounters the corruption of over-ripeness:

>One bush of berries so ripe it is a bush of flies,
>Hanging their blue-green bellies and their wing
>panes in a Chinese screen.
>The honey-feast of the berries has stunned
>them; they believe in heaven.

The positive mood of the picker immediately gives way to an obsession with decay and death. The bush that grew blackberries now seems to grow flies, which are associated with rotting flesh. The speaker does full justice to the "blue-green bellies and their wing panes" which seem to form "a Chinese screen," but the truth is that they are feasting on death. With bitter irony, the speaker comments, "they believe in heaven," but it is not the flies that have died but the over-ripe blackberries which are decomposing.

The speaker comments, "One more hook, and the berries and bushes end." On the literal level, she means that she has reached the end of the lane; she is almost at the point where it gives way to the sea shore. The only thing that holds her back is "One more hook." (Compare the "snags and eddies" in the air in "Tulips".) This recalls the description in stanza one of the "blackberry alley, going down in hooks, and a sea." The hooks symbolize life trying to hook onto her, to keep her from reaching the sea: they are a manifestation of the loving "blood sisterhood" which the blackberries feel for the protagonist as another living being trying to stay alive.

The final stanza begins with what amounts to an admission of defeat: the death principle, or mortality, or nihilism (call it what you will) slaps the protagonist in her face like wet laundry flapping on a washing line. She feels impelled towards the sea by "a sudden wind [that] funnels at [her]"; by the path that the sheep have trod before her; even by "the last hook" that brings her face-to-face with the orange rock of "the hills' northern face." The northern face would, of course, be the coldest face since it would get less of the sun. It is a stark contrast to the "hills [that] are too green and sweet to have tasted salt": the contrast is between the warmth and vibrancy of life and the cold, hardness of death. The view is of "nothing, nothing but a great space" which represents the great emptiness of death – the death of someone who has no belief in heaven. In that vacancy, she sees only "white and pewter lights, and a din like silversmiths / Beating and beating at an intractable metal." This is a complex and ambiguous metaphor. On the literal level, it described the sound of the pounding of the waves against the "intractable" wall of rock: a battle between life and death which will go on forever. It is vital to remember, however, that the speaker has not entered the sea: the last two lines are not a description of death, for death is "nothing, nothing." The lines describe an epiphany – the moment when the speaker realizes that she cannot live in the false security of "blackberry alley" for the rest of her life: she must face the reality that life is finite. All that is left to her is a "space" within which she, as an artist, can try to make art out of the "intractable metal" of the reality of the human condition as a silversmith struggles to make beauty out of the raw metal ore.

This is, of course, exactly what Plath has done in this poem, which means that fundamentally her subject is the role of the poet and the function of poetry. "Blackberrying" begins as a celebration of the fruitfulness of nature, but it quickly rejects the temporary comfort this brings and forces the reader honestly to face the ultimate meaninglessness of life in the face of mortality. Hall is making the same point when she writes, "The plain description of the external landscape in this poem is powerful and lively. But beyond that, rhythms and word sounds afford to the experience a distorted quality suggesting that this landscape is internal as well" (Bloom Ed. *Views* 110).

(Nobel Laureate Seamus Heaney has a beautiful little poem called "Blackberry-Picking" which, though it has none of the complexity of Plath's poem, makes much the same point. You should read it.)

Selected Poems by Sylvia Plath

FINISTERRE

Written in October 1961. Cape Finisterre is a headland in NW Spain, the westernmost point of the Spanish mainland, which looks down on the Atlantic Ocean. Finisterre is a very famous fishing port much loved of tourists, and as described in the poem, there is a statue dedicated to sailors lost at sea. The poem, which has received relatively little attention from critics, may owe much to Wallace Steven's "The Idea of Order at Key West" another poem set at the extreme point where land meets sea.

1. Stanza one describes the sea and the cliffs. Is this presented as a place of beauty?
2. Why are the "trefoils" (small flowers) said to be "close to death"?
3. In the last two lines of stanza two, how does the speaker describe the experience of walking in the mists generated by the waves crashing against the rocks?
4. To the speaker, the statue of Our Lady appears to have taken on a significance different from that intended by its builders. Can you explain?
5. Stanza four describes the inevitable tourist traps - the stalls which sell trinkets (made somewhere else and imported) and food. How do the final lines of direct speech reflect the themes of the poem?

I have no way of knowing whether Plath had the following passage from "Place-Names: The Name" (which is the final section of *Swann's Way*, the first book of Proust's *Remembrance of Things Past*), but it makes a great introduction to this poem:

> 'You feel there [Balbec], below your feet still ... far more even than at Finistère ... you feel that you are actually at the land's end of France, of Europe, of the Old World. And it is the ultimate encampment of the fishermen, precisely like the fishermen who have lived since the world's beginning, facing the everlasting kingdom of the sea-fogs and shadows of the night.' ... I tried to form a picture in my mind of how those fishermen had lived, the timid and unsuspecting essay towards social intercourse which they had attempted there, clustered upon a promontory of the shores of hell, at the foot of the cliffs of death.

The poem presents nature as harsh and antagonistic to human life. The landscape is allegorical: a scene from nature representing an inner state of mind. Religion affords no relief: the statue of Our Lady of the Shipwrecks is venerated by the people but shows no interest in the plight of her devotees.

The setting of the poem is the interface between the realm of the living and the realm of the dead. The rocks of the headland are personified: they reach into the sea as "rheumatic" hands, "Cramped on nothing." Life is already seen as inextricably linked with disease and suffering. The cliffs are, "Admonitory," they give a warning that here the land ends giving way to the "exploding" sea which has "no bottom, or anything on the other side of it." This suggests that death is the great nothingness, the ultimate negation, and the whitened skulls of the drowned testify to this reality. The speaker now turns her attention to the "dump of rocks" at the foot of the black cliff – the ruin to which the sea has reduced it. They are "gloomy" and like, "Leftover soldiers from old, messy wars" because they have lost their war: the battle with the sea has only one conclusion. The sea is constantly "exploding" and its sound "cannons" into the speaker's ear, two metaphors that present the sea as an invading army. Sunken rocks, presumably the dead, "hide their grudges under the water." Land's end appears also to be the end of hope.

Stanza two describes the vegetation clinging to the cliffs. The "trefoils [three overlapping rings], stars and bells" describe the shapes of the tiny plants in terms of graphic forms that the village women might embroider. They are "close to death" because of their precarious position on the cliff edge. These forms of life are, however, "Almost too small for the mists to bother with." The mists are generated by the beating of the waves against the headland. They seem to the speaker to be the ghostly spirits ("souls") of the dead, trapped for eternity in "the doom-noise of the sea." The in-coming waves "bruise the rocks out of existence," and then, when they recede, the rocks reemerge as though resurrected. To the speaker, the waves crashing against the rock sound like hopeless sighs, for they have nothing positive to offer. The plants may be unaffected, but when the speaker walks among the mists she is almost suffocated by them, unable to breathe because "they stuff my mouth with cotton." (The image of suffocation is a repeated one in Plath's poetry that has its origin in the severe sinusitis from which she suffered.) When the mists free her (notice that she seems incapable of freeing herself), she finds herself "beaded with tears," mourning for the dead and for the death she much face.

The marble monument depicts Our Lady of the Shipwrecked with a sailor kneeling before her; yet the Lady is "striding toward the horizon" acknowledging nothing and the sailor "kneels at her foot distractedly." There seems to be no evidence of connection between the two. Ironically, a black-clad peasant woman is venerating the monument, leading to the almost comic paradox that she is "praying to the monument of the sailor praying." Our Lady has nothing human about her: she is "three times life size"; she is a divine figure not a mortal; and "She is in love with the beautiful formlessness of the sea." Far from representing life, she is unmoved by the suffering of the living people around her. The only thing for which she feels emotion is "the beautiful formlessness of the sea" which she loves. The land in the poem represents order, structure and firmness, but Our Lady is a devotee of the chaos of the encroaching sea.

The final stanza marks a sudden and unexpected change of subject. The speaker now describes the tourist stalls and shops of the nearby, unnamed, village. Here, life is trivial. The "sea drafts" only "flap" the ties that (presumably) hold the canvas on the stalls. The speaker, previously a philosopher, if a manic depressive one, is now simply a tourist subject to the inane chatter of one of the locals. The souvenirs are cheap and tasteless "necklaces and toy ladies" made out of shells, but the shells do not come from "the Bay of the Dead." They are imported from "another place, tropical and blue" that no one on Finisterre has ever visited, so the only really positive description of nature in the poem is of a place no one has ever been to. The trite, banal language in the last line is striking: the speaker has been moved from considering the great questions of life and death, of mortality and eternity, to the purely practical issue of eating her crêpes before the wind cools them. More importantly, she has given up: she has accepted the refuge which people find in the trivia of everyday life in order to avoid the big questions, the implications of which are too frightening.

THE MOON AND THE YEW TREE

Dated October 22nd. A yew tree stood in the churchyard near the Devon house in which Plath and Hughes lived and was visible from the bedroom window. This is one of Plath's most difficult poems.

Once again the landscape is allegorical. Bassnett states confidently, "The moon and the yew tree of the mind coexist with the moon and the yew tree that Sylvia Plath could see from her bedroom window in Devon" (*An Introduction* 55), but Kendall is more circumspect when he writes, "The point where this mindscape ends and the physical world begins can no longer be discerned ... [I]t remains unclear whether the journey through this cold and planetary environment is real or imagined" (*Ibid.* 46). This lack of clarity accounts for most of the poem's difficulties, which are considerable. Perhaps the best thing that I can do is to offer a tentative overview.

The dominant impression is the speaker's feeling that she is trapped and that she "cannot see where there is to get to" from the point she has reached. She is trying to understand her relationship with the cosmos in order to be able to take her place within the community of the village and more specifically of her family. Two possible escapes from her existential angst (the despair of a meaningless life) are offered, first by the moon and second by the Church "affirming the Resurrection," that is, hope of life in triumph over the despair of mortality. How desperately the speaker would like "to believe in tenderness," but she cannot. What happens in the Church has no impact upon her and the moon offers only a terrible reality with no hope of salvation. The speaker is left with no way out.

1. Describe, or better still sketch, the setting of the poem.
2. Explain the symbolism of the final two lines of stanza one.
3. Explain the meaning of the speaker's statement that "The moon is no door." What evidence of this is provided in the first half of stanza 2?
4. What comfort to the speaker does the church seem to offer?
5. How does the moon as a deity differ from the Virgin Mary?
6. In the course of the poem, the speaker looks to the yew tree, the moon and the church for meaning and consolation. With what result?

The consensus of critical opinion takes the yew tree to represent the male principle ("cold," "black," "silent," "deathly") and the moon to represent the female principle ("bald and wild", "terribly upset" and in "complete despair"). Bassnett writes, "The moon and the yew tree of the poem are ... not partners but antagonists, symbols of the struggle between female and male that pervades Plath's work" (*An Introduction* 61). Writers who place emphasis on Plath's biography and psychology go further seeing the moon as a personification of her mother and the yew tree as the symbol of her father. Thus, Rosenblatt comments on the significance of color in the poem, "Black is the father's color, indicating the silence of the dead ..." (97). For a long while, I followed this basic interpretation of the poem, but I have finally rejected it. I have two reasons: first, while the speaker identifies the moon as her mother, she does *not* identify the yew as her father; and second, this identification simply does not allow me to make sense of the poem.

The situation is that the speaker is standing close to a village church in the graveyard wherein there is a yew tree. It is night, and the light from the moon illuminates the scene. The protagonist feels herself to be trapped by the "row of headstones" that are between her and her house. If the house represents 'normal' family life (a reasonable assumption), then clearly the speaker feels incapable of taking her conventional role (in Plath's case wife and mother) in that life. In an urge to get rid of her desolation and isolation from her fellow humans, she begins to commune with nature and to try to understand the elements of nature that surround her, but she finds no answer there.

The speaker begins by describing the two poles of her own mind: blue light and black. The opening line echoes Jesus' statement, "Then spake Jesus again unto them, saying, I am the light of the world: he that followeth me shall not walk in darkness, but shall have the light of life" (*Gospel of Saint John* 8:12 KJV). The "light of the mind" is clearly very different: it offers no warmth; it is not emotional but purely scientific and rational; it offers no hope or vision of anything other than a "cold and planetary" world. The color blue is (as often in Plath's poetry) associated with coldness and depression (as it was in early American culture). Perhaps even worse are the "trees of the mind" which represent the speaker's own thoughts which branch out, reaching for meaning, but do not bear leaves or fruit because they lead her to despair. It is important to say again that, at this point, the speaker is *not* describing the moon and the yew tree: she will later take these two features of her nocturnal landscape as symbols of the division *in her own mind* that she has just described.

The grasses are a form of life just as is the speaker, though they obviously lack consciousness (which the speaker gives them through personification), so to them the human being is equivalent to a God. Theirs is also an existence of darkness and despair, so they turn naturally as humble supplicants "murmuring" prayers to their God. Since the speaker knows that she is *not* a God, and that she has no answers for the grass, she is somewhat irritation by the grasses "Prickling my ankles." The description of the place she is in as "Fumy, [with] spiritous mists" suggests unpleasantness and uncertainty. It is just possible that the grasses are an extended metaphor in which the speaker compares humans to grasses: people who cannot handle their own problems lay their "griefs" at her feet because she is a poet (though, of course, the speaker does not identify herself as such). Absurdly, they have placed her on a pedestal "as if I were God" which is ridiculous because the protagonist feels even more intently than they the hopelessness all around her. For the speaker, mind has

71

come to the end of its tether (to coin a phrase from H. G. Wells), and she is at a complete impasse. Death, represented by the headstones, stands between her and being able to form a conception of anything in life that is worth pursuing. The speaker is certainly in need of a way out.

Immediately she tells us that the moon is not that answer to her existential despair. The "moon is no door." The moon does not represent Plath's biological mother; it represents the female guiding principle – the goddess Selene in Greek mythology and in Roman mythology the goddess Luna. The moon is traditionally linked with the female (just as the sun is linked with the male). The cycles of the moon control the tides and the woman's menstrual cycle. However, there is no connection between the speaker and the moon: the moon has its own identity and agenda, "It is a face in its own right." Normally thought of as 'the man in the moon,' here the face that the speaker discerns in the moon is definitely female. She looks at the face, as one does, to interpret its feelings and intentions, but it appears to be lost in its own despair, "White as a knuckle and terribly upset." The white knuckles suggest that the moon's hands are coiled into tight fists in her mourning. Rosenblatt identifies white as "indicating despair and the fear of death" (97). Some commentators see this as a sardonic reference by Plath to her own mother's insincere grief at the death of Plath's father, but such a psychological reading of the line is not essential (and is questionable biography). What is clear is that the moon is so wrapped up in its own despair that it can spare no time to comfort the speaker.

The moon "drags the sea after it like a dark crime." In Plath's poems, the sea is always associated with death, so the moon's despair is linked to mortality – the moon brings death. The moon makes no contact with the speaker because it is in a trance-like state contemplating its own sorrow with "the O-gape of complete despair." This is a bitter pun on the word 'agape' meaning selfless, sacrificial, unconditional love, the highest of the love described in the Bible. In contrast, the mother/moon has her mouth open in a wide circle of horror, incapable of loving the speaker who comments "I live here." She means both that she lives in this village and that she lives in the same despair that has paralyzed the moon. The speaker's thought has been brought back to the real landscape in which she is standing; she does, after all, live amongst other people (the villagers). She reflects that the eight church bells ring twice each Sunday (for Morning and Evening Service) their tongues (or clappers) apparently "affirming the Resurrection," their affirmation of agape over "O-gape." Despite the personification, there is something mechanical in the way this ritual is described, so that it appears to the reader to be a dutiful routine devoid of real meaning. To the protagonist, the bells are doing no more than sounding out their names (presumably the name of the note that the bell makes). She describes how they "soberly bong." The adverb suggests a lack of passion and the verb (which might have been 'sound', 'chime', 'ring' etc.) is both ugly and meaningless – it is almost childish language. Evidently the protagonist's attempt to connect with God (and therefore to find meaning) through the rituals of religion fails her. (Sylvia Plath soon stopped attending services in the village because she objected to the tone of the vicar's sermons.)

The yew tree is actually mentioned *for the first time* only in the third stanza. Yew trees are common near churches because "ever since people arrived in force upon these shores they have been in the habit of planting yew trees in acts of sanctification, close to where they eventually hoped to be laid to rest" ("Plant-Lore"). In Celtic lore, this evergreen tree became a symbol of death and rebirth: "Both Druids with their belief in reincarnation, and later Christians with their teaching of the resurrection, regarded it as a natural emblem of everlasting life" ("Tree Lore: Yew" Mara Freeman). Here it "points up" suggesting that it is trying to reach beyond the "planetary" realm to some divinity.

The yew tree is described as "Gothic," a word which has multiple connotations. It suggests the Gothic cathedrals of Medieval Europe built at the high watermark of the Age of Faith, but it also means "belonging to or redolent of the Dark Ages; portentously gloomy or horrifying" (Oxford Dictionary). As a writer, Plath would also have in mind Gothic fiction which combines horror, death, the supernatural and romance. (*Wuthering Heights* would be an example.) To the protagonist, the yew seems to point upwards to the moon to which is looks for rebirth just as the speaker has. The speaker clearly identifies the moon as (not *with*) her mother, but it is a mother from whom she can get no consolation because, "She is not sweet like Mary." The child-like nature of the adjective "sweet" suggests that the speaker is aware that the conventional image of Mary is a gross simplification. Mary's traditional blue garments conventionally convey her purity, but here they are simply cold. Out of her garments fly "small bats and owls," beasts associated with the Gothic horror genre, as are frightening, dark churchyards. (Compare the opening of *Great Expectations* by Charles Dickens.) Yet there is a desperate need in the speaker to "believe in tenderness" and to feel the gaze of her divine mother, "gentled by candles," and focused only on her. (Contrast this description with that of the statue of Mary in "Finisterre" which, fascinated by the ocean, appears to look away from her devotees.)

The final stanza brings together the two forces to which the speaker might look for consolation: the pagan moon/mother and the Christian church/religion. Neither of them provides solace for her feelings of loneliness and emptiness. Bassnett comments, "The dichotomy of this poem is between two sets of mental images – the images of the Christian faith, with its belief in resurrection and its effigies of the mother of God, and the images of nature, personified in the yew tree and the moon … that offer no prescription for salvation, nothing but silence, blackness and themselves" (*An Introduction* 56). Christianity holds no attraction for the speaker, but the pagan deity offers nothing but despair.

A Study Guide

The protagonist thinks of herself as one of the angels who fell with Lucifer after his rebellion (see *Paradise Lost* Book 1 by John Milton). She writes, "Clouds are flowering / Blue and mystical over the face of the stars." Of this statement, Jilly Birks comments, "The imagery is complicated and confusing, and subject to multiple interpretations" (genuis.com), which is true but does not get the reader very far. The stars now also have faces for they, like the moon, have power over the fate of individuals (remember that astrology occurs in several Plath poems). The clouds serve only to obfuscate: I think they represent the failed attempts of man over the centuries to find meaning and significance in the night sky – in which case the verb "flowering" is intended ironically, since human mysticism has served only to hide the truth (which may be that our lives are controlled by the stars and there is nothing we can do about it).

Having dismissed communion with nature as unproductive, the speaker turns again to the church inside which "the saints will all be blue." We have already seen the conventional association of blue with purity and the speaker's own association of blue with the cold and unemotional and depressing. However, the speaker is here making a rather bitter joke. The saints will "be blue" in the American colloquial sense of 'feeling blue' or 'having the blues' which means to feel depressed, sad and listless. (Think of the genre of music called 'The Blues' which emerged from the black experience in America.) The saints know that they too have failed to bring consolation to the people with whom they have no connection since their "delicate feet [float] over the cold pews" and their "hands and faces [are] stiff with holiness." They are as incapable of empathy as is the moon and for the same reason: both are entirely wrapped up in their own being. Yet the moon is the antithesis of Mary: "She is bald and wild" and does not make even the pretense of offering consolation, while Mary at least stands as a spiritual alternative to the world of death, however ineffectively. The last word is given to the yew tree which, like the speaker, was seeking for a meaning beyond the "planetary" world and has found only "blackness – blackness and silence." The speaker is utterly isolated and alone, incapably of taking her place in the house in which she lives because that place exists in a context that makes it meaningless.

There is salvation in neither the pagan goddess of the night, nor in the Christian Virgin Mary: desperately in need of warmth and empathy, the protagonist finds only coldness and indifference in both. This poem is both an embodiment and a justification of what Plath wrote in one of her letters home to her mother in the U.S., "Now stop trying to get me to write about 'decent courageous people' … I believe in going through and facing the worst, not hiding from it."

Selected Poems by Sylvia Plath

MIRROR

This is a reasonably straightforward poem cast in the form of a medieval riddle, except that the title supplies the solution! (A typical medieval riddle begins, "My house is not quiet, I am not loud ...") The poet anthropomorphizes the mirror which speaks directly to the reader describing its function and situation and also its owner, a woman whose transition from "a young girl" to "an old woman" the mirror has faithfully reflected. The poem was originally titled "Mirror Talk". It is written in two nine-line stanzas that have no rhyme scheme.

1. In stanza 1, how does the voice of the persona seek to establish the objectivity of the image that the mirror gives?
2. The woman searches "for what she really is." Why does the speaker regard "the candles or the moon" as "liars"? Is the speaker right to do so?
3. Explain the image in the last two lines.

The mirror claims to be objective and uninvolved. It makes no judgments, merely reflects back what it swallows without emotion. It is "truthful" and "exact," but not "cruel" – or at least not intentionally so. The metaphor of it having the "eye of a little god, four-cornered" is comic hyperbole for the mirror is, in fact, merely a mechanical device of "silver"

Most of the day, the mirror looks across an empty room and meditates on the opposite wall which is pink speckled. It has looked at that wall for so long that it describes it as "part of my heart." However, the image of the wall "flickers" because, every so often, it is obscured by the faces of by people who stand in front of the mirror to look at themselves and by the darkness that comes with night. The phrase "over and over" introduces the theme of the passage of time – the days quickly mount up.

In the second stanza, the mirror images itself as a lake. In an action reminiscent of the Greek myth of Narcissus, who is so transfixed by the beauty of his own reflection that he dies and is turned into a flower. The woman is similarly obsessed: she looks into the water trying to discover more than simply what she looks like: she is trying to discern "what she really is" by studying her reflection. Discontented by what she sees in the lake, the woman "turns to those liars, the candles or the moon" because their gentle light is flattering; it obscures imperfections and wrinkles. In contrast, the mirror/lake gives her a faithful reflection of herself as she is. The woman cries and wrings her hands for the image shows her beauty ebbing away. Nevertheless, it is important to her to look in the mirror; every morning hers is the first face that the mirror/lake sees. This suggests a life of routine and tedium. The last two lines are an extended image: over time, the woman has "drowned a young girl" in the mirror/lake, a metaphor of ageing, and now it is the face of an old woman that floats into view "like a terrible fish." The fish obviously represents the

75

woman's wrinkled face, but it may also represent the wasted potential of her life because she never discovered who she really was or what she really wanted out of life.

The conflict being described in this poem is between devastating truth and reassuring illusion. As Dyne writes, "As the poem progresses, the mirror's exactness comes to seem a cruel tyranny; the woman's dependence, a hopeless compulsion ... Bound to the mirror that claims to contain her entirety, the woman cannot retreat from the threat of the final lines ... The terror of this vision is its reduction of woman to inexorably aging flesh" (88). Even though she knows that it will upset her, the woman continually returns to the mirror for the truth. She does so because she is looking for some truth deeper than the physical. She is looking for her true self, some core of her being that transcends outward appearance. Unfortunately, her search appears to be fruitless.

Selected Poems by Sylvia Plath

THE BABYSITTERS

Dated October 29th. The main theme of this poem is time: time the inevitable destroyer of a happiness which, before it was lost, we simply took for granted and so didn't even think of as happiness. The poem is written in five nine-line stanzas with no rhyme scheme. The last line of each stanza is end-stopped making each stanza a separate unit.

1. What is your impression from stanza 1 of the age of the two "sisters"? How did you reach your conclusion?
2. The family certainly lived in style. Give examples of their luxury.
3. Why did her friends leave behind "a borrowed maid named Ellen" when they went off on a cruise?
4. In many ways the speaker envied her sister's situation. Why?
5. What did the two find on their jaunt to Children's Island?
6. How have the lives of the speaker and her friend changed in the decade since the summer described?

The setting is quite precise and, since the reader may not be familiar with this part of the Massachusetts coast, a little explanation may help. Marblehead is a historic coastal New England town in Essex County, Massachusetts, about seventeen miles north of Boston. It is noted for its quaint narrow streets and 17th and 18th Century buildings. Children's Island, known as "Cat Island", is an island about a mile north-east of Marblehead, which is named for the Children's Island Sanitarium which existed there from 1886 to 1946. The Sanitarium offered a healthy environment based on fresh air and sea bathing to children with a variety of chronic (but not contagious) complaints. Beginning in 1955, the YMCA operated a children's day camp on the island. Swampscott is an up-scale seaside town almost four miles to the south of Marblehead.

The first stanza establishes a tone of nostalgia for a vanished seaside summer vacation: a boat trip to Children's Island, the hot sun flaming down (no one used sunscreen back then), sunglasses to protect the eyes (quite an innovation), and "huge, white, handsome houses in Swampscott." The speaker seems to have been a young mother's help (nanny) working at the house of a rich and numerous family. She is reminiscing to a friend who shared one particular holiday working in a similar capacity for the family in the adjacent house. The two were like sisters that summer and the speaker indulgently describes herself and her friend as "always crying, in our spare rooms, little put-upon sisters." They were two young women, struggling to fulfill their role and meet the expectations that others had of them. The arrival of, "the sweetheart from England … with her cream skin and Yardley cosmetics" meant some inconvenience for the speaker since she had to move into the baby's room and sleep on "a too-short cot" and the seven-year-old could be irritating. The overall tone is, however, of an idyllic time because of her friendship with her 'sister'.

The second stanza opens with details of affluence: a house with eleven rooms, a yacht with steps of "polished mahogany" that let down into the sea, and servants (not least a cabin boy who can "decorate cakes in six-colored frosting"). The only problem was that the speaker felt inadequate: she "didn't know how to cook," and couldn't iron clothes without leaving small burn marks. More significantly, "babies depressed [her]" (not ideal in a babysitter!). Her only sanctuary and outlet was her room at night where she could be on her own and where she wrote in her "diary spitefully." Nor did her inadequacy pass unnoticed, for when friends were away, "They left me a borrowed maid named Ellen, 'for protection,' / And a small Dalmation." Is there also a suggestion here that the speaker might have been in need of a chaperone?

The speaker now makes a contrast between herself and her friend whose accommodation was superior, and had "a cook and a maid." Also, the friend secretly gained access to the whiskey. Life in the main house was more fun: her friend played "Ja-Da" (a hit song written in 1918 by Bob Carleton) on the piano "when the 'big people' [the older generation] were out." Even the servants were more fun, from the pool-playing maid, who (scandal of scandals) smoked, to the walleyed cook from Ireland who was finally fired for burning cookies. The reader has begun to sense an undertone of resentment in the speaker which never quite reaches bitterness.

The speaker returns to the event with which she began her reminiscence. She and her 'sister' acted more like children than adolescents, which is why the speaker asks rhetorically, "O what has come over us, my sister!" Having got a "day-off" (a day of freedom to be themselves), they stole a ham and a pineapple "from the grownups' icebox," hired a row boat and set off for Children's Island – which suggests a symbolic attempt to recapture (or simply to hang on to) the innocence of youth. As the speaker rowed her friend read, and what she read is highly significant. "*Generation of Vipers* is a 1943 book by Philip Wylie. In it Wylie criticizes various aspects and beliefs of contemporary American society, including Christianity; prominent figures such as politicians, teachers, and doctors; and 'momism' or the adoration of mothers" (Wikipedia article). The 'sisters' seem to have been enthusiastic early feminists!

On the island they found not their childhood, but the deserted, abandoned buildings associated with the Sanatorium. (Compare "The Burnt-out Spa" and "Wuthering Heights".) The "creaking porches and still interiors" were, the speaker says, "Stopped and awful as a photograph of somebody laughing / But ten years dead." [The image put me in mind of Dylan Thomas' line, "The yellowing dicky-bird watching pictures of the dead" from *Under Milk Wood*.] The abandoned buildings seem to be a symbol for the lost childhood of the two young women.

Selected Poems by Sylvia Plath

The speaker continues with a detailed description of what the two did on the island in the time they had completely to themselves. As she remembers it, it seems as though the ten years between then and now have been obliterated, "I see us floating there yet, inseparable – two cork dolls." And yet the two *have* been separated, and separated by the very ocean in which they bathed: the speaker now lives in England, while her friend still lives in the U.S.A. Time has not stood still – the "shadows of the grasses [that] inched round like hands of a clock" on that day have now measured a decade. The speaker feels like Alice who, in the children's classic *Alice in Wonderland*, falls down a rabbit hole where she finds a tiny key to a door too small for her to fit through. Eventually, Alice floats out through the keyhole in a sea of her own tears. For the speaker, "Everything has happened," and there is no going back to that wonderful day.

The title of the poem is ironic. The speaker and her friend were the "Babysitters", inexperienced and unprepared for their role, but now they are mothers with their own children, their freedom limited by the roles they must play as wives and mothers. Their little act of rebellion brought some relief (as did the occasional shot of bourbon!), but they could not stop the progression of time.

LITTLE FUGUE

Dated April 2nd, 1962, this poem was composed, through many drafts, following an extended period when Plath had written little poetry. Kendall points out that, "The manuscripts ... show Plath beginning to explore – often for the first time – many of the themes and images of her mature poetry" (71). The yew tree is the same described in "The Moon and the Yew Tree" and many of the phrases recall the earlier poem. The masculine yew is traditionally the death tree and Plath seems determined "to explore the nature of the 'blackness and silence', regardless of the psychological cost" (Ibid. 73). The poem's subject is the persona's father, or rather her failure to communicate with him in death as in life, and her attempt to come to terms with his death by opening up communications with the dead and (ultimately), by wishing to join the dead.

The poem comprises twelve unrhymed stanzas. Except for stanza five (which has eight lines) they all have four lines.

1. Several of Plath's poems use World War II Holocaust imagery to describe her personas' feelings about the loss of the father lost at about the age of eight (the age at which Plath lost her own father). The personas identify themselves, and the suffering they have experienced as a result of their personal loss, with that of the Jews persecuted by the Nazis. This has proved unacceptable to many readers and critics. Susan Gubar, for example, says categorically, "Plath's non-Jewishness as well as her lack of a personal stake in the disaster made her speaking on behalf of the victims appear [to be] a desecration." Where do you stand on this issue of Plath appropriating for her persona's images from mass slaughter to describe their feelings of personal loss, victimization, anger, etc.?
2. The poem is full of puns (starting with "yew" / "you"), some of which are darkly comic. Find as many examples as you can.
3. How do you feel about poems which are so difficult to understand? (I actually find some of the literary criticism on this poem completely obscure!)

This must be one of Plath's most difficult poems, so I suggest that you leave it until you have read all of the other poems in the book. The themes explored are very similar to those in "Daddy" though that poem has a clarity and coherence which this poem does not have. The poem follows the speaker's stream of consciousness as she makes connections which are personally meaningful but not immediately clear to the reader. As with much of Plath's poetry, we sense that the writing is heavily symbolic but the symbolism is also deeply personal and therefore hard to 'unlock.' I am going to offer a tentative reading of the poem on which I hope you will be able to build.

The word 'fugue' has a number of meanings. Perhaps the most relevant to this poem is "a polyphonic composition, developed from a given theme, according to strict contrapuntal rules" (wordnik); Plath was at the time interested in Beethoven's later works, including the *Grosse Fugue*. However the word can also mean "a pathological disturbance of consciousness" (Webster's dictionary), or "A flight from one's own identity, often involving travel to some unconsciously desired locality. It is a dissociative reaction to shock or emotional stress in a neurotic, during which all awareness of personal identity is lost though the person's outward behavior may appear rational" (OED). This helps to explain the poem's conclusion where the speaker "begins to question whether the tortured past or the outwardly 'rational' present constitutes her 'personal identity'" (Kendall 78). In "Little Fugue" the two meanings come together to describe the protagonist's failure to move beyond mourning, so that grief, guilt or other negative emotions are constantly recycled. The closing four lines settle the ambiguity, "the present, with its trappings of family life, constitutes an escape from selfhood. The speaker's self-conscious deliberation, and her focus on immediate surroundings, suggests a struggle to establish a new domestic identity. She is describing a 'fugue state', a 'dissociative reaction' to the loss of her father, by which she has escaped into the 'unconsciously desired locality' of normal family life. This state is highly precarious ... Despite trying to establish a new identity, the speaker cannot avoid eventually being drawn back through the yew towards what she perceives to be her real self – a self which belongs with the dead father buried among the tree's roots" (*Ibid.* 79).

The poem opens with opposites: the black of the "deaf and dumb" yew tree and the white of the "cold ... / blind" clouds, and the absolute failure of communication between the two. This may, of course, simply be a description based on observation of the yew in the Devon churchyard. If there is a symbolic meaning, it is not made explicit. Most obviously, the yew represents human mortality and the clouds the indifferent universe, but the main point seems to be the failure of the yew tree to unite (in any sense) with the clouds. Yet the blind pianist, who could only feel for his food, was able to "hear Beethoven" and somehow managed to bring the two realms together in the form of the black and white keys of the piano. Despite the "horrific complications. / [and] Finger-traps," he produced music. That is why the speaker "couldn't stop looking" – because she cannot make this kind of contact. The *Grosse Fugue* (composed in 1824 by Beethoven who was by that time becoming profoundly deaf) is a "yew hedge" presumably because of its technical difficulty. Out of the "tumult of keys," the pianist manages to make a big noise that the speaker envies because since her father's death she has been left only with silence.

She figuratively describes herself as a deaf person with a "dark funnel" (an ear trumpet) desperately trying to hear her dead father whom she addresses personally ("my father") for the first time. She is thus led specifically to childhood memories (which she 'sees' in her mind's eye) of her father, "A yew hedge of orders, / Gothic and barbarous, pure German. / Dead men cry from it. / I am guilty of nothing." These lines describe her father figuratively as a

German soldier in World War II, a soldier who was guilty of the massacre of Jews, whose cries she hears in her horrific memory of his voice. The speaker claims to be, like the Jews, an innocent victim.

She associates herself with the yew tree and the yew tree with Christ, for both suffered on earth to redeem the dead. The speaker is trapped in a cycle of perpetual mourning. The father is described figuratively as a butcher, "Lopping off the sausages!" in a California delicatessen during World War I. The images of him recur in her dreams. This is another metaphor of the Holocaust: the father might not have been directly involved, but his butcher mentality implies his guilt. The dead animals are silent, but a silence "of another order" is caused by the death of the father leaving her with only a "lame ... memory" of a Prussian man with one leg. (Plath's father, who was, of course, a scientist and university lecturer, had a leg amputated because of diabetes before his death.)

The speaker feels that death has opened to her once and may again, "Now similar clouds / Are spreading their vacuous sheets." As death once came for her father, the speaker senses that it is about to come for her, but he has nothing to say to offer her comfort. All she has are her imperfect memories of him: all his life added up to was "a blue eye, / [and] A briefcase of tangerines." Nothing else remains because death took everything else.

In the final stanza, the speaker presents herself as a survivor:
>I survive the while,
>Arranging my morning.
>These are my fingers, this my baby.
>The clouds are a marriage of dress, of that
>pallor.

She takes refuge in the conventional roles of wife and mother, but almost everything in the stanza has ominous undertones. The pun on "morning" / mourning shows that her life is dominated by her sense of loss. She speaks of her fingers and her baby in a strangely detached way as though trying to convince herself that they actually are connected to her. Her marriage is merely one of "dress," appearance not reality, and the "pallor" suggests the whiteness of a shroud.

Selected Poems by Sylvia Plath

AN APPEARANCE

Labeled one of Plath's 'transitional' poems, "An Appearance" has received relatively little attention from critics. Britzolakis provides important insight into its theme noting that in the manuscript it was titled "The Methodical Woman", and that the following words were written at the side of the page: 'index, file, order, tidy, symmetrical, system, discipline, rank, neat, systematic.' Britzolakis concludes, "The figure of the organized, 'efficient' housewife is at once a manipulable mask and a *doppelgänger* who threatens to usurp the speaker" (Bloom Ed. *Views* 130).

1. In the first line, the speaker associates iceboxes (the American word for refrigerators which had become pretty common by the 1950s) with death. Explain the connection.
2. Line two refers to "my loved one!" To whom do you think the speaker is referring? Explain your answer.
3. What are the "contradictions" to which the persona refers in stanza three? Again, explain your answer.
4. In what ways could embroidery (or sewing) be seen as an expression of "love"?
5. The last two stanzas clearly contrast two different personalities with different concerns. Describe each.

Readers familiar with Plath's poems will know that the theme of the reflected image which shows the other 'you' (the alternative 'you', the 'you' that you might become) occurs again and again. In this poem the "Appearance" indicated in the title refers to the persona's sudden confrontation with her alter ego which is connected (in some way) to "iceboxes." The double seems to take the form of the perfect, stereotypical wife and mother described in the women's magazines – the efficient, methodical, unpoetic manager of the domestic realm. This is an image (or ideal) to which the speaker feels she cannot measure up. Part of the speaker appears to want to become this 'wife-and-mother', but another part of her rejects being subsumed by this role.

The icebox (refrigerator) is the ultimate symbol of modern domestic efficiency; it is also a symbol of death (being associated with both cold and white) which is why the persona feels annihilated. Because of its absolute, unemotional efficiency, it is a perfect image of the persona's double – indeed, it appears to embody that double or to give birth to the rival "my loved one" – the woman the speaker desperately wants to be (and desperately does not want to be). In the icebox, the speaker sees herself dead with "blue currents in the veins" not the red blood of the living. This explains why Britzolakis comments that the double in the poem is:

> a persecutory figure. The image of the mech -
> anized woman, conjured out of the landscape

83

> of domesticity, sharply refutes the Romantic nostalgia for an organic or 'natural' femininity ... She is an allegorical cypher of femininity, reducible to the domestic appliances she operates and the repetitive functions she performs, a peculiarly willed, deliberate, and written construction." (Bloom Ed. Views 130).

The gentle hum of the refrigerator motor emits "ampersands and percent signs" instead of kisses. There is no love here, only cold efficiency.

The 'other' (the persona's alter ego) judges the speaker: in the *doppelgänger's* mind it is *always* Monday (traditionally laundry day in Britain) when she will judge the speaker by her harsh moral standards and find her wanting – literally wash out her defects. Aware of the "contradictions" between her own feelings and personal values and the lack of emotion and individuality in the alter ego, the persona is at a loss to know what to do. Finally, she bows down as before an idol or a god, pushing her contradictory feelings aside.

Needlework (or stitching) is both a precise activity and one traditionally associated with the 'woman-as-homemaker'; it is also a tedious, repetitive, mindless activity – depending on how you feel about it. It seems to be the persona who is engaged in this task, which is perhaps her act of homage and/or submission to the values of her double. The persona is unconvinced, however. She asks skeptically whether "the red material / Issuing from the steele [*sic.*] needle" is love. This "material" might be the cotton with which the sewer's needle is threaded, but it also suggests blood that the needle had "blindingly" drawn from the sewer. The question the speaker asks "Is this love then ...?" is rhetorical. The skepticism is evident in the addition of the word "then" (compare the question, 'Is that it then?'). For the persona, even covering "a dynasty" with "little dresses and coats" does not mean love – duty, perhaps, but not love.

In the last two stanzas, the persona and the alter ego are again quite separate and the persona again observes her double describing her mechanical nature: her body "opens and shuts" as efficiently as does the refrigerator door, and her movement is as perfect as that of a "Swiss watch." In contrast is the "disorganization" of the persona's heart. For the speaker, "The stars are flashing like terrible numerals," as though some catastrophe is at hand, but the *doppelgänger* is unflustered. She calmly flutters her eyelids as though everything to her is as easy as "ABC."

Selected Poems by Sylvia Plath

CROSSING THE WATER

Dated April 4th, this is the first poem in the posthumously published *Crossing the Water* which Hughes prepared for publication. The poem is written in four unrhymed three-line stanzas.

The title indicates that this is a poem of transition, but the symbols defy a simple meaning. The most obvious connotation of crossing the water is of dead souls crossing the River Styx that in Greek mythology separates the world of the living from the world of the dead (Hades). Plath herself crossed the waters when she and Ted Hughes decided to live in England.

1. What do you understand by the image of "cut-paper people"?
2. Explain the setting and action described in stanzas one and two.
3. The image of the pale hand rising out of the water recalls the hand which rose out of the lake to take back Arthur's sword, Excalibur, following his final defeat. What threat does the "snag" pose to those crossing the water?
3. In classical myth, the Sirens called sailors to destruction on rocks. Who are the sirens in this poem and what is their dangerous message?
4. What do you make of the final line, and, in particular, of the word "This"?

On the literal level, the opening of the poem offers few difficulties: two people are out in a small boat (either a rowing boat or a canoe) on a lake somewhere in the north-eastern U.S.A. It is either dusk or dawn because there is still enough light to reflect off the white water lilies. The only mystery on this level of interpretation is why two people should be out so early or so late.

Clearly, however, the description is meant to be read symbolically. The word "black" is repeated four times in the first two lines and is echoed in the words "shadows" in line three and "dark" in line six. Inevitably, this suggests death. The two travelers themselves are "cut-paper people," black, two-dimensional shadows against the "little light," but the image also suggests that they are not fully human; they are, perhaps, only the remnants (or spirits) of human beings. The personification of the trees close to the water suggests that the two travelers are being watched by trees which cast huge shadows. The reader may be reminded of the valley of the shadow of death ("Yea, though I walk through the valley of the shadow of death, I will fear no evil: for thou art with me; thy rod and thy staff they comfort me" *Psalms* 23:4 KJV.), but death appears to "cover Canada" – its domain is vast.

The only positive element of the description is the light that appears to be emanating from the "water flowers" and the fact that these flowers seem to express concern for the fate of the two people in the boat. The lilies wish to slow the progress of the boat (presumably their thick leaves stems and flowers are impeding it). The lilies offer their "dark advice," but there is no explanation of what that advice is. Logically, it would be that the two figures should *not* cross the water at all or, at least, that they should do so very slowly. The lilies may be warning, darkly about what is on the other side of the water.

As the description continues in stanzas three and four, the poem is again easy to follow on the literal level. It is now evident that the two people are in a rowing boat. As the oars are lifted out of the cold water, little drops are shaken from them and fall back into the lake. The limb of a dead tree rises from the water, but it appears to pose no danger of entanglement. It is also now clear that the setting is evening (another suggestion of death as opposed to dawn which would have suggested rebirth) since more and more stars are becoming visible and their light is reflected in the water alongside the lilies.

Symbolically, the two travelers appear to have become one with their surroundings, "The spirit of blackness is *in* [them]" (emphasis added). Thus, blackness must define their nature too as it does that of the fishes. The snag is personified as "a valedictory, pale hand." Since the hand is acknowledging their departure, it seems that it is the land of the living from which they are departing. The reference to the hand brings to mind that of The Lady of the Lake which rises to take back Arthur's sword Excalibur after which the dying king crosses the water to the Isle of Avalon. His death marks the dissolution of the ideal society of Camelot.

The reflections of the stars among the lilies seem to one of the occupants of the boat to be "expressionless sirens." Whilst the lilies were trying to impede the passage of the boat, the stars appear to be calling it forward. In Greek mythology, the Sirens were beautiful women whose songs lured sailors to their doom by causing their ships to crash on the rocks of their island. The phrase "expressionless sirens" is an oxymoron meaning something like 'the silent song of the stars.' One person in the boat asks the other if he/she is "not blinded" by the call of the stars, which seem to be beckoning the two onwards to death with the promise of something beyond death. The companion does not answer, and the one who asked the question comments "This is the silence of astounded souls." It seems that the companion is fully under the influence of the sirens.

The two people in the boat represent two aspects of the same person. Only one of the two speaks in the poem. She is obviously cautious from the start about the journey that the two are making; she notices all of its ominous aspects. Finally, she is driven to challenge her alter-ego by warning of the danger of the course that the boat is taking toward death, but the other is so set on this course that dialogue is impossible.

Kendall comments, "She [Plath] has now entered the domain of the yew tree, where everything has been contaminated with the same sinister blackness … The poem's conclusion draws on imagery from previous poems, emphasizing that the journey begun in 'Little Fugue' is still ongoing" (82).

AMONG THE NARCISSI

This poem has few difficulties. It "depicts Plath's Devon neighbor, Percy Key, walking on a nearby hill" (Kendall 83). Key had suffered a stroke and is apparently recuperating, but "the hill of the new dawn is also a hill of danger and fatality" (*Ibid.* 84). In reality, Percy died, and Plath was one of the mourners who followed his coffin at the funeral. In the poem, however, Plath shows her admiration for the power of the life-force. Rosenblatt finds the poem ultimately unsatisfying, "The situation of the octogenarian Percy is equated with that of the narcissus flowers ... The 'attacks' from the wind and from the external world unite the vulnerable man with the vulnerable flower. Unfortunately, Plath does not develop the connection in any substantial way in this poem" (103).

The poem consists of four three-line unrhymed stanzas. The writing is in coherent sentences and each stanza ends with a period making it a separate unit.

1. What similarities do you find between Percy and the man described in "The Hermit at Outermost House"?
2. How would you describe the "big thing" against which both Percy and the narcissi struggle?

Percy is a part of nature: he, like the narcissi "are bowing to some big thing" on the side of the same hill. Of course, we could simply identify the "thing" as the prevailing wind and leave it at that: certainly the wind "rattles ... [the] stars" (that is, the tiny flowers) of the narcissi and buffets Percy so that he is forced to nurse (protect) "the hardship of his stitches" as he walks – a clear indication this of the way in which Plath adapts biographical detail to the needs of her poetry.

The key word in the poem is "dignity," not a common concept in Plath's poetry. Life may be suffering, but one has to admire man's resilience. The narcissi are "vivid as bandages," and indeed being amongst the flowers does help with Percy's healing because they are fighting the same battle for survival. The final image is of the old man as loving shepherd to the "little flocks" of narcissi, and the narcissi as children looking up to him.

Nevertheless, the final stanza has ominous undertones. Percy is "quite blue" and the narcissi look "whitely," two cold colors which here (as elsewhere in Plath's poetry) suggest bloodlessness and death. The wind is "terrible" and "tries his breathing." The clear implication is that for both the man and the flowers, the fight against the "big thing" is a losing battle, for it is the fight against mortality itself.

It is something of a relief to come across a poem that communicates its meaning so readily. Nevertheless, had Plath always written like this, her poems would have been forgotten long ago and she would have been remembered, if at all, as a minor poet.

A Study Guide

ELM

Dated April 19th, a time when Plath was still struggling to come to terms with her husband's infidelity. The feminine elm represents rebirth. Unlike the yew tree that was to the west of Plath's cottage (and therefore associated with sunset), the elm was to the east (associated therefore with sunrise). Hughes wrote, "The house in Devon was overshadowed by a giant wych-elm, flanked by two others in a single mass, growing on the shoulder of a moated prehistoric mound." The drafts included the positive aspects of rebirth, but in the final version it is death that dominates. The result is a poem that portrays the mental turmoil of a suffering woman. The result is one of Plath's most difficult poems.

The poem fourteen three-lined unrhymed stanzas with lines of unequal length.

1. What does the elm mean when it says, "I know the bottom"?
2. What is the truth about love that the elm has discovered and tries to impart to the woman who is listening?
3. How does the metaphor on line nine attempt to illustrate this truth?
4. Stanza 6 begins, "I have suffered ..." Make a list of the things that the elm says she has suffered in the rest of the poem.
5. What is it that turns a woman's will to stone and then splinters and breaks that stone down?

In this dramatic monologue, originally titled "The Elm Speaks," the voice is that of a personified tree (indicated by the pronoun "she") speaking to an innocent victim (indicated by the pronoun "you") who reports the wisdom that the elm attempted to impart. The poem starts with the words that the elm tree spoke. The elm is a woman whom Britzolakis describes as "a witchy, primeval mother figure, governed by the deathly moon-mother figure" (Bloom Ed. *Views* 120). Through personal experience, she knows the fundamental truth about life ("the bottom"): her roots have gone deep into the earth to find this truth – a truth that humans fear to know. This knowing the bottom is an image for getting to the bottom of one's own psyche. (Elm trees are noted for their deep roots. The "tap root" is "the largest, most central, and most dominant root from which other roots sprout laterally" [Wikipedia article].)

The tree asks whether the listener hears in her sighing (presumably the sound of the wind through the branches) the "dissatisfactions" of the sea, or perhaps "the voice of nothing, that was your madness." The sea is here a negative symbol representing a deep void, a great nothingness that had formerly caused the speaker to lose her sanity. (This would seem to be based on Plath's nervous breakdown and suicide attempt ten years previously.) The tree tries to teach the listener the truth of what she knows about love: it is merely "a shadow" that the listener hungers after, and it has been irretrievably lost. This is depicted metaphorically as the distant sound of the hooves of horses galloping away. The tree admonishes the speaker to "Listen: ..." which implies that the loss of love which has devastated her has occurred quite recently so that its reverberations can still be heard.

It appears that the sound of impetuous galloping is being made by the tree as a way to calm the listener, presumably by convincing her that love really has gone and there is no point deluding herself that it might return or that it was worth having in the first place. The tree will continue with the sounds, she tells the listener, "Till your head is a stone, your pillow a little turf"; that is, until she falls to sleep. Alternatively, the tree offers her "the sound of poisons." The rain (which may symbolize the victim's tears) falling on the leaves of the elm makes a sound like a "big hush" and its fruit is "tin-white, like arsenic." The elm is pointing out the brutal truth to the victim: either she gets over it or she kills herself. The tree states that she similarly has "suffered the atrocity of sunsets" (being abandoned by the sun); that is, she has been set on fire by the red color of the setting sun, leaving her "Scorched to the root," her branches left as bare as wires, her veins ("red filaments") reduced to "a hand of wires."

Stanza seven begins with the elm describing the effects of a terrible windstorm which causes her to "break up in pieces that fly about like clubs." She assumes the part of a revengeful woman seeking to strike back at the cause of her suffering because, under such suffering, she cannot play the part of the calm bystander but "must shriek." Next, the elm feels herself to be at the mercy of the moon influencing her by its cruel "drag" (a reference to the moon's pull on the tides of the sea, and its supposed connection to a woman's menstrual cycle). The elm being barren brings down the wrath of the moon, the "radiance [of moonlight] scathes me." Perhaps, the elm speculates it is she who has captured the moon in her branches. She releases the moon, but feels that she is "Diminished and flat, as after radical surgery."

The elm, which began by separating herself from and trying to comfort the victim, now appears to have become one with the listener. Rather than the elm having calmed the victim, the latter's fears have taken possession of the tree, "How your bad dreams possess and endow me." The word "endow" suggests a gift (as in an endowment to a hospital or university). In some way, the elm feels that to have the victim's bad dreams possess her is a privilege: perhaps she is acknowledging their shared femininity. The female tree removes its barrenness, symbolized by the moon, and becomes pregnant with the dreams of the victimized woman, merging with her spirit. What she carries in her womb, however, is not a physical child but an artistic cry for love as well as a phobia about the ephemeral nature of love.

Stanza ten begins with a description of (perhaps) an owl, a predatory "dark thing" that terrifies the elm because it "sleeps in me" – which suggests that the "dark thing" is part of the elm's psyche, not something distinct from it. Each night the owl "flaps out / Looking, with its hooks, for something to love." This is an oxymoron; it is a strange and cynical description of love. The owl is actually searching for prey which it will consume. This implies that love is about possession, literally getting one's claws ("hooks") into someone. (It reminds me of the very sexist phrase, "She's got her hooks in him," which describes the female as predatory.) "All day" the elm feels the presence of the owl "its soft, feathery turnings, its malignity." This is another oxymoron suggesting that love appears soft on the outside but is actually motivated by selfishness. (This may be based on Plath's own resentment against Assia Wevill, the woman for whom Hughes eventually left her.) The elm looks up at the clouds and asks whether love is no more than these insubstantial appearances, these "pale irretrievables." If so, then love is not worth agitating one's heart over because it is something of an illusion. The distinction between the elm and the victim has completely disappeared.

In the final two stanzas, the elm says it is "incapable of more knowledge." At the beginning of the poem, the elm asserted "I know the bottom," and we realize now that the poem has been about *how* the elm came to know the fundamental truths about life and love. This is also a reference to the Tree of Knowledge in the Garden of Eden, the fruit of which Adam and Eve were forbidden by God to eat. The elm knows all about good and evil in life and cares to know no more. The face, "So murderous in its strangle of branches," seems to be the Serpent which tempted Eve; it was the Serpent that brought into Eden awareness of sex and thus sexual love. Its very existence "petrifies [turns to stone] the will" making action of any kind impossible. Having been turned to stone, fissures slowly emerge in the woman's psyche as the acids of betrayal and jealously burn into the rock and cause it to disintegrate. Thus we die slowly, one disappointment or deception at a time.

"Elm" is about the loss of love and a woman's subsequent suffering which fragments her psyche and leaves her a helpless victim of abandonment (as the sun, always a male symbol abandons the elm). The elm tree bears witness to this repeated atrocity (it seems to be part of being a woman, an inevitable fate), and shrieks and cries for the inarticulate victim.

Selected Poems by Sylvia Plath

POPPIES IN JULY

During April and May 1962, Plath began to suspect that Ted Hughes was being unfaithful. Not surprisingly, this is one of the most controversial periods of Plath's biography. That the bitterness of this discovery found expression in Plath's poems is undisputed, though how the poems of this period should be read in relation to her eventual separation is less clear. Kendall notes that "The eight poems she saved between May and August all reflect, more or less obliquely, a sense of betrayal and abandonment, even though the better poems manage to distance and transform such things" (104).

Dated July 20th when her marriage to Ted Hughes was breaking up. The theme of the poem is the speaker's inability to be touched by the poppies: she can neither feel the pain of their flames not can she enjoy the dulling sleep of their opiate. The speaker actively seeks pain and seems disappointed when she cannot achieve it. Bassnett writes, "The sight of poppies in a field in July is transformed into a string of sinister images that hint at domestic violence and pain, made almost explicit with the two lines that start with the conditional 'if'" (*An Introduction* 30)

The poem has seven unrhymed two line stanzas and an eighth stanza of a single line.

1. Why would the speaker want to put her hands in the "hell flames"?
2. Why do you think that it exhausts the speaker to watch the poppies?
3. What two images (one metaphor and one simile) are used in the third and forth stanzas to describe the petals of the poppies?
4. In stanzas five, six and seven, the speaker described three ways in which she might imbibe the tranquilizing poppies. What are they?
5. What do you make of the last line?

The poem immediately establishes a contrast, a complete disconnect, between the field of poppies and the protagonist. They are lively and colourful, but she is entirely lifeless; they grow in masses, but she is alone and feels isolated. It becomes clear that the speaker is in a kind of limbo: something has happened that has hurt her very much, and she feels detached, as though perhaps whatever it was has not really become real yet. (It is not true to say, as many critics do, that the protagonist feels 'numb'; she just feels 'out of it', which is not at all the same thing.) She sees two ways out of her impasse: either by experiencing intense physical pain or by falling into a drug-induced sleep.

Although the repetition of the word "little" on the first line is almost affectionate, the first four stanzas are filled with violent images. The speaker addresses the poppies as "little hell flames" (suggestive of the punishment of some sin), "the skin of a mouth / A mouth just bloodied" (someone has been punched in the mouth) and "Little bloody skirts" (which may symbolize menstrual blood). Evidently, the protagonist feels that she should be punished in Hell because she puts both "hands among the flames," but the paradox is that "Nothing burns" and she feels no pain. This failure further alienates protagonist and poppies. What does affect her is the energy and life-force that the poppies embody (compare "Tulips"), "Flickering like that, wrinkly and clear red." Their color suggests life and vigor which "exhausts" the watching woman who feels enervated. Then there is a change. For all of their life, it is the poppies that now seem to be suffering because the speaker is desperately trying to "touch" them, to find something in them with which she can identify. They have been punched and their mouths are bleeding and the speaker empathizes with their suffering. (Plath almost always wore dark red lipstick.) If the bloody skirt does represent menstrual blood, then it is a sign of a failure to conceive. In England, a 'skirt' is a slang term for a woman, so the blood may more generally represent the suffering of women at the hands of men.

Notice the use of long vowel sounds (a, o, u) which embody the poet's lethargic and numbed state in lines like, "I cannot touch you" and "it exhausts me to watch you." In contrast, lines which describe the poppies use short, sharp vowel sounds which capture their movement and energy in lines like, "Little poppies ..." and "Flickering like that, wrinkly and clear red ..."

The last four stanzas introduce another aspect of poppies, their association with opium and therefore sleep; the protagonist craves the numb feeling they create which would allow her to escape her despair. Unfortunately for the speaker, she is no more susceptible to the "fumes" of the poppies than she was to the "flames." Even in the form of "nauseous capsules" or "liquors ... in this glass capsule" (liquid tranquilizer or sleeping pills), they have no effect on her. She desperately seeks their, "Dulling and stilling" effect (more long vowels), but it evades her.

In stanza six, the protagonist sets out the two courses that might lead to recovery, "If I could bleed, or sleep," but she can do neither. She cannot, "marry a hurt like that!" If she could, she would become a part of it (husband and wife are one flesh); the bloody hurt symbolized by the poppies would be something tangible, while her own suffering is more psychological.

In the end she feels like the speaker in "Tulips" who says, "The tulips are too red in the first place, they hurt me." The difference is that in the earlier poem the color of life finally does reawaken in the protagonist the will to live in the real world, while in this poem, the speaker concludes by wanting a world that is "colorless. Colorless" – the very antithesis of the poppies. The ultimate colorless world is, of course, death.

The way that the protagonist comes upon the blooming poppies recalls the opening of "Daffodils" by William Wordsworth:

> I wandered lonely as a cloud
> That floats on high o'er vales and hills,
> When all at once I saw a crowd,

Selected Poems by Sylvia Plath

>A host of golden daffodils;
>Beside the lake, beneath the trees,
>Fluttering and dancing in the breeze.

Readers might also compare "Ode to A Nightingale" by John Keats, a poem in which the speaker similarly seeks to escape a world of suffering. The second and third stanzas seem particularly appropriate to "Poppies in July":

>O, for a draught of vintage! that hath been
>>Cool'd a long age in the deep-delved earth,
>
>Tasting of Flora and the country green,
>>Dance, and Provençal song, and sunburnt mirth!
>
>O for a beaker full of the warm South,
>>Full of the true, the blushful Hippocrene,
>>>With beaded bubbles winking at the brim,
>>>>And purple-stained mouth;
>>
>>That I might drink, and leave the world unseen,
>>>And with thee fade away into the forest dim:
>
>Fade far away, dissolve, and quite forget
>>What thou among the leaves hast never known,
>
>The weariness, the fever, and the fret
>>Here, where men sit and hear each other groan;
>
>Where palsy shakes a few, sad, last gray hairs,
>>Where youth grows pale, and spectre thin, and dies;
>>>Where but to think is to be full of sorrow
>>>>And leaden-eyed despairs,
>>
>>Where Beauty cannot keep her lustrous eyes,
>>>Or new Love pine at them beyond to-morrow.

A BIRTHDAY PRESENT

A recording of Plath reading this poem is on YouTube.

The poem is dated September 30th after Plath had separated from Hughes. This was a period of intense poetic creativity resulting in thirty poems written during the month of September. The birthday in question would be Plath's thirtieth.

The title has a double meaning: "A present I will get on my birthday," and "The present reality of my life on my birthday." The protagonist is a woman who feels trapped by her role as mother and wife. There is very little left over ("surplus") for herself in this life. In fact, the woman regards herself as slowly being suffocated or poisoned. At the age of sixteen, Plath wrote in her Journal, "I am afraid of getting older. I am afraid of getting married. Spare me from cooking three meals a day – spare me from the relentless cage of routine and rote."

The voice heard in the poem is that of the woman. The speaker imagines the voice of the present itself and also the presence of the giver of the gift whose thoughts she paraphrases, but the bestower of the gift is never given a voice, or a name, or even a gender. This is one of Plath's more difficult poems.

The poem is written in unrhymed couplets.

Stanzas 1 - 5

1. Which details fit with the conventional idea of a birthday present and which do not?

2. Explain the activities that the speaker is described as doing? What seems to be the attitude of the present to what it sees her doing?

Stanzas 6 - 10

3. Why does the speaker feel that she does not want (perhaps does not deserve) "much of a present, anyway, this year"?

Stanzas 11 - 15

4. A second character is addressed by the speaker in these stanzas. What do we learn of the identity of this character?

Stanzas 16 – 20 and line one of 21

5. How does the speaker seek to reassure the giver of the gift?
6. What does the speaker tell the giver of the gift about the life she is currently leading?

Selected Poems by Sylvia Plath

Line two of stanza 21 - 31

7. The speaker addresses the giver of the gift as "O adding machine –" What clue does this give about the giver's identity?
8. What gift does the speaker appear to want? Why?

Commentary:

Stanzas 1 & 2

The opening stanza presents a rather grotesque version of a person's natural curiosity about what their wrapped birthday present is: naturally they ask a series of short questions in an effort to guess what is concealed in the package. From the very start, however, the questions asked by this speaker are strange and disturbing. The present is not wrapped but "behind this veil" which suggests that it is human. That it is wrapped not in bright paper but a "veil" introduces sinister connotations of concealment. A "veil" suggests either a bride or a widow in mourning for the death of her husband. The personification is continued in the conception that what is behind the veil might be "ugly ... [or] beautiful ... [have] breasts," but what kind of present is "ugly" and what kind of present is human? The other two concepts, that the gift is "shimmering" and that it might have "edges," appear to contradict the idea that it is human. The reader is completely confused, as though the poem were a riddle, and that is precisely the intention.

The first line of the second stanza again comes close to the sort of response that is expected of a birthday girl: she expresses confidence that the gift (whatever it turns out to be) will be "unique" and just what she wants. That's the sort of thing that you are *supposed* to say. However, the repetition of "I am sure," while it may convey certainty, might equally suggest that the speaker is trying to convince herself. The continued personification of the mystery gift is ominous and threatening, for as she goes about her routine jobs as homemaker she feels it "looking [at her and] ... thinking." There is something sinister in this description of a voyeur and plotter. In contrast, the picture of the protagonist "quiet at my cooking" suggests someone unassertive and conventional: she is performing the functions of her role submissively.

Stanzas 3 – 5

These stanzas are placed in speech marks. They are words spoken by the gift as the woman imagines them to be. The tone is mocking – evidently the gift is convinced that the recipient is unworthy of it. The woman is described as a conventional housewife using a recipe for her baking and following its instructions precisely, doing everything by the "rules." This one activity is clearly representative of the dull, unadventurous life that the woman lives: her life leaves her no "surplus," nothing for herself. In this context, the gift's

95

questions are ironic. How can this woman, worn down by the drudgery of her existence ("with black eye-pits and a scar") be "the one ... the elect one, the one ... the one for the annunciation?" This is a reference to the announcement of the Incarnation given by the angel Gabriel to Mary (*Luke* 1:26–38). The idea that this woman has been chosen by God to bear his child (compare "You are the baby in the barn" from "Nick and the Candlestick") is, to the gift, an absurd joke. There is nothing worthy about this woman. The reader might speculate that the gift is the protagonist's artistic self, her inspirational self and that the stanzas are asking the question of whether the protagonist can combine the roles of writer and single mother.

Stanzas 6 – 10

Stanza six exposes the naiveté of the speaker who still thinks that the gift is shimmering to attract her because "it wants me" – an expression that suggests its power and desire to possess the woman (perhaps sexually). In contrast, the woman seems passive and accepting. She will take the gift no matter what its form, "I would not mind if it were bones, or a pearl button." This line is the first explicit reference to death in the poem. The pearl recalls "Ariel's Song" of the dead father:

> Full fathom five thy father lies.
> Of his bones are coral made.
> Those are pearls that were his eyes.
> (*The Tempest* 1.2)

The woman is self-deprecating: she does not feel that she deserves "much of a present" since she is only alive because an earlier suicide attempt failed. Having failed to kill herself, she lives on "by accident." Suddenly, and without explanation the singular veil obscuring the present becomes a plural, the transparent, delicate "veils," like satin curtains at "a January window / White as babies' bedding and glittering with dead breath." There is a troubling connection of opposites here: "white" suggests purity and innocence, and babies suggest birth and generation. The veils she is describing here separate her from any valid form of life. They are ubiquitous since they are evident in aspects of her role as wife and mother. Ivory also combines the idea of value and purity with death; it is inanimate, like the pearl. Again the speaker repeats that she does "not mind what it is"; that is, what form the gift takes because compared with the wasted death-in-life of her current existence it must be better.

Stanzas 11 – 13

The second line of stanza ten has introduced a third 'character' – the giver of the gift – whom the speaker addresses directly. With rising impatience, the woman entreats this person to give her the present and so end her suspense. She

Selected Poems by Sylvia Plath

reassures the giver that she is prepared for whatever the gift proves to be whether it is "small" or an "enormity," and suggests that the two of them sit down on either side of the present "admiring the gleam, / The glaze, the mirrory variety of it." Once the gift is unveiled, the two can "eat our last supper at it, like a hospital plate." This contains two references to death: Jesus held the Last Supper knowing that he was about to be betrayed by Judas and crucified, and hospitals carry connotations of sickness and death (not to mention unappetizing food!)

The identity of the giver is important, but it is left tantalizingly vague. At times it seems to be her husband which would suggest that the gift might be a divorce that would allow the speaker to begin her life anew, to become her real self. Plath might have had Hughes in mind, but such a reading goes outside of the poem which does not even mention a husband. It appears to me that the giver is not a person at all but a part of the protagonist's psyche: if the gift is death, then it is a gift that the woman will give to herself, but part of her is, quite naturally, hesitant and reluctant. This part of her consciousness needs to be convinced by the other part that she does not need to be afraid to raise the veil and see what is on the other side – that she needs not to be afraid of dying.

Stanzas 14 – 16

The woman suggests that the giver is reluctant to hand over the gift, and thus to join her in the death ritual, because this other is terrified that she will not be able to deal with the reality of death and the "world will go up in a shriek." In these lines, the speaker becomes Salome who, after her dance, asked Herod for the head of John the Baptist. The image then switches to the shield which Perseus used in order to observe, by reflection, the head of Medusa without being killed by the sight. The precise meaning here is obscure (at least to *me*), but the speaker seems to be reassuring the giver that he is in no danger in handing over the gift.

Stanzas 17 – 18

The woman reassures the giver, saying calmly that there will be no drama: there will not even be the sound of paper; she will not even drop the ribbon on the floor; and certainly not "scream at the end." In the first lines of the stanza that have a defiant, aggrieved tone, the woman tells that giver, "I do not think you credit me with this discretion." There is real resentment in this statement.

Stanzas 19 – 25

In stanza nineteen, the veils (note the plural) do not hide the present (i.e., what is beyond death); they have been hiding from the woman what life has to offer, and they have been doing so for years. Her life has become a sort of living death because she has fallen into the stereotype of wife and mother, and it has destroyed her sense of self. To the giver, the speaker is sure that this does not seem like a big deal: the veils are "only transparencies," but to the woman they are suffocating "clouds ... like cotton," and there are, "Armies of them" – she feels under attack. The clouds are composed of "carbon monoxide," and simply by breathing she has been progressively, "Filling my veins," with the poison. In order to convince herself that death is her only way out, she has to prove to herself that she is gradually dying anyway. Poison gas also occurs in other Plath poems, such as "Poppies in October":

> A gift, a love gift
> Utterly unasked for
> By a sky
> Palely and flamily
> Igniting its carbon monoxides

The doses that the woman is inhaling are microscopic, but together the "million ... motes [specks of dust]" are taking years off her life. (Contrary to what you will read, Plath did not die of carbon monoxide poisoning. She *did* put her head in the oven and turn the gas on, but in those days domestic gas was coal gas [also called 'town gas'] which contained a variety of poisonous gases only one of which was carbon monoxide.)

The giver is "silver-suited for the occasion" of the woman's birthday, but this leads her to see the giver as a calculator – totally rational, unemotional and lacking empathy. This suggests that the giver is time itself, or the years, or life – it amounts to the same thing. If the giver is, indeed, a part of the speaker's being, then it is a part that is not willing to let go; it will fight against the idea of suicide even if it means bruising the woman (stamping "each piece purple"), even if it means condemning her to a slow death-in-life. Only the woman herself can give herself the "one thing" she wants for her birthday – her ultimate freedom from life. (Of course, this could equally apply to her husband's unwillingness to mark the clear end of their relationship which would lead the speaker to denounce him as calculating.)

Stanzas 26 – 28

The speaker feels that her death is all around her, at her window "big as the sky," which makes it sound powerful and threatening, and in her bed sheets, "cold dead center" of her existence. The use of the singular possessive pronoun "my" suggests that the woman sleeps alone, her former relationship having already "stiffen[ed] to history." She begs that the will to die should come to her quickly, not like a letter passed from hand to hand or like a message passed on through word of mouth. If that happens, she will be sixty before her present finally reaches her, and by then she will be "too numb to use it."

Stanzas 29 – 31

Once again the woman begs the giver to reveal the gift by letting down "the veil." The triple repetition of this phrase indicates the speaker's longing. If the gift is the will to kill herself, then that would have a timelessness, a gravity and a nobility which would really make it "a birthday." This is, of course, a paradox: her birthday would be her death-day. Then the knife would "not carve" but go straight in, "Pure and clean as the cry of a baby." Once again, paradoxically, she connects the idea of birth ("cry of a baby") with suicide after which she will be free of her connections to "the universe."

Conclusion

This is a poem about transition: the movement that will purify the protagonist. She must die in order to attain her true self. This may mean no more than that it order to be the artist she aspires to be she will have to 'kill' the woman who spends her time cooking and reading recipes.

THE BEE MEETING

In June, Plath and Hughes became, like many of the villagers, beekeepers. There is an irony in this because Otto Plath, professor of Biology at Boston University, wrote a thesis called *Bumblebees and their Ways* that was published in 1934. Perhaps because of the link to her father, bees seemed to hold a fascination for Plath given the frequency with which bee imagery appears in her poems.

The poem is based on an entry in her journal titled "CHARLIE POLLARD & The Beekeepers" dated June 7-8th. Plath also wrote to her mother on June 15th giving a full account of the incident described in the poem. The letter begins jauntily, "Today, guess what, we became *beekeepers*!" Though Plath calls the experience "thrilling," her account describes nothing frightening or oppressive in wearing her mask to watch, "Mr. Pollard make three hives out of one," or the setting up of their own hive. Plath even comments that, unlike Hughes "I didn't get stung at all, and when I went back to the hive later, I was delighted to see bees entering with pollen sacs full …" The poem, dated October 3rd, was the first of a sequence of five bee poems that were written over the next week. A significant difference from the earlier prose versions is the sense of being threatened that the persona conveys, and another is the fact that in the poem the protagonist is alone – there is no husband-figure. This reflects the couple's bitter separation.

The poem is largely descriptive, and these aspects present little difficulty. The incident, however, becomes symbolic of the speaker's fear at once of being isolated *and* of being assimilated into the group, with the resulting loss of her individual identity. This introduces surrealism into the description which recalls nothing quite so much as the paranoia of Franz Kafka's *The Trial* and *The Castle*. It is a complex poem that has been interpreted in various ways, so please regard the following commentary as tentative. My aim is to provide a consistent, not a definitive, reading.

Structurally, the poem is composed of eleven unrhymed five-line stanzas.

1. Explain the process by which the speaker becomes assimilated into the group of villagers and indistinguishable from them.
2. What is it that the villagers are doing to the hive and why *should* the old queen be grateful for their intervention?
3. Why is the speaker so cold at the end of the poem?

The poem opens with a question (it will be followed by ten more before the end) which immediately suggests the speaker's uncertainty and fear of the very process that she seems to have initiated – after all, it is she who comes to the bridge where the villagers are merely waiting. The bridge symbolizes that the speaker will be crossing over from one state to another: what is about to happen is a ceremony, a communion, a rite of passage. Dyne identifies the villagers' integration of the speaker into their intervention with the hive as symbolizing, "her own initiation into the received meanings of female gender ... She participates simultaneously as a willing accomplice and unsuspecting victim in a village ritual that seems to require female sacrifice or at least sedation" (105).

The villagers lack individuality and personality: each is identified by his or her role, "The rector, the midwife, the sexton, the agent for bees." In contrast to them, the speaker feels exposed and vulnerable since "they are all gloved and covered" while she wears a "sleeveless summery dress" that offers "no protection." She has, as yet, no role in the village. Immediately, the speaker is suspicious that the villagers have kept the need for protection secret from her in order to do her harm. The reader senses paranoia. The speaker feels "nude as a chicken neck," a simile which suggests vulnerability since chickens are killed by wringing their fragile necks. The simile calls to mind the visual image of a plucked chicken hanging upside-down with its long neck exposed.

In reality, the villagers have brought along protective clothes for her; they have no sinister motives. The "secretary of bees" helps the speaker into a "white shop smock." The protagonist is reassured comparing herself with the fluffy milkweed silk (a plant native to Plath's home, North America). However, though the smock seems to offer the protection she sought, it serves only to hide, not to allay "my fear, my fear, my fear." Her meeting, particularly with the rector and a midwife who together suggest marriage and childbirth, and her robing in white, though with a black veil, suggests a symbolic marriage ceremony. The presence of the sexton, however, suggests a symbolic burial. The two ideas are not, of course, incompatible since in marriage a woman gives up her family name and takes her husband's name – her spinster identity dies.

In the third stanza, the anonymity of the villagers becomes vaguely threatening. The black worn by the rector (if it *is* the rector), suggests death. (In real life, Plath did not approve of the village rector. His sermons she found so grotesque that she quickly stopped attending church.) The individuals have metamorphosed into a unit acting in unison, "Everybody is nodding a square black head," but it is a unit from which the speaker is excluded. She is merely an observer. Their invulnerability makes them "knights in visors" with "Breastplates of cheesecloth," and their feeling of security (so different from the speaker's evident insecurity) makes them smile. Their confidence is also evident in their changing voices. We are not told *how* their voices change, but immediately the unit seems to take possession of the speaker, "I am led through a beanfield." The reader senses that the protagonist feels like a victim being led to sacrifice, but also that the villagers appear menacing only because her paranoia distorts her perception.

Stanza four describes what the speaker sees as she is led through the allotment gardens of the villagers. Notice the use of personification, "tinfoil winking like people, / Feather dusters fanning their hands," and the bean flowers with eyes, hearts and (perhaps) "blood clots." Kendall comments, "Such anthropomorphising of the plants transforms them into monstrous hybrids; the reference to 'blood clots', in particular, implies sickness and fatality" (136). Right at the end, the speaker is able to take a more rational view: she is, after all, merely looking at "scarlet flowers that will one day be edible." Such a viewpoint is not, however, easily arrived at, for the speaker has to almost bully herself into it, "No, no …"

The use of the word "grove" is particularly important for it carries connotations of a religious ceremony recalling the sacred groves in ancient times where sacrifices were performed, and the "circle of hives" resembles a temple or altar. Bassnett explains, "[T]he poet has become a sacrificial victim, the borrowing of a smock becomes part of a ritual in which it appears that she is being prepared for sacrifice. The villagers appear part of a grotesque ceremony that the speaker of the poem cannot understand" (*An Introduction* 32-33). Now the speaker, who earlier was worried because she was *not* part of the group, is fully integrated into it. Her reaction is ambivalent: the Italian straw hat is "fashionable," but the black veil "moulds" to her face immediately robbing her of her identity and threatening to suffocate her (a very common feeling in Plath's poetry). She feels that she has lost control of her own future and that she is now in the hands of the villagers who "are making me one of them." Stanza six ends on yet another question: the speaker is out of her depth.

The use of the word "operation" recalls Plath's earlier hospital poems (see "The Stones"). It carries connotations of the speaker as a helpless, unconscious victim (etherized by the hawthorn scent). The anonymous "apparition in a green helmet, / Shining gloves and white suit" may be the life-changing surgeon, but again the speaker makes an effort to think rationally: it may also be someone familiar, someone benevolent, someone unthreatening.

The protagonist evidently feels the urge to break away and by so doing reassert her individuality. She is, however, "rooted" to the spot (compare "It took root at my coming" in "Night Shift"), held there by the thorns of the gorse bushes. There is a deeper reason why the protagonist cannot run: she tells us, "I could not run without having to run forever." She instinctively feels that she must go through with this ceremony of initiation into the group, through which she will establish for herself a place in the village, or alternatively remain isolate, and 'on the run' for the rest of her life. Kendall notes that, "A letter to Plath's mother, dated 9 October, refuses the prospect of return to America because 'If I start running now, I will never stop'" (136).

The initial description of the hive suggests innocence and purity, "The white hive is snug as a virgin." It is self-contained, self-sufficient and calm, "Sealing off her brood cells, her honey, and quietly humming." The intrusion of the humans, however, shatters the world of the hive which "thinks this is the end of everything." The "outriders on their hysterical elastics" fly out erratically to defend the hive, but calm has been replaced by fear and hysteria. The threatened bees now pose an active threat to the speaker whose defense is to disassociate herself from the attackers by becoming part of the natural environment so that "they will think I am cow-parsley." Only by relinquishing all claims to the human can a person avoid the pains of being human. Her defense against the bees' "animosity" will be anonymity, becoming "a personage," not a person, "in a hedgerow."

The speaker now describes the intervention which the villagers make in the hive. Once again, she is ambivalent about what they are doing. On the one hand, she describes them as predators "hunting the queen" who is very wisely hiding, but on the other hand, the entire point is to save the life of the queen, something which the queen is wise enough to know, "She is old, old, old, she must live another year, and she knows it." The new virgins wait "in their fingerjoint cells" separated from the queen they must kill by only a "curtain of wax." Having killed the queen, one of the virgins will take her place and will take "the bride flight, / The upflight of the murderess into a heaven that loves her." This describes the death of the male bee once it has inseminated the queen whose triumph is described by reference to the myth of Medea, the wronged wife of Jason, who killed her two children before ascending in triumph into the sky in a chariot. In this moment, the queen has become both female and male in one body (since the queen carries his sperm).

The "new virgins" will inevitably kill the queen unless they are moved, so the queen should be grateful for the villagers' intervention, but she does not seem to be so, "The old queen does not show herself, is she so ungrateful?" The symbolism of the intervention on the hive is as ambiguous as is the speaker's reaction to it. The disruptive sexual potency of the "new virgins" is neutralized, and the order of the hive is secured, just as the community of the village is securing itself from the intrusion of the protagonist by defining and circumscribing her role within it. On the other hand, the protagonist clearly identifies with the queen who is being protected from the "new virgins" who symbolize the younger women who will attract the husband away from his wife and tempt him into infidelity (a clear reference to Ted Hughes' adultery).

The operation having been concluded, the final stanza returns the focus to the speaker's feelings. It is as though she has been the subject of the intervention – she is the queen whose life the villagers have attempted to save by integrating her into their community. In doing so, however, the queen has been confined to the hive, her role limited to giving birth to further generations of bees. The protagonist uses a metaphor of herself as "the magician's girl who does not flinch." The reader will perhaps have three images: the girl in white around whom the (male) knife-thrower throws his knives; the girl who enters the magician's box which is then pierced by swords or by a saw (the phallic symbolism of knives is impossible to miss); and the girl who enters the magician's box and is seen, seconds later, to have disappeared. In each case, agency resides in the male and the "girl" is acted upon. The 'trick' has been performed successfully, and the villagers, in jubilant mood "are untying their disguises, they are shaking hands." The speaker's role, like that of the queen, has been passive acceptance of their manipulation.

The reader is left with the ambiguous "long white box in the grove." (In a draft, it is explicitly identified as "that coffin, so white and silent.") The speaker is no help at all in defining its significance since she can only ask, "what have they accomplished, / why am I cold." There are no question marks now because questions are *all* that the protagonist has – if every statement is a question then no statement needs a question mark. Is the box a coffin, in which the protagonist's former self has been buried? Is it a grave stone on which the protagonist's former life is recorded? Is it the 'box' of her role as mother – stereotypical roles which, though limiting, will keep her safe? The fact that the reader is left with these unanswered (and perhaps unanswerable) questions is *the whole point*.

Selected Poems by Sylvia Plath

DADDY

(See Appendix 2 for an alternative way of approaching this poem.)
A video of Plath reading this poem is on YouTube.

In a letter to her mother dated October 16th, 1962, Plath expressed exuberant confidence in the way her poetry was developing, "I am a genius of a writer; I have it in me. I am writing the best poems of my life." The next four months would prove to be a period of quite exceptional achievement. "Daddy" is perhaps Plath's single most famous poem, her most popular and most vilified poem, and one of the most commented upon short texts in modern literature. Few works of comparable length have elicited such divergent and passionate responses.

The poem, originally titled "A Birthday Present," is dated October 12th, the day Plath learned that Ted Hughes had agreed to a legal separation. This is one of Plath's most obviously autobiographical poems in that many (though by no means all) details of the life of the speaker are identical to those of Plath. The reader should, however, as always, resist identifying the voice in the poem with that of the poet (any more than readers associate Robert Browning with the murderous megalomania of the speaker in "My Last Duchess"). Otto Plath was not a Nazi, her mother was not Jewish, and Hughes did not have the look of Adolf Hitler. The persona who sees her own suffering (real or imagined) at the hands of the two dominant men in her life as being equivalent to that which the Jews suffered under the Nazis is engaging in childish fantasies, as she is when the compares her sufferings to nursery rhyme situations and stereotypical vampire stories. This is the speaker's coping strategy: by creating an image of what she fears, she seeks to exorcise her fear. In a BBC program Plath, introduced the poem by saying:

> Here is a poem spoken by a girl with an Electra complex. Her father died while she thought he was God. Her case is complicated by the fact that her father was also a Nazi and her mother very possibly part Jewish. In the daughter the two strains marry and paralyze each other – she has to act out the awful little allegory once over before she is free of it.

Clearly, Plath has based the presentation of her protagonist on Freud's theories of infantile sexuality, of transference of feelings from one person to another, and of compulsive repetitive behavior and language as a sign of neurosis. One point that seems to have escaped most critics is that Plath identifies the persona as "a girl." This in itself separates the speaker from Plath, for though both are chronologically roughly the same age (thirty), the relative psychological immaturity of the speaker is an important factor in the reader's reaction to and evaluation of what she says.

Axelrod points to the "childlike speaking voice ... The 'I' articulates itself by moving backward in time, using the language of nursery rhymes and fairy tales ... Such language accords with a child's conception of the world, not an adult's" (55-56). Dyne makes the same point when, having accepted descriptions of the poem's tone as adolescent, even childish, and hysterical, she argues that most of the criticism of the poem makes the mistake of "conflating the voice in the text with the voice of the author" In contrast, Dyne argues that the "excesses [of the poem] are part of Plath's conscious strategy of adopting the voice of a child" (48). Britzolakis is even firmer asserting, "The elements of caricature, parody, and hyperbole in 'Daddy' are so blatant that only a very determined misreading could identify the speaker with the biographical Plath," or (we may add) with the actual Otto Plath and Ted Hughes (Bloom Ed. *Views* 133). In this regard, it is relevant that Anne Stevenson reports that Plath once read the poem aloud to a friend "in a mocking, comical voice that made both women fall about with laughter" (quoted in Kendall 153) and that Plath said that the poem was intended as "light verse." Plath appears to be writing comic parody, and once this is understood many of the problems of interpretation are resolved.

Representative of critics who take a different view is Bawer who argues that in both "Daddy" and "Lady Lazarus":

> [R]ather than trying to turn homely objects and settings into objective correlatives for her emotions, she embraces wholeheartedly the idea of poem as subjective (and highly surrealistic) effusion ... nowhere else in her verse does Plath more bluntly address her most fundamental psychological conflicts ... [They] are the most arresting of Plath's verses, and it is their hate, really., that makes them so – a hate communicated, often quite effectively, by way of natural language and rhythms, manically insistent repetitions and multiple rhymes, and sensational, often surrealistic images, all of which are designed to grab the attention of the most impassive reader. (Bloom Ed. *Views* 16-17)

The poem has sixteen five-line stanzas with no set rhyme scheme. However, as Bassnett points out, "Forty-one of the 80 lines repeat the same rhyme: you/do/shoe/Jew/blue/screw/etc. The effect of this is to create an impression of great speed and furious energy accentuated by the use of other devices – broken sentences, incomplete sentences, sentences without main verbs, repetition of certain words, use of German words" (*Women Writers* 88).

Selected Poems by Sylvia Plath

It is noticeable, however, that as the poem proceeds, the speaker expresses herself more clearly and coherently, in more complete sentences indicating *the protagonist's* growing confidence that the exorcism has worked and she is free.

1. Having read the poem a number of times, write a paragraph giving your initial reactions and your first impressions of its meaning. Share your initial impressions, discuss them and write a paragraph on what you have learned from this sharing.
2. There are a number of references in the poem to the role of Germany in World War II (e.g., "Dachau ... Luftwaffe ... Aryan ... Fascist" etc.) and to Vampirism and the Occult ("Taroc ... a stake in your ... heart" etc.). Find as many of these types of references as you can and by discussion and research try to understand them. Give an account of your efforts to understand the meaning of these references. What became clearer about the meaning of the poem and what remains obscure?
3. Read and discuss the sheet on Freud (see Appendix). What light does it shed on the poem? Construct two parallel timelines, one for the life of Sylvia Plath and the other for the woman who is speaking in the poem. Mark off the significant events for each. Highlight any differences.
4. You should now be in a position to explain the theme of the poem and to explore at least some of the ways in which this theme is developed (e.g., the significance of the references to World War II and to Vampirism and the Occult should be clear by now).
5. Much of the poem is devoted to expressing the speaker's feelings about her father. This is done in a series of images, mainly metaphors (e.g., "black shoe," "a bag full of God," etc.). Make a complete list of these images and discuss what feelings they suggest.
6. Listen to Sylvia Plath reading this poem. What does her reading of the poem add to your understanding of it and your feelings about it?
7. Read the work of a range of critics on the poem. With what did you agree/disagree?

Stanzas 1 - 3

The voice of the speaker is assertive and her judgment final. She speaks in the simplest of language (all of the words in the first three lines are monosyllables). The first line, ironically, sounds like a parent scolding a naughty child, which makes sense given what we learn of the speaker's feelings about her father. Even her use of metaphor is simple: the father is a shoe in which she, a foot, has been crushed and stifled for thirty years. The reference is to the nursery rhyme:

> There was an old woman who lived in a shoe.
> She had so many children, she didn't know
> what to do;

> She gave them some broth without any bread;
> Then whipped them all soundly and put them
> to bed.

The speaker is "white" because the constricting shoe has cut off the circulation of blood, and she hardly dares it to breathe or sneeze because of the tightness of the shoe around her. The father is, by contrast, "black," a color that will be consistently associated with him in the poem. (Plath suffered severely with recurring sinusitis, and images of suffocation and of being mothered occur in many poems.)

    By the end of the first stanza, the reader has got the idea that the protagonist is convinced that her overly-dominant father has made her feel like a victim of oppression and that she has finally gained her freedom. Stanza two adds the information that it is not primarily the living father that did these things but the fact that the father died before his daughter could grow out of the stage in which she was in awe of him:

> Daddy, I have had to kill you.
> You died before I had time –

Notice that the second statement in this quotation is cut off, as though the speaker is unable or unwilling to verbalize the essence of her dilemma – that her father died before she had time to grown out of her Electra phase. His image, frozen in time, is what has oppressed her, and it is this image that she has had to "kill." The statement above is an oxymoron ("kill ... died"): paradoxically, by dying relatively young, the father has attained a status akin to immortality (at least in the mind of his doting daughter). There follows a succession of images which define the image of the dead father: a marble colossus, "a bag full of God" (I do not discount the possibility that this line might be a joking play on the idea of 'a bag full of marbles' which are quite heavy. Either way, the implication is that the father thought of himself as God, or at least that this was the daughter's perception of him. The line may also be a play on the common expression 'wind bag' for someone who talks too much.); a statue so large that its toe is "Big as a Frisco seal." (The seals in San Francisco Bay are huge. The statue reference reminds me of the Colossus of the Roman Emperor Constantine and the Colossus of Rhodes which are also huge. "Ghastly" is presumably a memory that Otto Plath's foot was infected with gangrene due to untreated diabetes; his leg was eventually amputated.) The next image of the father is of a disembodied head floating in the waters off Nauset (where a warm current meets a cold current which accounts for the different color of the waters). This final comparison is evidently one drawn from the speaker's own experience of beach holidays when she was a child and her father was alive. After he died, the speaker admits she "used to pray to recover" him. "Ach, du" is German for "Oh, you." This introduces the father's German

Selected Poems by Sylvia Plath

origins. It is also a play on the French word 'adieu' meaning 'goodbye', so it again affirms the protagonist's belief that she is free of her father.

Stanzas 4 - 7

The use of German at the end of the previous stanza is explained by the daughter's belief in her father's Polish-German origins. The first line of stanza four refers to the German re-naming of towns conquered during the occupation of Poland (a notable example being the town of Oświęcim which was renamed Auschwitz, the site of a network of Nazi concentration camps). This continues the theme of an alien identity being imposed on a helpless victim, in this case a country "Scraped flat by the roller / Of wars, wars, wars." Once again violence and oppression are associated with the male. She refers to her "Polack friend," a derogative term for Polish, but she is using the language of the Germans not her own language here. Having failed to trace her father to his origin (presumably in the hope that this would allow her to come to terms with him and move on), his "root," because all she had was the name of a town that was very common, the daughter tried to learn German to communicate with him, but found she quite literally could not speak the language. She is describing a psychological inability first to speak (in English) to her father when he was alive and later to learn his native language. Her tongue, "stuck in a barb wire snare. / Ich, ich, ich, ich," and she could only stutter 'I, I, I, I.' This image brings to mind pictures of the liberation of the concentration camps by the Americans at the end of the war. For the first time, the speaker introduces the idea that her awe before her father's image led her to project that awe onto others, "I thought every German was you." This is the first indication of the scope of the psychological damage that the speaker has suffered.

The German language and the father become a railway engine, "Chuffing me off like a Jew" to one of the concentration camps. (For a chilling description of the reality, read *Night* by Elie Wiesel.) The verb recalls the child's expression 'chuffer-train.' The callousness belongs, of course, to the oppressors (Nazis/father) not to the speaker, who identifies herself with the persecuted Jews and by implication identifies her father with the Nazis. There is something flippant about the statement, "I think I may well be a Jew." This metaphor has excited endless controversy. Seamus Heaney writes, "A poem like 'Daddy', however, brilliant a tour de force ... however its violence and vindictiveness can be understood or excused in light of the poet's parental and marital relations ... [nevertheless] rampages so permissively in the history of other people's sorrows that it simply overdraws its rights to our sympathy." The heart of the objection is that, whatever Otto Plath may have done to his daughter (in actuality or in her imagination) does not justify Plath in comparing her suffering with the deaths of millions of Jews. Such criticism makes the mistake (you can find it in the Heaney quote) of equating the persona of "Daddy" with the author. The metaphor is one that Plath *puts into the mouth of her persona*, not one that she herself endorses. For the speaker, "The extermination camps ... typify, albeit in extremis, a universe of intense suffering, of eating and being eaten, where God is the ultimate torturer" (Kendall 122). This is a description of the speaker's psychological obsession not of what the poet takes to be the reality of her situation. The question about the poet's right to use holocaust metaphors can still be asked, but at least we are now asking the question in the right way.

Stanzas 8 - 10

These stanzas elaborate on the comparison of "daddy" to the Nazis. That the speaker sees equivalence between her own suffering and that of the Jews tells us a great deal about her mental state. The first two lines of stanza eight contrast the pure white snow of the Austrian Alps and the pure beer of Vienna, capital of Austria, (a sort of picture postcard deception) with the reality of the actions of the Germans during the Holocaust. (Hitler lived in Vienna from 1907 to 1913, and the reference to beer recalls The Beer Hall Putsch [November 8-9th, 1923] which was a failed coup attempt by Hitler, then leader of the Nazi Party, to seize power in Munich.) The daughter now identifies herself with the Gypsies, another minority group persecuted by the Nazis. Jew and Gypsy are indistinguishable to the daughter, she identifies with both indiscriminately.

The images in stanza nine become more specific as "daddy" is compared to various branches of the German military: the Luftwaffe, the German air force, and the Panzers (Hitler's elite tank divisions), both of which were elements of Blitzkrieg ('lightning war'). The "neat mustache" identifies the father with Hitler himself, and his "Aryan eye, bright blue" describes him as the physical embodiment of the Aryan Master Race. One of the reasons the speaker could never talk to her father was that he spoke in "gobbledygook." Far from being childish speech, the term refers to the sort of obscure language used in technical and government reports – more a device to obfuscate than to communicate. Stanza nine ends with another incomplete statement as though the speaker's anger is just about to get the better of her, and she bites the word 'bastard' back just in time.

Earlier, the father was compared with God, but now he is "a swastika" (a black symbol within a white circle on a red background). The blackness of the symbol blocks out the sky (as the "Black shoe" of stanza one blocks out the light). The next three lines are ambiguous (and controversial):

> Every woman adores a Fascist,
> The boot in the face, the brute
> Brute heart of a brute like you.

The speaker is obviously the daughter, but the aphorism, "Every woman adores a Fascist," belongs to the father (and to all those who justify male violence against women on the grounds that 'they secretly like it' or 'they were asking for it'). The daughter has internalized the basic belief that men use to dominate women, but the reader may find in her language mockery of the belief that she states so that the lines are most accurately interpreted as a parody of man's justification of the unjustifiable.

Stanzas 11 – 14

The images that the speaker uses to describe the father change. They begin with the relatively unthreatening image of "daddy" as a teacher standing at the blackboard. The status of teacher is, naturally, above that of student: the teacher can be seen as a kind of dictator. The blackboard continues the theme of color: black imposed upon white. His blackboard obscures the daughter's view of the world – she must see the world through the lens of his instruction. The imagery soon changes, however, from domestic to demonic. The devil is often described as having cloven hooves. Her father has a cleft in his chin, but he is "no less a devil for that." He is "the black man who / Bit my pretty red heart in two." The "black man" is another way of referring to the devil, who was traditionally described as wearing black clothes and riding a black horse. The reference to biting her "heart in two" suggests that she now sees her father as a vampire seeking to steal away her lifeblood. A more symbolic interpretation would be that the daughter feels her psyche to have been split by, on the one hand, her devotion to her 'self', and on the other by her devotion to her father's image.

The speaker now gives biographical background which does something to explain the stalled Electra Complex from which she has suffered. There is no doubt that Plath draws on her own suicide attempt for the details of this crisis in the life of her persona, but the reader should not assume that the details of motivation or the attitudes are Plath's. The persona seems equally angry with her father and with herself. She speaks angrily about her obsessive attempt to "get back, back, back" to the father because it was based on what she now sees as the absurd assumption that "even the bones would do" – a delusion from which she feels herself to have recovered. At the same time, she recalls and reflects her anger at those who saved her. Their actions are described as mechanical, automatic and heartless, "they pulled me out of the sack, / And they stuck me together with glue." The second line is absurd: it reflects the failure of the psychologists to cure her and their arrogance in thinking that they had. The result was that the speaker made the same mistake again, marrying a man who was the "model" of her father. Briefly, she recaps the imagery used to describe the father. The husband is the devil, a Nazi and a torturer, "A man in black with a Meinkampf look / And a love of the rack and the screw."

There is heavy end-stopping after the repetition of the daughter's marriage vows, "I said I do, I do." This represents the turning point in the poem: the fight-back starts here. She declares herself free of her father: she is 'over him.'

To convey this she uses a macabre but humorous metaphor, "The black telephone's off at the root, / The voices just can't worm through." She's pulled the telephone cable out of the socket (a symbolic castration of the father) so that it does not receive any more messages. Her father is in his grave, food for worms, and the worms have no way of reaching the speaker. She is free.

Stanzas 15 – 16

The daughter asserts her freedom from both her father and her surrogate father, the "vampire who said he was you." She is finally laying her father's spirit to rest. Her closing image of him is as Count Dracula killed by the villagers who never really liked him and "always *knew* it was [him]." (Plath evidently has in mind the village in Devon where she lived with Hughes.) In a scene that seems to be right out of a 'B' horror movie (and deliberately so), they have hammered a stake through his heart and are dancing on his grave. The speaker wants the poem to be a celebration of her liberation from the hold which her idealized father has had on her, but the poem makes it clear that her victory is not as clear or complete as she wants to believe. The simple statement "I'm through" carries several possible meanings: "I'm finished with you and free of you"; "I'm finished with what I have to say about you"; "I'm defeated, exhausted with fighting you"; "I've finally got through to you (on the black telephone)"; or "I'm dead." Which of these meaning the speaker has in mind is unclear; perhaps she does not herself know.

The style in which the poem is written is a reflection of the mind of the daughter confronting its own suffering. The simple language, rapid rhythm and obsessive rhyming are the ways in which she attempts to convince herself that she is now in control of her life. Uroff writes that the poem is, "a demonstration of the mind confronting its own suffering and trying to control that by which it feels controlled … the speaker is caught in her own strategies. She can control her terrors by forcing them into images, but she seems to have no understanding of the confusion her wild image-making betrays … The pace of the poem reveals its speaker as one driven by a hysterical need for complete control, a need that stems from the fear that without such control she will be destroyed." The reader is left doubting the victory that she claims, and this ambiguity is the surest indication of the distance Plath establishes between persona and poet.

MEDUSA

A recording of Plath reading this poem is on YouTube.

Dated October 16th, this poem (originally titled "Mum: Medusa") is in many ways a companion piece to "Daddy." In that poem the persona seeks to announce her liberation from the influence of the father and in "Medusa" the persona, a tortured narrator attempting to shed an identity that she feels has been imposed on her and to find her true self through abandonment of the mother-figure, makes much the same declaration about her independence from her (still living) mother. Dyne calls it, "her most extreme poem of matricidal rage" (93). A reading of the *Journals* shows that Plath's relationship with her mother, Aurelia, was not so positive as she portrayed it to be in her *Letters Home*. Undoubtedly, Plath felt the need to attain some distance from Aurelia in order to become her own person, and never more than when she was left alone with her two children after Hughes moved out. Nevertheless, as always, Plath is not writing autobiography but using autobiography as the basis for creative writing. Bassnett comments, "The umbilical relationship between daughter and mother/medusa binds them both together and the daughter cannot do anything except declare in the last line of the poem that 'there is nothing between us', which in view of what has gone before seems to be more of a wish or a hope than a statement" (*An Introduction* 93).

The poem is amongst Plath's most difficult largely because of the complexity of the imagery which links the Medusa jellyfish with the Medusa gorgon in the Greek myth, and with related religious and maritime imagery. In Greek mythology, Medusa was one of the three Gorgon sisters. She had the face of an ugly woman with snakes instead of hair, and anyone who looked into her eyes was immediately turned to stone. Jellyfish also belong to the genus of creatures known as 'Medusozoa' because of their generally rounded shape and tentacles (the equivalent of the snakes of Medusa). The name of the saucer or moon jellyfish, the most common jellyfish species on British shores, is 'Aurelia Aurita' (the "white sticks" of stanza one) which links it to the name of Plath's mother.

The poem has eight unrhymed five-line stanzas (quintains) and a concluding single-line stanza. The lines have no set length or meter.

1. At the start of the poem, where does the speaker appear to be and what is she doing?
2. What do the sea and the creatures in the sea appear to represent? (Clue: The speaker describes herself as a boat.)
3. The speaker asks, "Did I [by coming to live on the European side of the Atlantic] escape, I wonder?" What evidence is there that the mother still manages to 'keep in touch' – perhaps more easily than the daughter would want?

A Study Guide

4. Stanzas 5 and 6 describe a visit that the mother paid to the daughter. In what ways does the daughter now regard the visit as a personal disaster for her?
5. In stanzas 7 and 8 what images does the speaker use to assert her total independence of her mother?
6. In stanza 8 what motive does the speaker attribute to the mother to explain her constant interference?
7. What does the speaker mean when she says, "There is nothing between us"? Is she right?

Rosenblatt offers the following observations that are relevant to this poem, "To address someone else in a poem is to include the other [the person addressed] as an actual presence within the poem ... But in Plath's case particularly, the address to the other has violent consequences: the other is almost always a persecutor, who threatens the speaker's existence. By choosing to use dramatic address and dramatic monologues, Plath places her personae in direct contact with a figure who threatens them with death" (148).

Stanza one opens with the speaker looking out (either actually or in imagination) from the beach toward the sea. Medusa is located beyond the landspit of stones – stones just large enough to stop the Medusa's speech, so that the landspit is a defensive bulwark protecting the speaker. The word 'spit' also suggests a grilling spit, a sharp steel spike for impaling meat which here metaphorically impales the sea. The mother seems to be at the mercy of the sea, her eyes and ears "rolled by ... the sea's incoherences." Nevertheless, the sea is her "house." Where the father in "Daddy" is "A bag full of God," here the mother's head is a "God-ball" (the shape is suggested by the shape of jellyfish) and the effect on the speaker is equally "unnerving." The highly original word suggests 'eyeball' representing the mother's all-seeing nature and the speaker's inability to escape. The problem for the protagonist is that everything has to be seen through the "Lens of [her mother's] mercies" so that she feels smothered by apparent sympathy and pity.

In the second stanza, "stooges" "refers to the small commensal animals called medusafish that look like tiny heart-shaped muscles and swim near the larger medusa, unharmed by its tentacles" (Quinn, Lane Ed. *New Views* 100). From the context, these seem to be the mother's spies, those whom the mother 'employs' to keep an eye on her daughter and to keep her safe in the mother's absence. The speaker compares herself to a small boat shadowed by these "wild cells" which take the form of "hearts" representing the suffocating love of the mother for the daughter. The "Red stigmata at the very center" links the mother's love and sacrifice to that of Christ (stigmata being the bloody marks of the crucifixion left on Christ's body). The "Jesus hair" refers to the way Jesus is usually depicted (particularly on the cross) with long, straggly hair; to the snakes that are Medusa's hair; and to the tentacles of the jellyfish: the mother sees herself as her daughter's savior, but to the daughter such love is as

Selected Poems by Sylvia Plath

deadly as Medusa's gaze and as painful as a jellyfish sting. Notice how the Medusa has been described as a series of body parts: mouth, eyes, ears, head, cells, heart and hair. The mother is ubiquitous in the sea, "Riding the rip tide to the nearest point of departure." A rip tide is a strong undertow which drags swimmers out from the beach as the tide recedes. (They are more common on the east coast of America than in the U.K.). This suggests that the mother is awaiting any opportunity to pull the daughter away from the land in order that the two can be reunited.

It now becomes clear that the Atlantic Ocean separates the protagonist from her mother (as it did Plath and Aurelia), yet the speaker clearly doubts whether she has escaped her mother's influence and control since she is constantly drawn back to think of her. Medusa is "Old barnacled umbilicus" a metaphor that combines nautical imagery with imagery of her mother's body. Barnacles are small, grayish-white crustaceans that live on rocks, pilings, and boat hulls, and the umbilicus is the navel, the point at which the umbilical cord, which connects a baby in the womb to its mother, is attached to the fetus. Linking this to the marine imagery, the word "umbilicus" is also applied to the depressed central area on the coiled shells of some mollusks. The speaker feels connected to her mother by the umbilical cord of the "Atlantic cable" which carries telegraph and telephone communications between the U.S and the U.K. It seems to the speaker that she has not really escaped because the cable linking her to her mother (whether biological, psychological, mystical, or technological) seems to be "Keeping itself ... in a state of miraculous repair." (There can be no doubt that Plath is drawing on her tense relationship with her own mother at the time she was struggling to set up house in London. The evidence for this is in the *Letters Home* for this period.) The words "it seems" may suggest the speaker's belief, or hope, that the connection is not as mysteriously indestructible as it appears to be. The question, "Did I escape, I wonder?" may have an affirmative answer.

In any case, the voice of the mother is "always ... at the end of my line" because the two are literally only a telephone call apart. The daughter is clearly irritated by her mother's, "Tremulous breath at the end of my line," a description that suggests the mother's quivering, timid or nervous manner, which the speaker feels is designed to make her (the daughter) feel guilty. The next lines are ambiguous. The persona's "water rod" seems to be something like the forked stick or rod[s] that dowsers use to locate ground water. Plath may also have in mind Aaron's rod which had miraculous power over water:

> And the LORD spake unto Moses, "Say unto Aaron, 'Take thy rod, and stretch out thine hand upon the waters of Egypt, upon their streams, upon their rivers, and upon their ponds, and upon all their pools of water, that

> they may become blood; and that there may be blood throughout all the land of Egypt, both in vessels of wood, and in vessels of stone.'"
> (*Exodus* 7:19 KJV)

and also the rod of Moses:

> And Moses lifted up his hand, and with his rod he smote the rock twice: and the water came out abundantly, and the congregation drank, and their beasts also. (*Numbers* 20:11 KJV)

These references clarify the meaning of these lines: the mother rushes toward the rod (the daughter) in a way the speaker describes as "upleaping ... / dazzling and grateful, / Touching and sucking." The verbs begin by being positive and even beautiful, but they change. Touching, when not welcome, is a form of assault, and the reference to sucking reminds the metaphor of the father as vampire in "Daddy." The fact that the rod seems to be in the daughter's hand is interpreted by some to show that she has the power to attract or to repulse her mother, but there is nothing really to support this idea in stanza four, and stanza five entirely contradicts it. The image does, however, suggest a mutual dependence.

Stanza five begins with an assertion which recalls the statement, "The black telephone's off at the root, / The voices just can't worm through." In this case, the phone (it would have been black Bakelite because all phones at that time were) is still functioning, but the speaker is adamant that she did not use it to contact her mother. Despite this, the mother got on a ship and "steamed to me over the sea." (Plath's mother visited her daughter and her husband in Devon in the late summer of 1962 at the time when Plath's suspicions about Hughes' adultery were growing. Plath later wrote to her mother of that visit, "The horror of what you saw and what I saw you see last summer is between us and I cannot face you again until I have a new life.") The mother is compared in a metaphor with the placenta which provides nourishment for the fetus through the umbilical cord. Thus, the mother is asserting possession of the daughter, reclaiming her, and denying her individuality. The description "Fat and red" is pretty repulsive, and the effect of the mother's arrival is to paralyze "the kicking lovers" – evidently a reference to the daughter's sexual relationship, which the mother comes close to wrecking.

"Cobra light" is an oxymoron. It equates the jellyfish sting, which can occasionally be fatal (depending on the species) with the world's most venomous snake. The image suggests that the impact of the mother was subtle but deadly: she squeezed "the breath from the blood bells / Of the fuchsia [evening primrose]." The site "Living Arts Originals: Enrich Your Life With Symbols" states that "The flower symbolism associated with the fuchsia is confiding love." Assuming that this is what the speaker has in mind, then the suffocating impact of the mother is clear. This leads to the description of the daughter fighting for breath, "Dead and moneyless" (at least in the mother's eyes), and feeling not only that her mother can see through to her very essence, but that her mother has exposed her to the same scrutiny from everyone else. (When Plath and Hughes first determined to live on the proceeds of their writing alone, they were taking a tremendous gamble and money was tight. After the break-up with Hughes, Plath was emotionally "Dead" and even more strapped for money since she had published relatively little. Again, Plath is writing *out of* her own experience but not *about* her own experience.)

The persona feels that her mother sees through her as effectively as an X-ray, exposing all of her vulnerabilities. For the first time in the poem, the daughter addresses the mother directly rather than speaking about her. With the metaphor of a "Communion wafer" the imagery switches from maritime to religious. A communicant takes the wafer in recognition that Christ sacrificed his life for mankind; the speaker is angrily sarcastic in asking whether her mother is arrogant enough to see herself as Christ. (Again, Plath is drawing on her own experience. Years before, Plath wrote to her brother Warren, "You know as I do, and it is a frightening thing, that mother would actually kill herself for us if we calmly accepted all she wanted to do for us. She is an abnormally altruistic person, and I have realized lately that we have to fight against her selflessness as we would fight against a deadly disease" [quoted by Quinn, Lane Ed. *New Views* 103].) The speaker rejects the essence of the mother-baby bond, feeding: she will not eat of her body as a Christian eats of the body of Christ in the form of the communion wafer, and as a fetus 'eats' of the mother through the umbilical cord, and as a baby does by sucking at the breast. She rejects the mother's identification of herself as the Virgin Mary crying (blubbering) over the crucified body of her child because the daughter does not regard herself as defeated. This is not, of course, the same as rejecting the real Mary, the transcendent mother offered by Christianity. Nevertheless, she admits that her mother is the "Bottle in which I live, / Ghastly Vatican." The first metaphor is clear enough. It recalls the title of Plath's novel "The Bell Jar." (It may also be a reference to the British fairy tale *The Little Old Woman Who Lived in a Vinegar Bottle*.) The second (a rather shocking oxymoron, at least to readers who are Catholic, which Plath was not) refers to the Vatican City which is a walled enclave within the city of Rome and to the absolute power which the Pope has over the faith and lives of Catholics. The speaker wants to encounter the world as herself, free and independent.

The next stanza returns to the sea imagery. The "hot salt" to which the daughter refers is both the mother's tears and her amniotic fluid, the protective liquid contained by the amniotic sac of a pregnant female which provides nutrients ('salts') and is, for obvious reasons, at body temperature. The daughter accuses her mother of the jealousy of a sexually impotent eunuch.

(Compare Iago, "Oh, beware, my lord, of jealousy! / It is the green-eyed monster which doth mock / The meat it feeds on" [Othello 3.3].) All the mother can do is impotently try to direct the way that her daughter lives. Metaphorically, her wishes will be snakelike (an image which recalls the umbilical cord and the cobra mentioned earlier) and "Hiss at my sins" out of envy – the suggestion being that the mother is trying to live vicariously though her daughter. Finally, the speaker shouts, "Off, off, eely tentacle!" The "eely" tentacle represents her mother's possessiveness, her all-enclosing clinginess, in an image that draws on earlier references to the snakes of Medusa, the cobra, and the tentacles of the jellyfish. She asserts, "There is nothing between us" in what at first reading seems to be an unambiguous declaration that there is neither love nor connection between herself and her mother. However, just as in "Daddy", there are ambiguities, for if there is nothing between mother and daughter then they are *one*, attached and inter-dependent. In the light of this interpretation, the reader may go back to these lines:

> I didn't call you at all.
> Nevertheless, nevertheless
> You steamed to me over the sea

Originally the repetition of the word "nevertheless" appears to be a sign of the speaker's frustration, even anger, at her mother's intrusiveness, but might it not also be interpreted as a sign of relief that the mother did not abandon her? This raises the question of whether the speaker does not secretly long for the very thing that she seems to be rejecting – an inconsistent attitude probably typical of adolescents (or either sex) but not of an adult woman.

Once again, the deliberate ambiguity of the entire poem, the way in which the speaker's ostensible meaning is undercut by the very words she uses, shows the poet's conscious desire to re-imagine her personal situation into impersonal art. In support of this view, Dunning suggests a much more universal interpretation of the poem:

> There is an additional possibility that the mother-figure in 'Medusa' is symbolic of the female, rather than a literal representation of a parent. If we accept this reading, the poem becomes wholly different, exposing Plath's feelings of entrapment by her gender, societal expectations and the need to conform. A submissive loss of identity caused by gender can also be read within 'The Applicant,' 'The Jailor,' Plath's journals and her letters home.
> (Mari Ellis Dunning *Wonderful Words and Book Reviews*)

Selected Poems by Sylvia Plath

In contrast, however, Dyne argues that this is one of those poems in which Plath "fails to create a metaphoric narrative that safely exteriorizes the threat that her mother's gender embodied. Several narrative lines are generated by the psychodrama of the mother's parasitic solitude that consumes what it nurtures, but none are dramatically coherent or entirely intelligible" (95). This relative failure (if one accepts Dyne's judgment) may go a long way to explaining the obscurities of the poem.

LESBOS

This poem, dated October 18th, is based on an incident that happened at the time of the break-up of Plath's marriage. She took her two young children and some pet kittens in the car to visit her friends, Marvin and Kathy Kane, who lived in Cornwall. Unfortunately, The friend insisted that Frieda (Plath's daughter) leave her kittens outside, and the visit became tense and embarrassing. It is important to stress, however, that Plath only took the basic situation as the germ of the scenario developed in her poem much of which is purely fictional (e.g., Frieda was certainly not "schizophrenic").

The basic situation seems to be this: the speaker has two young children but there is no reference to a father. The speaker's friend has one child and a husband who appears to be unfaithful and unable to satisfy her sexually. The friend is trying to dominate, bully, or manipulate the speaker who finally rejects her. If this overview is accurate, it should help you to understand some of the details of the poem.

Lesbos is a Greek island. Bassnett states, "The title of the poem is ironic; Lesbos was the center of female intellectual activity in ancient Greece, presided over by the poet Sappho, but here it is used to indicate both the common experience of suffering at the hands of men that women share and the failure of the two women in the poem to communicate with one another and help lessen the pain" (*An Introduction* 108). Sappho was said to have "loved women," but the relationship between the Sappho/Plath persona and the other female is adversarial. Britzolakis describes the poem as "a pseudo-dramatic monologue addressed to a female interlocutor, explores a rivalrous and perversely eroticized relationship between two women" (Gill Ed. *Companion* 113).

This poem is written in long, unrhymed stanzas of varying length with irregular length lines.

Stanza 1

1. How does the speaker feel about the way her friend's home is decorated and furnished?
2. Why does the friend regard the speaker as a "pathological liar" and her infant daughter as "schizophrenic"?
3. What has happened that has upset the speaker's daughter.
4. Explain the friend's different attitude to the speaker's two children and how she feels about her own husband.

Stanza 2

5. What further details of the friend's house are given and what mood is created?

Selected Poems by Sylvia Plath

6. Explain why the husband "slumps out for a coffee" and why the speaker would rather he had stayed.

Stanza 3

7. The speaker remembers a time when she and her friend were not at each other's throats. Where were they? What were they doing?

Stanza 4

8. In this stanza the speaker packs up her stuff and leaves. What is important about the manner in which the two women part?

Stanza 5 and 6

9. The speaker gives her final thoughts as she leaves. What has destroyed the genuine friendship that once existed between these two women?

Commentary:

Stanza 1

The opening of the poem describes a domestic scene in a way that foreshadows conflict. The reader can hear the hostility in the sibilants of "viciousness" and "potatoes hiss," and the short, hard vowels in the first line. The potatoes (frying or boiling) foreshadow the hissing anger of the two women. The speaker finds fault with the décor of the room which appears to be 'contemporary American' with the new florescent tubes that buzz, and "paper strips" instead of doors, which suggests flimsiness and deception. All in all, it looks fake – like a film set. The reference to the friend's "widow's frizz" may anticipate the failed state of her current marriage (i.e., she is effectively already a widow). 'Frizz' means tightly curled but since it also means "to fry or sear with a sizzling noise" it recalls the cooking sounds already referred to. The word can also mean "the condition of being frizzed" which may indicate how close the friend is to a nervous breakdown (Free Dictionary).

The speaker turns to address her friend and to describing what she assumes her friend thinks of her. She calls her friend "love" (a common term of address in England) and has undoubtedly praised the décor (because that's what one is *supposed* to do), hence she is "a pathological [i.e., compulsive] liar." The infant daughter appears to the friend (remember that the speaker is putting these words into her mouth) to be having an uncontrolled tantrum lying face down on the floor kicking, because her kittens have been put outside where she can't hear them. It's clear to the friend that the child is "schizophrenic." In turn, the speaker finds her friend's action insensitive: she has "stuck" (not, for example, 'placed', or 'taken') the kittens in "a sort of cement well." This echoes the tragic fate of kittens in fairy tales and nursery rhymes, such as:

121

>Ding, dong, bell,
>Pussy's in the well!
>Who put her in?
>Little Tommy Green.
>Who pulled her out?
>Big Johnny Stout.

With its harsh monosyllables, the description of the kittens is hardly cute, "they crap and puke and cry," but the speaker seems to be blaming her friend for that. Now the hostess says outright that she cannot stand the speaker's daughter, mainly because she is a girl (as though it would not be so bad if she were a boy). If the reader is still under any illusions, it ought finally be clear that this is not an account of a real conversations that actually happened; it is an imaginative reconstruction by a very biased protagonists of what was unsaid during the visit.

Now it is the turn of the speaker to be 'catty'. She compares the voice of the friend with a "bad radio" – a fairly common insult. Before the invention of transistors, radios (and televisions) depended on fragile tubes to control the electric current: when the current surged, or when they got old, the tubes would blow and you would need to call the repairman. The woman's voice is thus no longer audible to Plath. The "staticky noise of the new" is an apt description of the tinny sound of a radio getting a poor signal. The phrase "blown your tubes," however, suggests another interpretation: if this is seen as a reference to the woman's fallopian tubes (which carry an egg from the ovary to the uterus), the speaker is implying that the friend's resentment against her daughter may be because she has herself lost the ability to have children. She has literally blown her chances of having another baby.

The speaker's account of the conversation becomes increasingly surreal and farcical – a point that commentators seem, almost universally, to miss. The idea of one woman saying to another, an old friend and guest in her house, that she should drown her kittens because they smell and drown her daughter because, "She'll cut her throat at ten if she's mad at two," is absolutely absurd. The speaker describes her own baby as a "fat snail" which is hardly complementary, but is probably meant to be affectionate. It is probably be a reference to the nursery rhyme "What Are Little Boys Made Of?":

>What are little boys made of?
>What are little boys made of?
> Snips and snails
> And puppy-dogs' tails
>That's what little boys are made of.
>
>What are little girls made of?
>What are little girls made of?

Selected Poems by Sylvia Plath

> Sugar and spice
> And all things nice
> That's what little girls are made of.

The friend loves the baby (who is also on the floor on the orange linoleum) because he is a boy, "[She] could eat him" – which is a joke when we remember the earlier description of him as a "fat snail."

The friend complains about her husband who is "just no good to [her]," a phrase that suggests sexual inadequacy, which is explained by his oppressive "Jew-Mama [who] guards his sweet sex like a pearl." He has been emasculated and made impotent by the smothering love of his mother. The casual racism and venomous bitchiness of the remark is shocking, but the speaker locates it in her friend's unspoken resentment at the fact that she only has one baby – and obviously does not expect to have another at least with her current husband while the speaker has two. The friend then begins a list of things her visitor "should" do and should wear. The reference to sitting on a rock would make the speaker Lorelei, the female siren who sat on the cliff above the River Rhine combing her golden hair, unwittingly distracting shipmen with her beauty and her song, causing them to crash on the rocks (Wikipedia article). I assume "tiger pants" (tight-fitting pants sometimes with a tiger print) were all the rage at the time. The stanza ends with the friend's vision of the two as spirits together "in another life," which is ironic given all the bitterness the two have shown toward each other. The last four lines of the stanza have a rapid movement because of the short, repetitive phrases and the rhyming "hair," "affair," and "air."

Stanza 2

The second stanza contrasts the present life of the friend with her glamorous former life in America. In the present there is "a stink of fat and baby crap" (the monosyllables and hard vowel sounds are uncompromising) and the "smog of cooking." Life is "hell" for both women who are trapped in hell by the "smog" and trapped into being "venomous opposites" for always at each other's throats. The speaker is "doped and thick" from her last sleeping pill and the friend is an "Orphan, orphan" because she is cut off from her family in the States, ill with ulcers and tuberculosis (more comic hyperbole, albeit black comedy), nostalgic for her days as a belle in "New York, in Hollywood" with the men admiring her. (Apparently Kathy Kane, Plath's hostess, had lost her parents at a young age, but I think that it would be wrong to assume that this is what the line 'means.' It is another example of Plath taking details from her life and reimagining them. Similarly, to argue that the speaker in the poem is irritated by her friend's focus on her own issues when Plath needed her empathy, is to use biography to provide information that is *not* in the poem.)

The speaker's focus turns to the "impotent husband [who] slumps out for a coffee." He is both sexually impotent and impotent to save his wife from the hell in which she is trapped. The images in the rest of the stanza come thick and fast, and are difficult to interpret. It seems that the speaker tries to prevent the husband from leaving because he acts as a lightening conductor protecting her from the spite of her friend. She uses the image of "acid baths, [and] the skyfuls off of you" to convey how much she feels helpless and hurt by her friend's viciousness. The husband, however, leaves: he is like a horse-drawn tram, his movements contained and the horse "flogged" by his wife's dominance. The image changes to an electric trolley. The sparks are a realistic description of the point where the trolley polls connect with the electric cables overhead. The closing image recalls the colloquial phrase 'the sparks flew' to describe a tense encounter. It is also an image of disintegration, "Splitting like quartz into a million bits," for the lives of all three people seem to be disintegrating.

Stanza 3

The opening line of the third stanza appears to be addressed by the speaker to her friend, and if so it marks a radical change of tone. This is explained because the verse harks back to an incident in their youth when the two women were happily together. The description of the friend as a valuable jewel is a reference to Proverbs 3:15, "She is more precious than rubies: and all the things thou canst desire are not to be compared unto her" (KJV). The protagonist recalls a night when the moon rose red "over the harbor lights" appearing to drag "its blood bag, [like a] sick / Animal." The reference to blood links the moon with the woman's menstrual cycle, but this moon appeared to have no connection with the two women because it soon grew, "normal / Hard and apart and white." The speaker admits to having been scared to death by its "scale-sheen on the sand" – a description that links it to the silvery color of fish. However, the companionship of the two women transformed the scene into one of delight and fun, "We kept picking up handfuls [of sand], loving it." The sand is compared to "dough" and "silk grits," and the experience was obviously positive – this seems to have been a time when cooking (referenced in these images) was a pleasure, unlike now. The sand is a "mulatto body" transformed into a thing of beauty. The husband, having no part in this shared communion with nature went off with the dog, though the speaker humorously suggests that it happened the other way round, "A dog picked up your doggy husband. He went on."

Stanza 4

The stanza begins with a sad acknowledgement of how much things have changed for both women since the night on the beach. Now the speaker is in silent "hate" up to her neck (a reference to the common practice of burying people up to the neck in sand), and the hatred is "Thick, thick." The speaker is preparing to leave after this less than successful visit, packing everything she will take with her: potatoes, babies, and sick cats. The parallel structure of these three lines, which begin "I am packing the ...," together with the hard vowel sounds, suggests the speaker's anger and frustration. Perhaps frightened by the loss of control she perceives in her own emotions, she takes refuge in a compulsive act of ordering. She describes her friend in an oxymoron, "O vase of acid, / It is love you are full of." The 'enemy', the one who is worthy of "hate" is the friend's husband "hugging his ball and chain down by the gate." The image of a ball and chain, as worn by prisoners, is a common one to convey the idea that marriage is a form of confinement, at least for men. Its use here implies that the man is trapped in a failing marriage. The image of the sea driving in "white and black" and then spewing it back (like the sick kittens puking) suggests that he finds no comfort there.

The speaker turns again to addressing her friend directly describing how she daily fills her man "with soul-stuff, like a pitcher." She is obviously saying that the husband lacks spirituality, but she also seems contemptuous of her friend's spirituality referring to it dismissively as "soul stuff" that she mechanically tries to pour into the empty vessel that is her husband. (The Kanes were Buddhists.) The result is that the friend is simply exhausted and her voice rings in the speaker's ear (recall the earlier comparison of the voice with a tinny radio) buzzing, "Flapping and sucking, [like a] blood-loving bat." The friend's unhappiness is sucking the life out of the speaker.

Finally packed, the speaker takes her leave. There are no words exchanged unless the words "That is that," which indicate that the friendship between the two women is over, are spoken (and there is no indication that they are). The woman simply watches from her door, and the speaker thinks she is a "Sad hag." The final speech seems to belong to the speaker: women (including herself) are no more than men's whores; there is nothing left to say because women seem to have lost their sense of self and so their ability to communicate.

Stanzas 5 and 6

The final long stanza gives the speaker's verdict on her friend and on their friendship. The protagonist sees the other woman being stifled by domesticity and marriage. The "cute décor / Close on you like the fist of a baby." Babies are noted for their instinctive ability to grip tightly onto things. In this case, the image also indicates that the woman has been suffocated by her motherhood (perhaps because it keeps her with a husband she no longer loves). It is as though she is enclosed by "an anemone, that sea / Sweetheart, that kleptomaniac." The manner in which the sea anemone captures its prey is described in this *National Geographic* article:

Their bodies are composed of an adhesive

> pedal disc, or foot, a cylindrical body, and an array of tentacles surrounding a central mouth. The tentacles are triggered by the slightest touch, firing a harpoon-like filament into their victim and injecting a paralyzing neurotoxin. The helpless prey is then guided into the mouth by the tentacles. ("Sea Anemone")

In another oxymoron, the anemone is both "Sweetheart ... [and] kleptomaniac": The other woman has been lured in by domesticity which has stolen her soul, her identity, and her freedom. Some element of independence and rebellion still survives in the speaker. As she leaves, the protagonist tells her friend that she "may be back" (a conventional politeness), but she won't, and they both know that she won't. She concludes, "Even in your Zen heaven we shan't meet." Female companionship and love appears to have been destroyed by the male.

Conclusion

This poem is a prime example of the way in which Plath entirely reworked (re-imagined might be a better word) the autobiographical incidents on which she based much of her poetry. Even the literal reading offered above makes it clear that this is *not* an account of an actual visit made by Sylvia Plath to Marvin and Kathy Kane, who do not appear as characters in the poem any more than the author does. (What the Kanes thought about the poem I have been unable to discover!) The speaker, friend and husband are, rather, generalized, figures representative of different life styles and life values which are now incompatible. Ironically, it is the single mother, struggling to cope and messy as she is, who embodies the ideals of motherhood better than the married, thoroughly modern wife. If the reader steps back a little, however, it becomes clear that the speaker and the friend might actually represent, not two different people (old friends whose lives have changed them in irreconcilable ways), but two aspects of a single divided personality. As Grant saw in his 1971 review of *Winter Trees*, this poem is a dramatic monologue in which "[a] woman is addressing her separated self' and trying desperately, but fruitlessly, to achieve reintegration and become whole as she once was (Wagner Ed. *Essays* 54). The struggle described is between woman as wife (bitter, dissatisfied wife) and homemaker (cooking in the modern kitchen and keeping a tidy house for her husband) and the independent woman trying desperately to create order in her life in a way that will allow her successfully to juggle the conflicting demands of being a loving mother to two young children and fulfill her own creative instincts.

FEVER 103°

A recording of Plath reading this poem is on YouTube.

Dated October 20th. In her introduction to a BBC reading of the poem, Plath wrote that it "is about two kinds of fire – the fires of hell, which merely agonize, and the fires of heaven, which purify. During the poem, the first sort of fire suffers itself into the second." The poem describes through complex imagery a hallucinatory descent into hell (which references Dante's *Inferno*). Fever is the body's way of purifying itself: as the speaker descends further into the fire, her former selves (the artificial roles she has had to play), are purged away and is pure enough to enter Paradise. (Plath was frequently ill during the last months of her life and she is drawing on that experience here.)

This monologue is variously addressed to "love" and "darling" but this person's identity is ambiguous. Indications in the poem suggest it is a man whose relationship with the speaker has been physically and psychologically painful. His adultery is linked to the horrors of nuclear war. The fever proves to be cathartic, releasing the speaker from her previous repressed life and helping her to form a new sense of who she is and the life she wishes to lead.

Kendall notes that the poem, "perfects, for the first time, the normally short-lined triplets which immediately become Plath's standard stanzaic pattern" (162). There is no formal rhyme scheme, although some of the lines are rhymed.

1. How does the speaker minimize, even trivialize, the traditional image we have of the fires of Hell?
2. What is threatening about the smoke that the speaker sees rising from the fires of Hell?
3. What realistic details are given of the course of the speaker's illness?
4. From the point that the speaker refers to herself as a Japanese lantern what do you notice about the things to which she compares herself?
5. What new identify (sense of self) has the speaker achieved by the end of the poem?

The first line asks a question the answer to which the protagonist will have discovered by the end of the poem. In Greek mythology, Cerberus was the monstrous, three-headed Hound of Hades. The heads of snakes grew from his back, and he had a serpent's tail. He devoured anyone who tried to escape from Hades and refused entrance to living humans. In this poem, however, he is fat and ineffective. The speaker describes him as "dull," a word that occurs three times to match the triple heads. The fires of the underworld seem incapable of "licking clean" the speaker's hurt and sin.

The "tinder cries" as the dead burn in Hell. The speaker detects the "indelible smell / Of a snuffed candle!"; that is, of a life snuffed out. The smoke of the fires seems to approach and enfold her so that she is "in a fright" that one

A Study Guide

might trap her like the scarf which killed the internationally celebrated dancer Isadora Duncan. (On the night of September 14th, 1927, Duncan was a passenger in an open-topped car. Her long silk scarf became entangled in the rear wheel breaking her neck and killing her instantly. Duncan's young son and daughter drowned while in the care of their nanny in 1913. She gave birth to a son in the following year, but the baby died shortly after birth. Understandably, Duncan suffered severe depression.) The speaker fears that she too will be caught by the scarves of Hell's smoke and dragged to her death. The "yellow sullen smokes" are like fog (or more properly 'smog', a mixture of smoke and fog) which stays close to the ground and "will not rise." (Smog was a consequence of the Industrial Revolution and the resulting air pollution. "The Great Smog of 1952 darkened the streets of London and killed approximately 4,000 people in the short time of 4 days [and a further 8,000 died from its effects in the following weeks and months]" [Wikipedia article].)

The protagonist feels relatively safe from the scarves of smoke; they "trundle round the globe," slow-moving, threatening the whole planet, but killing first "the aged and the meek" and the vulnerable baby "in its crib" (who is like a delicate orchid in a hothouse barely hanging onto life). The smoke killed the vulnerable orchid (a hothouse plant frequently grown in hanging baskets) making it "ghastly." The smoke is called a "Devilish leopard." (In *Inferno*, Dante encounters a leopard, a lion, and a she-wolf. The leopard symbolizes the sins of malice and fraud because its spots enable it to camouflage itself.) The "it" that was killed by radiation poisoning from an atom bomb "in an hour" is the baby/orchid (*not* the leopard). The bodies of adulterers have been roasted to ash, as at Hiroshima, but the final line is ambiguous: Is the sin the adultery of the victims or the mass murder of their destroyers?

A more realistic description of her situation is given by the persona: she has been in bed with a fever for three days and nights (the time Dante spent in Hell), alternately sleeping and waking. The damp sheets adhering to her "heavy as a lecher's kiss," which is a reference to the fact that she slept in the same bed with the lover who finally proved to be unfaithful to her. During this time, she has been unable to keep anything in her stomach, even lemon water and chicken broth. This section is addressed to "Darling." This seems to be a former lover. She has now learned the answer to her initial question. She feels that she is too pure for anybody: the presence of other people in her life only hurts her as the sinfulness of the world hurts the God who created and loves it.

The speaker feels herself transformed into a lantern – which seems to be a reference to the rumor that skin of Jews killed in concentration camps was made into ornamental lampshades. The speaker has gone through the cleansing fires of the crematoria attached to the death camps. However, the image immediately changes to the protagonist as a delicate and beautiful Japanese lantern (a white spherical paper lantern with a candle inside) like the moon. Her

Selected Poems by Sylvia Plath

skin of beaten gold feels, "Infinitely delicate and infinitely expensive." She feels herself to be "a huge camellia" a rapidly growing, flowering ornamental shrub. [The camellia originates in Japan as does the paper for the lantern, recalling the earlier reference to Hiroshima. Beauty has emerged through the purging fire.] The rapid switch from image to image suggests hallucination, but they all have in common value and beauty. The protagonist has found herself, and she has done so "All by myself," without the aid of the man who betrayed her.

Fever has purified the speaker, she feels ("beads of hot metal fly" refers to the mercury rising in her thermometer), and she thinks she will survive. There is a reference here to Medea, betrayed by her husband Jason, rising in triumph into the sky in a chariot. Now she is "pure acetylene." (Acetylene [C_2H_2] is a colorless gas used as a fuel which burns with an intense white flame.) She is reborn as pure spirit and thus a virgin (a contrast with the "adulterers" mentioned earlier) and ascends into Heaven accompanied by roses, cherubim and "whatever these pink things mean." The tone here is comic, almost self-mocking. The unnamed man who has been part of her life will not ascend with her "To Paradise," and neither will the other men with whom she has had (perhaps sexual) relationships. Kendall comments on the conclusion, "His punishment is to be reduced to the role of voyeur, spectating at a consummate sexual performance which renders him irrelevant, as the incandescence of fever merges with orgasm" (163). The speaker rejects her previous identity as sexualized woman, dressing herself in frills to be ogled and pawed by men.

A Study Guide

CUT

A recording of Plath reading this poem is on YouTube.

Dated October 24th. The poem begins with a simple and graphic description of something we've all probably either done or come close to doing – slicing the top off of a thumb whilst cutting vegetables. The remaining flesh at the top of the finger is compared to a hat and the blood running from the cut to the loose folds of skin in a turkey's neck. The poem was dedicated to Susan O'Neill Roe, Plath's nurse/nanny and a close friend during the period of her single motherhood.

The poem has ten unrhymed four-lined stanzas.

1. As you read the poem make a list, in two parallel columns, of the images that the speaker uses to describe her injured thumb. Head one of the columns 'Male comparisons" and the other "All other comparisons.' What do you notice?
2. The speaker describes her reaction to the injury as a "celebration." That seems odd. How do you explain it?
3. What actions does the speaker take to treat her injury?
4. How would you describe the speaker's mood at the end of the poem?

A woman has just cut off the very top of her thumb while slicing an onion. Her tone is initially a little frenzied, and her reaction, that it is "a thrill," unconventional. However, the cut is obviously not serious, and the speaker's elation may be explained by a combination of an adrenalin rush and relief. (I find not the slightest suggestion in the poem that the cut was anything other than a minor kitchen accident.) After the abrupt, and abruptly ended, first line, the protagonist takes a strangely calm and detached approach to her situation describing the result very precisely as though the thumb were not really part of her. She's obviously not in pain which is presumably being blocked by her natural endorphins. The images she uses to describe her thumb are comic: in a simile, the remaining flap of skin, which has no blood supply, is a white hat (the rhythm and language of the line is child-like); the blood is "red plush," a luxury fabric with a deep pile; the thumb is a Pilgrim scalped by an Indian; Pilgrims suggest Thanksgiving which suggests turkeys, so the blood oozing "Straight from the heart" is like a "turkey wattle / Carpet." Turkey wattle is the red protuberance that hangs from the beak, and the blood flowing is thick like a carpet; it falls onto the floor and she steps on it (presumably to wipe away the mark).

The string of humorous images continues: the thumb is like a bottle of pink champagne fizzing over, so that the event seems like a celebration. Then, the tone changes. The blood rolls out like a million "Redcoats" from the Revolutionary War. She does not know whose side they are on since bleeding is both a sign of injury and of the body healing itself; she wonders if her body is betraying her. For the first time she addresses her thumb directly. She calls it

Selected Poems by Sylvia Plath

"homunculus" (a very small human or humanoid creature often ugly or evil) and admits that she is "ill" and has taken a painkiller to get rid of the "thin / Papery feeling." This explains why she has been so detached about the cut: it has not actually become real to her yet.

Now the speaker lists a number of images to describe the thumb. The early humor has largely evaporated. These comparisons are more serious and more threatening: it is a saboteur (a traitor); a Kamikaze pilot (a Japanese suicide pilot in World War II); the blood seeping through the white gauze looks like a man in Ku Klux Klan robes (the speaker imagines the whiteness of the robes as stained by the blood of violent attacks against black people); the bandage is a babushka (in Poland and Russia, an old woman or grandmother and by association the large headscarf worn by these women). The blood soaking through the gauze in which she has wrapped the wound dries and loses its bright color, rather like iron rusting.

The next four lines are the most obscure in the poem. Dyne provides an explanation arguing that "The balled / Pulp of your heart" is a reference to the speaker's child, "the blood issue of her female sexuality ... a tarnished stain, dirtied through cultural pollution" (164). This makes sense of the following lines which describe her new-born as it, "Confronts its small / Mill of silence." Perhaps this is too specific, however. The pulp may represent any child born of any woman; it may represent the universal life-force.

The first line of the final stanza parallels the first line of the poem – perhaps the speaker has just felt a stab of pain. Certainly, the thumb is throbbing. Having recovered, the speaker's final three images are less threatening and progressively more realistic. The thumb is: a "Trepanned veteran" (a soldier with a head wound whose skull has been drilled to relieve pressure); a "Dirty girl" (this cut is very minor but very messy and she talks to her own thumb as a parent scolds a naughty child); and finally a "Thumb stump" (like the stump of a tree).

This poem seems to invite biographical and psychoanalytical interpretations: the thumb is a male phallic symbol, and the cut castration (the feminist revenge for oppression); it represents Ted Hughes and describes just what Plath would like to do to him to revenge herself for his adultery with Assia Wevill; trepanning is a reference to her own ECT treatment ten years before which has dulled her sensations; the poem is a response to the various crises (specifically the Cuban Missile Crisis) around the time it was written; the poem is about self-harming and a prediction of Plath's ultimate self-harming, suicide; the out-flowing of blood represents female gestation (menstrual flow) and, specific to Plath, her poetic creativity; the increasing blood flow symbolizes a world rushing to a nuclear holocaust. Alternatively, it is a quirky, humorously exaggerated account of the speaker's reactions to a minor cut in a kitchen accident. The obvious response is that the poem can hardly be about *all* of these.

What *can* be tied to the text? The thumb is obviously female, since it belongs to the speaker, but in roughly half of the images used (seven out of thirteen) the violent figures are male. If there is a phallic symbol in the poem, then it is the knife which has penetrated (raped) the female thumb, and the thumb is a "dirty girl" because she has lost her virginity to the man – hence the blood. ("The hymen can be stretched open the first time a girl has vaginal sex, which might cause some pain or bleeding" [planned parenthood.org].) This textual evidence certainly suggests that, whether consciously or unconsciously, Plath (and I *do* mean Plath not her persona) saw this as a poem about the hurt that men do to women.

Forgive me if I fall short of the language of critical discourse by stating flatly that I regard interpretations which see in the poem as a description of self-harming (what we now call 'cutting') and thus a prediction of Plath's future suicide as absurd.

Selected Poems by Sylvia Plath

BY CANDLELIGHT

Dated October 24th, this poem was written after Hughes had left their home in Devon but before Plath had moved from the cottage to London. Plath constantly strove to turn her subjective agonies into poetry with which her readers could relate. She achieved this by creating poetic personas whose voice is not her own voice. Most commentators believe that the more clearly this distinction is made in a particular poem the more successful that poem is, and conversely that when the distinction seems not to be clear the poetry becomes less an act of communication with the reader and more of a private expression of personal angst. That seems right to me. This poem has obvious similarities to "Nick and the Candlestick," and readers might compare the two with the above comment in mind. Dyne points out that the drafts of the two poems "reveal that Plath initially conceived them as two versions of the same poem" (161).

This is the first of the poems to her children included in this selection. They mark a considerable shift in the poet's focus and tone. Where earlier poems are inward-looking, these poems are child-centered. They are celebrations of motherhood and of motherly love. Bassnett identifies a further difference:

> In these poems there seems to be no I-persona, no intermediary fictionalised figure between the I-that-is-writer and the I-that-is-narrator within the poem. The mother who writes so powerfully about her children is also the speaker and the poems are like love letters to those children, messages without ambiguity ... [which] contrasts with the complex ambiguity of the poems about relationships between men and women. (*Women Writers* 94)

It may be so, but I still prefer to retain the idea of a persona. No doubt the voice of the mother in these poems represents a very important aspect of Plath, but it is only one aspect.

The poem is written in four stanzas of varying length within which lines have neither set length nor meter. Occasional rhyme is used without any fixed rhyme scheme except that the last two lines of each stanza rhyme (or in one case ["wall / ... real"] half-rhyme).

1. Describe the setting of the poem as it is given in stanza one.
2. The "fluid" in which the speaker and her baby meet is the fluctuating light on the candle. What does this light/fluid symbolize? (Think of *Macbeth*, "Out, out, brief candle! / Life's but a walking shadow, a poor player / That struts and frets his hour upon the stage / And then is heard no more. It is a tale / Told by an idiot, full of sound and fury / Signifying nothing" [5.5].)
3. Stanzas two and three could be seen as symbolically describing the birth of

133

the speaker's baby. What do you find important about the way that coming to life is described?

4. The "brass man" is Atlas - the candlestick is made in the form of Atlas holding up the candle. In mythology, it was Atlas who held up the heavens (i.e., the sky, not the globe of the world). Atlas "keeps the sky at bay, / The sack of black! It is everywhere, tight, tight!" What does night/blackness represent here? Who or what might Atlas represent in the life of the mother and/or the child?

5. Presumably, the five brass cannonballs at the feet of Atlas are another detail on the candlestick. What is the significance of the word "when" in the final line? (The final line makes me think of Nero playing the lyre while Rome burned!)

In this dramatic monologue, the speaker is holding her baby in her arms on a winter night. The opening stanza describes their environment in wholly negative terms: the night is cold, dark and "rough," lightened only by the weak, metallic light of the stars. The darkness is, "A sort of black horsehair, / A rough, dumb country stuff." Horsehair, which is coarse, was a common stuffing for furniture and mattresses – hence the playful pun on its being "country stuff." The darkness is the "steeled" light of the stars, a threatening metaphor which inevitably suggests a steel knife. The stanza gives a sense of the mother and baby being besieged in their home, surrounded by vague threat. Few of the potentially positive "green stars" make it to the gate of the cottage, which suggests that, if the two are going to find salvation, they will have to rely on themselves rather than on external aid. This point is emphasized by the description of the Church clock, "The dull bells tongue the hour." The use of the word "tongue" instead of "clapper" involves a personification of the bells which seem to be trying to communicate (at least by announcing the time), but the speaker dismisses their "dull" voice as having no relevance to herself or her child. In the reflection of the mirror, she sees their floating image illuminated by a single, flickering candle. Candlepower was a unit quantifying the intensity of a light source: against all this enclosing darkness, the protagonist's only protection is the smallest unit of light.

The speaker describes the light that fights the darkness as "the fluid in which we meet each other." This metaphor suggests amniotic fluid, the liquid that surrounds the fetus during pregnancy, which leads to the apparently paradoxical idea that in giving birth to her baby the speaker has herself been reborn. There is something holy about the light whose "haloey radiance that seems to breathe" as though it were blessing mother and child. It is the light that gives the two their reality for when it withers their shadows wither and when the flame recovers their shadows are "huge again, violent giants on the wall," an image that suggests self-confidence and power. The light gives them being; without it they are nothing. Fortunately only "One match scratch" (note the effective use of rhyme and onomatopoeia) is enough to make her baby real to the speaker. Yet that light is uncertain: the candle is compared to a flower that will not bloom but extinguishes itself, "snuffs its bud / To almost nothing, to a dull blue dud." However, though the candle initially sheds only cold blue light and the flame declines "To almost nothing," the language here is playful. 'Dud' refers to anything that does not perform as expected (like a dud firework that does not go off); the word suggests a minor failure rather than a significant one and this comic tone is supported by the full rhyme of "bud" and "dud."

The third stanza describes the awakening of the child in a similarly light-hearted tone. The baby is a "Balled hedgehog" because it is curled into the fetal position. The comparison recalls the benign hedgehogs of children's fiction, as in Beatrix Potter's *The Tale of Mrs. Tiggy-Winkle*. There is also a play on the word "Balled" since it sounds like 'bald' which the new-born baby is. The idea of a bald hedgehog is an oxymoron suggesting the baby's vulnerability. As the baby wakes, it is initially, "Small and cross" as babies tend to be, but at the same time (so that the two actions appear to be causally connected) the candle flame recovers and, "Grows tall." The metaphor of the flame as a "yellow knife" is reassuring not threatening since it is a 'weapon' on the side of mother and child: it is a knife to cut through the enveloping darkness; it is a yellow to replace the cold blue light. The baby clutches the bars of his crib and cries loudly as the mother rocks him and sings to calm him, suggesting that both are fully alive. The speaker sees herself as "like a boat" conveying her child across the ocean of the Indian carpet and the cold floor.

The closing description of the stanza is of the brass candlestick that holds the candle that the protagonist has just lit. It is in the form of Atlas, one of the Titans in Greek mythology who was condemned to hold up the sky for eternity. Here he is holding up the "white pillar with the light [the candle] / That keeps the sky at bay" and he is doing it "as best he can." Those four words mark the return to a darker tone in the poem.

In the final stanza, the brass figure becomes the child's sole heirloom, his only protector keeping "the sky at bay." The tone suddenly darkens: the positivity of the previous stanza evaporates suddenly when the speaker is again confronted by the night which she describes as, "The sack of black! It is everywhere, tight, tight!" The suffocating darkness suggests depression and/or death and the speaker's panicked helplessness in the face of these. (Compare "they pulled me out of the sack" from "Daddy" and note that, in a letter to her mother at about this time, Plath wrote of her life in the Devon cottage as like being, "Stuck down here as into sack, I fight for air and freedom.") All she can bequeath to her child is the candlestick which she knows will not offer protection for the sky *will* inevitably fall. I have been unable to determine the significance of the "pile of five brass cannonballs" which do not appear in any representation of Atlas I have seen – perhaps they were a peculiarity of that particular candlestick. One thing is clear, they are all that Atlas has, "No child, no wife" with which to fight the on-coming darkness – family will not save the child from disaster. It is insufficient and inappropriate ammunition, as the speaker indicates in her exclamation, "Five balls! Five bright brass balls!" They will provide only a distraction, to Atlas and to Nick, when "the sky falls."

The poem dramatizes the feelings of the persona that, much as she loves her child, and much as she longs to be able to do so, she will be unable to protect him from the enveloping darkness of the world beyond their cottage. The mood swings from fear, through elation to despair. By the end of the poem, the speaker has simply vanished, leaving the baby with its sole "Poor heirloom," a tiny image of the absent hero father. The tone of this poem is fatalistic; the speaker feels helplessly overwhelmed by life.

LADY LAZARUS

A recording of Plath reading this poem is on YouTube.

This poem was written between October 23rd and 29th, a period of creative intensity during which Plath wrote eight other poems. In her introduction to her reading for a BBC reading, Plath said:

> The speaker is a woman who has the great and
> terrible gift of being reborn. The only trouble
> is, she has to die first. She is the Phoenix, the
> libertarian spirit, what you will. She is also just
> a good, plain resourceful woman.

Bassnett explains that the poem develops the "idea of the woman who transcends her torments and exacts revenge for her suffering on men ... [S]he has come back once again into the world of male savagery" (*An Introduction* 111-112). Plath may have had in mind these lines from T. S. Eliot's "The Love Song of J. Alfred Prufrock" (1915):

> Would it have been worth while
> To have bitten off the matter with a smile,
> To have squeezed the universe into a ball
> To roll it toward some overwhelming question,
> To say: "I am Lazarus, come from the dead,
> Come back to tell you all, I shall tell you
> all"—

In this poem, the speaker certainly thinks it worthwhile to come back from the grave to tell her story. Unlike the Biblical Lazarus, the protagonist relies on no external savior to bring her back to life, "the center of power becomes the individual's ability to create the self" (Sanazaro in Wagner Ed. *Essays* 90).

In order to describe the experience of the speaker, Plath adapts specific incidents from her own life, in this case her suicide attempts, yet to associate the speaker directly with Plath, as many critics do, ignores the fact that Plath employs a whole range of creative techniques to distance herself from her protagonist. The persona in this poem emerges as a fantasy figure, a kind of superhero, who is able to control her own impulse to commit suicide. She is a performance artist (compare the story "The Hunger Artist" by Franz Kafka), a Holocaust survivor, a phoenix and a shape-shifting chameleon. In these guises, the protagonist is able not only to come back from the dead but to exact revenge on those who drove her to suicide. Throughout the monologue, the speaker is desperate (almost hysterical) in her compulsion to present herself as in complete control because the alternative would be to face up to the fact that she is quite evidently *not* in control. Her performance is thus an unrealistic and ultimately unconvincing defense against her own despair. That is the truth that the poem embodies. Plath shows that she has a deep understanding of the way

A Study Guide

in which people with suicidal tendencies think; she does not, however, endorse those ways of thinking.

The poem is composed of twenty-eight unrhymed three-line stanzas.

1. What exactly is it that the speaker has done again?
2. Why might her enemy be terrified when he peels the "napkin" off her face?
3. When the speaker says, "This is Number Three," to what is she referring?
4. Who are the "Gentlemen, ladies" who watch the protagonist's body being unwrapped? How do they react?
5. For what are the observers charged extra?
6. At what point in the poem does the speaker's extended metaphor of herself as a performance artist transition into an extended metaphor of herself as a Jewish victim of the death camps?

Dyne describes the persona in this poem as "searingly self-confident – a taunting, bitchy phoenix who appears to loathe her earlier incarnations ... almost as much as she does her present audience" (55). O'Hare, writing more generally of the *Ariel* monologues, stresses their comedy suggesting that Plath's intention is:

> to immerse her readers in dramatic situations, sequences of thought, or perceived events, uninterpreted except by the excited and abnormal consciousness reporting them ... The poems' central concerns are the personae themselves ... [It] is precisely the abnormality, idiosyncrasy, or downright wrongness of these personae that the poems display. (Lane Ed. *New Views* 82)

The tone of the first line is immediately ironic and self-mocking. It is by no means clear what the speaker has "done ... again," but the idea that she manages to do it "One year in every ten [years]" suggests that she regards it as nothing serious. Notice also the playful use of rhyme ("else/well," half-rhyme; "well/hell," full rhyme; "hell/real," half-rhyme; "real/call," half-rhyme). The protagonist's claim to be, "A sort of walking miracle," comes across as comic hyperbole. She then begins to itemize her resurrected body parts. Her skin is as bright as the preserved skin on "a Nazi lampshade." (The story that when U.S. troops entered Buchenwald they found a lampshade made from the skin of a dead Jew may well be apocryphal. Nevertheless, it was taken as fact and seen as symbolic of Nazi barbarism.) Her foot functions as a paperweight, and her face is like fine Jewish linen. We can see that the speaker associates herself specifically with the Jewish victims of the Holocaust and those against her with the Nazis.

Selected Poems by Sylvia Plath

She has been reborn (this is the miracle referred to earlier) and asks for the "napkin" (the burial cloth) to be peeled away from her face. Will her enemy be terrified of what he sees because it is evidence of the woman's indestructibility: a face with everything there and "sour breath" which will "vanish in a day" as she breathes normally again? Now the reference to Lazarus becomes clear: four days after his death, Jesus raised Lazarus of Bethany from the grave still bound in his grave clothes. Similarly, the speaker has been raised from the dead and her flesh, which had spent some time decomposing ("the flesh / The grave cave ate") will regenerate, and she will be again a "smiling woman" of "only thirty."

The flippant tone continues as the protagonist compares herself to a cat with nine lives: this has been her third killing of herself, so that leaves her another six lives (enough for her to make it to ninety). Each attempted suicide is a gesture to "trash" an entire decade, to obliterate it, because the speaker has found life so intolerable. She describes herself as a performance artist (think David Blaine and Criss Angel) drawing spectators to the unwrapping of her corpse. The crowd pushes in, crunching their peanuts, to see "The big strip tease." The verb "shoves" conveys how heartless and sensation-seeking the crowds are. The "million filaments" are the flash bulbs of reporters determined to capture the moment for the papers. Like a carnival barker she addresses her audience, "Gentlemen, ladies," and begins to show off, one by one, her newly uncovered body parts, displaying that they are really there and fully alive. ['Roll up, roll up, roll up! See the wonder of the age! The lady has been sealed in her tomb for four days. Watch as her funeral clothes are unwound and, body-part by body-part, see her come back to life! Roll up, roll up, roll up!' – or something like that!] Like a magician's assistant who has disappeared from a magic cabinet, she reappears assuring the audience, "I am the same, identical woman," despite the inevitable loss of weight ("I may be skin and bone").

Now the speaker gives an account of her previous two 'performances' (for which Plath is obviously drawing on her own suicide attempts). The attempt at ten was not seriously intended. It was an "accident," something that "happened" to her rather than something deliberate, but at twenty she really did mean, "To last it out and not come back at all." She rolled up in the fetal position, blocking out the entire world, "I rocked shut / As a seashell." (In 1953, Plath hid in the crawl space under her house and took an overdose of her mother's sleeping pills. She was there three days before she was found in a coma, pulled out and eventually resuscitated.) The reference to rock suggests the stone used to close the entrance to cave tombs in Jesus' time. However, they found her and through persistence they dragged her back to life. They even had to "pick the worms off me like sticky pearls" which is an oxymoron since pearls are shiny and smooth. Pearls are, however, associated with death in Plath's poetry (see "Full Fathom Five").

The speaker takes pride in her art: she gives a good performance. The whole art of dying is to do it like you mean it, so that it is "like hell ... / feels real," and that part is easy to do because you just "stay put." The escape at the last moment is the theatrical climax, the "Comeback in broad day," so that the audience shouts that it is, "'A miracle!'" It is that part which gives the speaker a real buzz ("That knocks me out"). However, the statement that she is 'resurrected', "To the same place, the same face, the same brute / Amused shout" reveals (perhaps despite her conscious intentions) her personal disappointment; it has been a great trick but nothing has changed (same world, same self, same unfeeling, brutal people), which is presumably why she will perform again in about ten years when life has again become intolerable. This is the closest the protagonist comes to facing her inmost fear that she probably will do it again. What she presents to the crowd as a miraculous return to health, the speaker knows to be merely a return to the perilous conditions that have driven her three times to suicide, but this is a truth that she *must repress*. It must be replaced by the fantasy of survival. Kendall points to this limitation, "[The speaker's] myth of rebirth relies on repetition. Her reborn identities are never able to establish themselves in a role they can accept, so they must recurrently undergo a new and painful transformation through death ... unlike the speaker of 'Daddy', who hopes to consign her trauma to the past rather than to continue to relive it in contemporary experience, she presents herself as fatalistically locked in this cycle ..." (158). (Note, in the original, Kendal begins the above quotation with the word "Plath's." My own analysis resists equating the protagonist with the poet.)

The speaker continues the performance metaphor: there are additional charges, on a steeply sliding scale, for the voyeurs who want to get a really intimate experience of the resurrected woman or a souvenir. She feels that she is on display: the people clamoring around her are desperate to get a piece of her (a gross parody of the idea of Christian relics), and she is equally determined (notice the repetition of the word "charge") to make them pay for it. This brings to the speaker's mind the death camps where the Jews were stripped naked before being taken into the gas chambers (which were disguised as showers) and everything of value, including their hair, clothes, jewelry, and gold fillings was taken from them. (Plath may also be drawing on the description of the crucifixion, "And they crucified him, and parted his garments, casting lots: that it might be fulfilled which was spoken by the prophet, They parted my garments among them, and upon my vesture did they cast lots" [*Matthew* 27:35].)

Now she addresses those who control her performance, "So, so, Herr Doktor. / So, Herr Enemy." In terms of the performance artist metaphor, this might be her manager and the barker. In terms of actual suicide, it would be the doctors who (as another persona says in "Daddy") "pulled me out of the sack, /

Selected Poems by Sylvia Plath

And ... stuck me together with glue." The doctors would be her enemy because they were thwarting her intention – putting her back together against her will. In terms of the death camp metaphor, the lines refer to the army doctors who supervised operations at the camps (men like Dr Josef Mengele, known as the Angel of Death, the SS officer and physician in Auschwitz who supervised horrific medical experiments on prisoners).

The imagery has now entirely changed. The speaker no longer sees herself as an expert performance artist, but as a victim being exploited by her enemies. In this extended metaphor, she explicitly identifies herself with the Jewish victims of the Holocaust. Her enemies have taken possession of her and made her *their* work of art, their "valuable" possession. The Nazis melted down the gold in their victims' teeth, but she is their "pure gold baby / That melts to a shriek." The next line is bitterly sarcastic, "Do not think I underestimate your great concern." The line refers to her persecutors and to those who look on: they have no human concern for her; their only concern is to make sure that they extract all of the melted gold they can.

The repetition of the word "ash" recalls the funeral service from the *Book of Common Prayer* (1662) which reads, in part, "we therefore commit his body to the ground; earth to earth, ashes to ashes, dust to dust; in sure and certain hope of the Resurrection to eternal life, through our Lord Jesus Christ." Having been incinerated, her enemies "poke" (a verb that conveys their lack of feeling) through the ashes and find no trace of flesh and bone. There are, however, the spoils: the gold wedding ring and tooth filling, and the fat that can be processed into soap. (The story that the Nazis made soap from human fat was widely believed, since after the horrors of the death camps came to light almost anything was believable, but this probably was not true.)

The final two stanzas end with a warning which is made more powerful by the rhyming of four of the last five lines, "Beware / Beware / ... red hair / ... like air." She names her enemies: Nazis, God, and the Devil – all male. What they do not know, however, is that she will rise from the fire like a Phoenix and then take her revenge, "And I eat men like air." This seems to be another reference to the liberating post-coital moment described in *The Bee Meeting*, "the bride flight, / The upflight of the murderess into a heaven that loves her." The last two words of the poem link the speaker with the chameleon. Chameleons were believed to eat air and subsist entirely on it. (Compare, "Chameleons feed on light and air," [Shelley "An Exhortation"] and Hamlet's statement to Claudius that he fares, "Excellent, I' faith, of the chameleon's dish. I eat the air, promise-crammed" [*Hamlet* 3.2].) Like the phoenix, this is another metaphor of transformation – in this case from victim to avenger. Bassnett concludes, "Lady Lazarus is a survivor, a woman who understands the nature of her enemy and returns to fight back" (*Women*

Writers 116). I would perhaps add only that this is how the persona desperately wants to think of herself.

As Uroff correctly points out, the persona "speaks of herself in hyperboles ... she is engaging in self-parody." In her increasingly desperate attempts to "manipulate her own terror," she fails to understand that:

> Her extreme control in fact is intimately entwined with her suicidal tendencies. The suicide is her own victim, can control her own fate. If she is not to succumb to this desire, she must engage in the elaborate ritual which goes on all the time in the mind of the would-be suicide by which she allays her persistent wish to destroy herself. Her act is the only means of dealing with a situation she cannot face. Her control is not sane but hysterical ... By making a spectacle out of herself and by locating the victimizer outside herself in the doctor and the crowd, she is casting out her terrors so that she can control them. When she says at the end that she will rise and eat men like air, she is projecting (and again perhaps she is only boasting) her destruction outward. That last stanza of defiance is in fact an effort of the mind to triumph over terror, to rise and not to succumb to its own victimization ... When she sees herself as a victimized Jew or Christ, she may be engaging in self-parody but the extremity of her circumstances does not allow her to realize it. The poet behind the poem is not caricaturing Lady Lazarus as she had Miss Drake; she is rather allowing Lady Lazarus to caricature herself and thus demonstrating the way in which the mind turns ritualistic against horror.

I cannot improve on that!

Selected Poems by Sylvia Plath

ARIEL

A recording of Plath reading this poem is on YouTube.

The poem is dated October 27th, Plath's 30th (and last) birthday. Many of the difficulties of this poem disappear when you know that Ariel was the name of Plath's favorite horse. She rode frequently during her time in Devon. The poem describes a woman riding in the countryside in the early morning. It explores the feeling of ecstasy and personal transformation that occurs to the speaker through the exhilarating combination of speed and contact with nature. The ride is uninterrupted when a child's cry is heard. The sun fully rises and burns off the dew. Rosenblatt comments, "[The poem] possesses power and importance to the degree to which the horse-back ride Plath once took becomes something more – a ride into the eye of the sun, a journey to death, a stripping of personality and selfhood" (16). This suggests that the 'meaning' of the poem is essentially symbolic.

The poem has ten unrhymed stanzas of three lines each, and a final single-line stanza.

1. Which lines in the first three stanzas clearly refer to riding a horse?
2. What time of the day is it and how do you know? What does the persona appear to be doing at the start of the poem?
3. As she rides through the air, what happens to the speaker as described in stanzas six and seven?
4. The speaker seems to change her physical state in stanza eight. To what?
5. What is the "red Eye"? What happens to the speaker?

The poem begins in the pre-dawn darkness. Everything is still since the darkness is unchanging. Presumably the speaker is waiting for there to be enough light to begin her ride. In the second line, she describes how the blue of hills in the distance come into being with the light of dawn. Notice the sibilance of the long 's' sounds throughout the first stanza. Together with the long vowels, the rhythm here is slow embodying the very stasis that the poet describes. The long vowels are particularly evident in the phrase "Pour of tor" which describes the way in which the dawn seems to pour out the distant hills.

The second stanza begins with the protagonist addressing her horse as "God's lioness." 'Ariel' in Hebrew translates to 'the lion or lioness of God' (See Isaiah 29:1, "Woe to Ariel, to Ariel, the city where David dwelt!" [KJV]. The city in question is Jerusalem. The Lion of Judah is the symbol of the tribe of Judah, the root of King David.) She begins her ride and immediately experiences the feeling of becoming one with her horse. Ending the stanza by splitting subject from verb in "The furrow / Splits and passes" embodies the rapidity of the horse's movement. The plowed furrow past which she rides is "sister to" the neck of her horse: nature is fully integrated, and while she rides she too becomes a part of nature. Yet the furrow is as elusive as the brown neck of her horse. Notice the hard 'c' sounds in the lines, "The brown arc / Of the neck I cannot catch," which convey the intensity of the speaker's feelings. The image suggests that the protagonist is striving for an experience that must ultimately elude her: she may feel at one with Ariel, but the horse has a freedom that she can never attain.

As she rides, the narrator observes black berries in the hedgerows. The metaphor "Nigger-eye" to describe the berries is likely to be found offensive by the contemporary reader, and, whilst I would argue that it is not intentionally racist, I will not defend it. The "hooks" or thorns on the berry bushes (they are mentioned in "Blackberrying" and several other poems) appear to grasp at her. Here they seem to be holding her back (as though they would ultimately pull her from her horse) which suggests that they represent the things in her life which the protagonist feels to be restricting her – preventing her from becoming the person she could be. The fact that they are, "Black sweet blood mouthfuls, / Shadows," may be seen as sinister, for it is "Stasis in darkness" from which the speaker seems to feel the need to escape. Perhaps they threaten, vampire-like, to suck her dry of her "sweet blood."

An unnamed "something else" forcefully pulls the protagonist through the air. (Only as we read on are we able to identify this as her own longing for freedom.) As she rides, it seems that she is stripped of her identity which flakes off her heels and is blown away. She is "White Godiva," the legendary wife of Leofric, Earl of Mercia, who rode naked on her horse through Coventry to save the people from her husband's unfair taxation. Like Godiva, the speaker is declaring her female independence from stifling patriarchal forces. The color white suggests virginity, purity, and freedom, and it stands in contrast to the black berries that want to trap and hold her back. Notice the speed of the verse at this point produced by a combination of short vowels and consonants, the absence of definite and indefinite articles, and the lack of grammatical structure as the speaker jumps from one (apparently) unconnected idea to the next. The dried up parts of her flake off, and she feels stripped of, "Dead hands, dead stringencies." These represent the people and the social rules that have constricted her development of her own identity. This is not, however, an involuntary effect – in fact the very opposite. The phrase, "I unpeel," implies that the speaker is in control of her actions and very conscious of what she wants to achieve.

Now she feels free; she is the foam on the sea of wheat in the fields, part of the sparkling of light on the seas, "And now I / Foam to wheat, a glitter of seas." The reader cannot miss the sexual connotations of this description. From the very start, the riding of the horse has been described in terms that might equally apply to sexual intercourse, "How one we grow, / Pivot of heels and knees!" It seems now that the point of orgasm has been reached. The foam may be suggested by the horse foaming at the mouth during the gallop, but it also suggests the ejaculation of the male during sex, and the rider's foam describes her vaginal discharge during orgasm. The word "glitter" in Plath's poems frequently suggests masturbation. The speaker is entirely unashamed of the sexual pleasure of her exhilarating ride.

The protagonist seems to hear a child's cry through a wall (evidence of one of those "Dead hands" that restrict her), but she ignores it: her priority now is her personal freedom, to pursue which she must reject the traditional female role of mother and care-giver. The idea of hearing the child through a wall suggests that she would accept enclosure and limitation if she responded to the cry. (It also suggests that she isn't actually outside riding a horse but is inside the cottage.) The protagonist is now "the arrow." She has become one with Ariel and has taken upon herself phallic masculinity that gives her total control of her own direction and destiny. (Compare this definition of the difference between the male and the female given by Mrs. Willard in *The Bell Jar*, "What a man is is an arrow into the future and what a woman is is the place the arrow shoots off from" and the reflection of the novel's protagonist, Esther, "I wanted … to shoot off in all directions myself, like the coloured arrow from a Fourth of July rocket" [Lane *New Views* 188].) More ambiguously, the speaker is also the "dew that flies / Suicidal, at one with the drive / Into the red / Eye, the cauldron of morning." She wishes to subsume herself not only by becoming one with the horse but by vanishing like moisture into the warming risen sun. In seeking to become one with the cosmos (the "I" of the narration *becomes* the "Eye" of dawn), she must relinquish her personal identity.

Evidently the poem explores far more than a simple morning ride – the reader should note that the one word missing from the poem is 'horse'. It has universal themes of spiritual freedom and re-birth through mystical union with a universal spirit. Dyne calls this, "The ecstatic translation of the flesh into other natural forms …" (120). The protagonist achieves religious ecstasy by the end of the poem, the sort of spiritual state that a person might attain through meditation. The title "Ariel" refers to the androgynous sprite from Shakespeare's play *The Tempest* who is imprisoned and subsequently released by Prospero. Similarly, the protagonist's spirit is liberated from those things that distort and limit it (a patriarchal society which manifests itself in all aspects of life including upbringing, marriage and even the reception of a writer's work). By the end of the, poem the protagonist has transcended gender and the limitations of gender. Before a person can create that person must create her self.

POPPIES IN OCTOBER

A recording of Plath reading this poem is on YouTube.

This poem was written on the same day as "Ariel." The unseasonal appearance of poppies so late in the year seems a staggering gift out of place with everything else. This links the poem to "Tulips" where vibrant red flowers seem similarly out of place. Plath uses her familiar unrhymed three-line stanzas with even more variation in line length than normal.

1. Stanza one contains two comparisons used to emphasize the redness of the poppies: one is beautiful and the other shocking. Explain them both.
2. In stanzas two and three the "sky" and the "eyes" are too dead to have asked for or to appreciate such a gift. How is this made clear?
3. The final stanza once again stresses the unlikely element of the poppies. How?
4. "O my God, what am I". This line and the two which follow seem to encapsulate the impact which the poppies have upon the speaker. Try to explain this in your own words.

"In the temperate zones, poppies bloom from spring into early summer" (Wikipedia article); hence, the title "Poppies in October" is, if taken to refer literally to flowers blooming, an oxymoron. It has been suggested that that the poppies might be the paper poppies worn in Britain at the approach of Remembrance Day, but that is on November 11 almost two weeks after the poem was composed so it seems unlikely – though not impossible. (The idea that the line refers to cut flowers offered for sale can be rejected. Poppies do not survive long once cut and so are not sold in this way.) Nevertheless, the symbolism of the poppies is ambiguous. Because of the poppy seeds (the source of opium), the flower has often been symbolic of sleep, forgetfulness and death. In the Great War, poppies grew in great profusion on the battlefields and came to symbolize the slaughter of a generation. On the other hand, the blood-red poppy symbolizes life-giving blood, and in Greek mythology the poppy symbolized the resurrection to life after death. It is clear by the end of the poem which of these symbolic meanings is intended by the poet.

The opening line is a description of dawn with the rising sun illuminating the clouds and tingeing them with red. The noun "sun-clouds" is not the oxymoron that it seems to be: the clouds are not obstructing the sun, rather the sun glows on and through them. The clouds suggest colorful frilly skirts worn by women, as do the up-turned petals of the poppies. However, though the dawn was beautiful, the cloud-skirts are easily outdone by the poppy-skirts. (There actually is a style of skirt called a 'poppy skirt' – a flared skirt normally with a floral pattern, though not necessarily poppies.)

The speaker jumps to another comparison. The poppies also outdo "the woman in the ambulance /Whose red heart blooms through her coat so astoundingly." There seems to be little point in trying to 'place' the speaker in a particular place where she saw a woman in an ambulance. Perhaps she did, but if so she does not say so in the poem: the incident may well be hypothetical. Nor is it clear if the woman is a patient (a woman whose heart is hemorrhaging) or a nurse (a woman whose heart "blooms" metaphorically with love and compassion as she treats the patient). There is also a religious association in that Jesus is often portrayed with a sacred bleeding heart to represent his love for mankind. The point is that the redness and life-force of the poppies is greater than any of these.

Whatever their origin, the speaker sees the poppies as, "A gift, a love gift / Utterly unasked for," either by the sky, which is still red enough to ignite "its carbon monoxides," or by the properly dressed men walking to work in their bowler hats. The former, though paler now, still has enough red to tinge the exhaust fumes from the cars. The latter have been "dulled" by the routine of their lives and are unable to appreciate the unexpected beauty of these flowers and, by extension, the richness of life's possibilities. Plath may have in mind these lines from T. S. Eliot's *The Waste Land* (1922):

> Unreal City,
> Under the brown fog of a winter dawn,
> A crowd flowed over London Bridge, so many,
> I had not thought death had undone so many.
> Sighs, short and infrequent, were exhaled,
> And each man fixed his eyes before his feet.
> ("The Burial of the Dead" 60-65)

The speaker, however, receives the flowers as an unlooked-for token of the beauty of the world and is joyful. It is a genuinely religious impulse that leads her to ask God what she has done to deserve this gift; she feels unworthy. The poppies have triumphed over "a forest of frost" that sought to deny them life so that now their "late mouths ... cry open." They may be crying in joy or perhaps in agony, but they are alive against all the odds. The poppies assert their will to life in "a dawn of cornflowers." Cornflowers are a rich blue, always a cool color in Plath's poems. Since cornflowers also bloom in summer, the speaker cannot be speaking literally. The poppies symbolize life and passion (compare "Tulips"), whilst the cornflowers symbolize the trials and adversities (the frosts) of life. The poem is a joyful assertion of the beauty and indestructibility of the urge to live.

A Study Guide

NICK AND THE CANDLESTICK

A recording of Plath reading this poem is on YouTube.

The poem is dated October 29th. Many of the apparent difficulties of this poem disappear when the dramatic situation is explained. The speaker, woken in the night by the crying of her baby son, Nicholas, takes a candle to light her way to the baby's room. (The rural cottage has no electricity). She enters his dark bedroom where she finds rugs on the wall, an aquarium, and her baby. In her imagination, familiar objects are transformed into hostile ones making the world appear to be a dangerous and hostile place. All is redeemed, however, by the child for he gives the speaker's life a purpose that she has not found anywhere else.

The poem is written in unrhymed three-line stanzas with variable line lengths. The vocabulary is very simple with a high proportion of monosyllables.

1. Explain the opening metaphor, "I am a miner".
2. In what ways is the metaphor of the stalactites made so negative?
3. In what ways is the metaphor of the "Black bat airs" made so negative?
4. Can you explain the reference to "holy Joes"? (Think religion.)
5. The lines, "And the fish, the fish - / Christ! ..." involves a rather bitter joke. Do you know why?
6. How is religion presented so negatively?
7. The recovery of the candle flame in stanzas seven and eight seems to be symbolic. Of what?
8. How does the description of the child establish its purity?
9. Examine the final stanza very carefully. It includes two images. Explain each

The speaker begins with the startling metaphor of herself as "a miner" negotiating her way along a tunnel. This is an uncharacteristically definitive statement for a Plath persona, one who will appear throughout the poem as engaged and proactive at least in the domestic world of her home. The light of the candle "burns blue": its pure flame casts only a cold light – the first ominous detail in the poem. In the protagonist's imagination, the mine becomes an ancient cave, and the wax melting from the candle flame forms "stalactites" (the ones that hang down from the roof of a cave). The mine/cave next morphs in her imagination into the "earthen womb" – the birthplace of all life. Yet the womb is crying tears "from its dead boredom." This line has produced a number of responses from critics including frank mystification. It may refer to the boredom of being pregnant, the helplessness of having to wait around for nine months for the baby to pop out so that the mother can start her life again. Perhaps the speaker felt this boredom during her pregnancy and now projects it onto the constantly pregnant "earthen womb." The metaphor is ironic and paradoxical since Nick has spent nine months in the speaker's womb, but is now very much born.

Returning to the cave image, the speaker imagines bats flying at her, wrapping their wings around her face and smothering her. It is not bats, however, but "Black bat airs" that enfold her. This could be a description of the clinging cold she encounters as she moves down the corridor, but it might also be a reference to depressive thoughts (unfortunately not so uncommon following a pregnancy) wrapping themselves around her like "cold homicides" (i.e.,, making her feel suicidal). However the reader interprets the "Black bat airs" we are told that, "They weld to me like plums." This simile has caused much confusion except to those who have ever eaten very hot stewed plumbs: if you try to eat a really hot stewed plum, it immediately welds (adheres) to the roof of your mouth burning it quite painfully.

By this time (if not before), it is reasonable to assume that the protagonist has made it to Nick's bedroom which may explain why she addresses the cave as though it were an old friend. The calcium icicles are the stalactites previously mentioned and a cave certainly echoes. In the room there is an aquarium which prompts the next observation. The "newts are white" because in the absence of light color pigments do not form; for the same reason, the fish are transparent "panes of ice." The speaker associates both life forms with Christianity: the newts are "Those holy Joes," an American colloquialism referring to a chaplain (particularly one in the US armed services), but also to a sanctimonious, holier-than-thou type of Christian (the kind Plath is known to have disliked intensely); the fish is associated with Christianity because the image of the fish was used by early Christians as a secret symbol with which they could identify themselves to other believers. It is now often called the "Jesus fish" which accounts for the speaker's apparently bitter exclamation "Christ!" The newt and the fish are described as being the opposite of redemptive. To the speaker they represent a "piranha religion" and a perverse form of communion in which the worshiper does not partake of the blood of Christ but has the blood sucked out of them by a religion that is anti-life. She imagines the ministers of Christianity, those sanctimonious kill-joys, biting into her toes like piranhas (omnivorous freshwater fish in South America which will devour just about anything) and sucking out her life-blood. The bitterness and negativity of the poem reaches its climax at this point: the world is cold and comfortless and Christianity offers no alternative vision. However, the tone of the poem is just about to change radically.

The candle, which has almost gone out, suddenly (and inexplicably) comes back to life and burns warmly for the first time bringing color and cheerfulness to the mine/cave/room. The protagonist happens upon her baby as though she is

149

seeing it for the first time. It is a wondrous mystery to her, like a gift she was not expecting. She asks in amazement, "O love, how did you get here?" The baby is curled up in the fetal position of an embryo, his legs still crossed as they were in the womb. This is a clear reference to Christianity: the legs of dead knights were crossed at burial to indicate that they died in the Christian faith. Unlike the bloodless newts and fishes, "The blood blooms clean," in the protagonist's child – he is the true religion. Reverting to the initial metaphor of herself as a miner, the speaker calls her son a "ruby." There is no trace of original sin or the fall of man (as in the story of Adam and Eve) in this precious gem of a child, who needs nobody's forgiveness for being alive.

The physical and moral perfection of the baby is, however, contrasted with the world into which it has been born which is characterized by "pain" of others' making. What stands out is the mother's devotion to her baby (whom she calls "love" three times) and her efforts to make his transition into this harsh world easier. The "cave" is now a space that she shares with him and which she has made as comfortable as possible with flowery fabrics in pre-modern style, "soft rugs – / The last of Victoriana." The description of the child as a "ruby" and the reference to "roses" (whether real or woven into the carpet) embody warm colors in strong contrast to the colorless, cold cave of the first half of the poem. (Compare the vibrancy of the flowers in "Tulips.")

The speaker turns again to the pain of the world and contemplates what we would now call two 'worst-case scenarios': that the world should end (because the movement of stars is already determined by their trajectory as the destination of a letter is determined by its address, and Atlas is unable to lift up the heavens) and that drinking water should be polluted by mercury (high levels of mercury can certainly have a crippling effect both on the mind and the body). The speaker certainly does not want these things to happen, but she acknowledges them as possibilities beyond her control, yet even if they happen this baby will remain for the protagonist the one stable point in a disintegrating world, the one certainty which all uncertainties "lean on, envious." This leads to the climactic final line, "You are the baby in the barn." This is a clear reference to the birth of Jesus, the leader in whose name a religion has developed which the protagonist has earlier rejected for its sanctimonious attitude. This child will be the speaker's savior, for in a real not a mystical sense this child gives meaning to an otherwise meaningless existence in a corrupt and dying world. The speaker's tone is defiant: let the world throw everything at her, she now has a reason for living and will survive it. (There is a similar optimism in Plath's *Letters Home* at this period.)

(Tragically, Nicholas Hughes committed suicide on Monday, March 16th, 2009, at his home in Alaska following a long struggle against depression.)

Selected Poems by Sylvia Plath

LETTER IN NOVEMBER

Plath wrote to her mother in November 1962:
> The next five months are grim ones. I always feel sorry to have the summertime change, with the dark evenings closing in in midafternoon, and will try to lay in some physical comforts these months – the best insurance against gloominess for me.

The speaker walks in the orchard near her cottage, squelching through the wet grass, happy but conscious of the wounds of past and future experience. As Kendall explains, the poem is based on an idea that underlies much of Plath's later poetry, "History is cyclical and (therefore) repetitive: it is a contemporary experience which cannot be consigned to the past. For all their obvious differences, the death camps of World War II, and the massacre of the Spartans at Thermopylae in 480 BC, are perceived as manifestations of this same essential underlying pattern. Amnesia becomes a desirable state …" (174-175).

The "wall of old corpses" refers to a graveyard close to the Devon cottage where Plath lived with Hughes that is also mentioned as a "row of headstones" in "The Yew Tree and the Moon".

The poem has seven unrhymed stanzas of five lines in which the lines have variable length.

1. In stanzas one and two, how does the speaker describe autumn and the on-set of winter?
2. What reasons does the speaker give for feeling "so stupidly happy"?
3. Can you explain the line, "O love, O celibate"? To whom is this line addressed?
4. Can you explain the lines, "The irreplaceable / Golds bleed and deepen, the mouths of Thermopylae"?

The letter is addressed to "Love," though the person to whom the letter is written is never definitely identified. (Having read the whole poem, the reader will most likely conclude that this is a letter by the speaker to herself. I take the line "O love, O celibate" also to be addressed to the speaker.) The setting is late autumn and the time is early morning. The colors of the vegetation have changed "Suddenly" and with it the speaker's perception of the world. Winter is coming. Much is often made of the description of the trailing branches of the laburnum (sometimes called golden chain) as "rat's tails." Since the laburnum flowers in May and June, and the tree is deciduous, it is perhaps an accurate description, though hardly a positive one. Since it is not mentioned, Plath might have expected her readers to know that the laburnum has a reputation for being poisonous.

When the speaker states, "It is the Arctic," she seems to be referring to the

151

cold weather outside, to the local countryside "with its tawn silk grasses." However, the "little black / Circle" could metaphorically be the speaker's sense of her own solitude and isolation in the countryside. The adjective "tawn" (tawny) means tan-colored, which is another sign of the coming winter. The grasses are like "silk" because of their fine texture (*not* because the grass is artificial), like "babies hair / There is a green in the air" which is a delightfully positive simile. The "green in the air" recalls the phrase "a certain meaning green" from "The Hermit At Outermost House". Despite the cold and the change to autumn colors, the speaker feels loved and cherished by nature.

The third stanza is very assertive: the first four lines each begins with the first person and makes a confident statement of well-being. The phrase "stupidly happy" is an oxymoron, but there is nothing negative in it; rather it captures the speaker's inexplicable joy in living. The description of "Squelching and squelching through the beautiful red [colors of Autumn]" is delightfully playful. The tone of self-confidence and self-assertiveness continues when the speaker states her ownership of, "This … property." Literally, she means the cottage and its orchard, but figuratively it is a statement about being entirely in control of one's life. At this point, however, a more negative tone is evident. She walks the boundary of her property "Two times a day" which at the very least suggests that she has fallen into a routine, or rut, but it also conveys a sense of confinement. She uses the verb "pace" (rather than, say, 'walk', 'stroll', or 'wander'). The word "pace" suggests impatience and even anxiety. She sniffs her territory like a dog does – a metaphor that suggests that she feels trapped. The holly is "barbarous" because its "viridian [bluish-green] / Scallops, pure iron" remind the speaker of barbed wire such as might enclose a prison yard. Now, the walls that confine her are "pure iron," implying that it will be difficult for her to break free. The final boundary is "the wall of the odd corpses," a row of gravestones in the churchyard which mark the ultimate boundary of her mortality. Ignoring the negative connotations of what she has said (and perhaps unaware of them), the speaker asserts her love for the grave stones and for the history that they encapsulate.

The speaker next turns to describe the orchard that forms part of her property. "The apples are golden," she states, which seems very positive. However, golden apples have many connotations related to mythology and fairy tales, by no means all of them positive. For example, in awarding the golden apple to Aphrodite, Paris caused the destruction of his city, Troy. It can be no coincidence that the speaker numbers her trees at seventy since this is man's life-span as given in the Bible, "As for the days of our life, they contain seventy years …" (*Psalms* 90:10). Perhaps she feels that the span of her life is reaching its close. Other references to death follow quickly. The "gold-ruddy balls" (they are no longer organic "apples" but inorganic "balls") hang from the trees, "In a thick gray death-soup," which would seem to be a description of the cold fogs of autumn. (A thick fog in England was called 'a pea souper.') The leaves on the trees remain "Gold" but are "metal and breathless" (like the holly), words which convey their unyielding and inhuman nature.

The cause of the protagonist's unhappiness is her isolation and loneliness since "Nobody but me / Walks the waist high wet." She has just addressed herself as "celibate" which is another result of her being alone. Walking "the 'waist high wet'" is a strong contrast with the earlier description of joyously "squelching" through the grass in her Wellington boots. Now the vegetation is higher and the wet overtops her Wellingtons, a metaphor of her rising despair. The beautiful golds are disappearing: the "irreplaceable" beauties of life are being lost as they bleed out and deepen to a dead brown. The reference to Thermopylae is to the mountain pass where, in 480 BC, a Spartan army of three hundred fought to the last man against a much larger Persian force. The speaker seems to be saying that her happiness will be slaughtered just as the Spartans were slaughtered – and just as permanently.

DEATH & Co.

Dated November 14th, this was the last of the poems Plath wrote that she intended to be in the collection *Ariel*. The opening line has its origin in a visit that Plath had in the hospital from two acquaintances.

The title suggests the name of a business (perhaps a firm of funeral directors) – an example of black humor. This sets the satirical tone of the poem which describes death as a business. There are two representatives of the firm so death takes two forms: on the one hand there is the traditional figure of terror and on the other a rather attractive and seductive figure. The speaker accepts the inevitability of death, but does not seek or welcome it. In fact, she shows considerable assertiveness and wit in evading the machinations of death.

The poem has six unrhymed stanzas of five lines and a final stanza of one line.

Stanzas 1 - 5

1. List the unattractive physical features which are associated with death in its traditional form.
2. In what ways does death make fun of the speaker?
3. On first impression, what makes death in its second form appear attractive?
4. How does the speaker make it clear that she has seen through this apparent attraction?

Stanzas 6 - 7

5. Why do the flowers created by the frost on windows and the glitter of a frozen drop of dew equally speak of death?

Death is personified in two very different personas. The speaker has just realized that death has two different forms, but as soon as she has realized this fact it seems "perfectly natural now." The first form that death takes is compared with the death mask of the poet William Blake (1757 – 1827) in which he appears with his eyelids closed and his eyes somewhat protruding. "The scald scar of water" is one of the visible "birthmarks that are his trademark." This seems to be a reference to the mark of the devil (such as was used to identify witches). The hairless head of the death mask suggests a second comparison with the bald head of the condor. ('Verdigris' is a green or greenish blue poisonous pigment.) The condor is a very large carrion bird native to the Americas (the Andean and California condor), and the speaker feels that she is its natural victim, "I am red meat." The bird seems to be in the very act of eating the speaker, but she asserts "I am not his yet." Death begins to mock the woman by exploiting her vulnerabilities: she photographs badly because she is unattractive. The juxtaposition of this petty jibe with the horrible image of dead babies in the morgue is shocking. He describes how sweet the babies look wearing Greek-style death-gowns, their two little feet sticking out of the bottom. The metaphor "their Ionian Death-gowns" compares the folds of the babies' shrouds with the flutings of columns in the Greek Ionian style. His point is, presumably, to convince the protagonist of the power of death: in death a sort of artistic perfection is possible that is not possible in life. This manifestation of death is all business and seriousness, "He does not smile or smoke."

The second manifestation of death is attractive and suave. Where the first is mocking, this death is "plausive" – flattering his potential victim. Yet the speaker sees through him at once. He is a "Bastard / Masturbating a glitter." The word "masturbating" implies that this man is altogether too much in love with himself. The word "glitter" is commonly used in Plath's later poems and always with negative connotations: it suggests superficial attractiveness only. The protagonist is not seduced.

The final four lines turn to a description of a winter landscape. The freezing temperature makes crystal flowers on the inside of the windows and frozen stars from drops of dew outside. She hears the tolling of a bell and concludes, in colloquial American, "Somebody's done for." On this occasion, at least, it is not the speaker who will live a little while longer. (Contrast the last three lines with John Donne, "Any man's death diminishes me, / Because I am involved in mankind, / And therefore never send to know for whom the bell tolls; / It tolls for thee.")

A Study Guide

MARY'S SONG

Dated November 19th. The narrator describes the Sunday lunch (roast lamb) cooking in the oven, but the heat of the roasting joint suggests associations of violence and murder related to Christianity, the persecution of heretics and the Holocaust. The result is a complex poem that explores one woman's feelings of persecution, betrayal, and impending destruction in the context of the vast sweep of history.

The poem has seven unrhymed stanzas of three lines.

1. Who is the "Mary" of the title? How do you know?
2. Stanza 1 is at once a domestic description of the Sunday lamb cooking in the oven and, **symbolically**, a reference to the death of Christ on the cross. Can you explain how this association is achieved?
3. What do you make of the line, "A window, holy gold"?
4. The idea of the fire which melts the fat (turning it the "precious" color of liquid gold), leads onto the idea of the fire which destroys. What specific historical examples are given?
5. In what sense do the victims of such inhuman destruction "not die"?
6. What important change in the voice of the poem occurs in line 13?
7. The gray birds bear the message of death from the past, but the last three stanzas make it clear that the speaker feels that she already inhabits a burnt, post-holocaust, world. How?
8. How does the final line of the poem, return the reader to the subject of the first line?

The poem begins in realism of the most domestic time. Sunday lunch is something of an English tradition and its centerpiece is roast meat, in this case a joint of lamb. Without mentioning the heat, its effects are described: the solid fat on the joint liquefies and becomes transparent; the meat is cooked in its own juices. Even in this stanza, however, the reader is aware of wider connotations. The "Sunday lamb" inevitably suggests Jesus, the Lamb of God, who sacrificed his life to save man from his fallen state (a result of the disobedience of Adam and Eve). There is also, however, the biblical concept of lamb to the slaughter as in "I was like a lamb or an ox that is brought to the slaughter" (Jeremiah 11:19) and "he is brought as a lamb to the slaughter" (Isaiah 53:7). This inevitably leads by process of association to the idea of religious persecutions and ultimately the ovens in which the bodies of gassed Jews were burned as the Nazis put in place their Final Solution to the Jewish 'problem'. Obviously, the reader might not consciously pick up on all of these possible associations but they are all latent in the stanza.

The transparent liquid fat suggests to the speaker a stained-glass in which the predominant color is "holy gold." The sacrifice of the lamb to the fire makes the gold produced (the liquid fat) "precious" like an icon or holy relic –

something entirely pure. It then occurs to the speaker that the same purifying fire of faith and passion that produced something holy and valuable, also produced the motivation for the burning of heretics. Tallow is a fat produced from cattle and sheep; the heretics are "tallow" because their own body fat makes them burn well. The line "Ousting the Jews" references centuries of persecution of the Jews from the first century, when Christianity broke away from its Jewish routes and later, by becoming the official religion of the Roman Empire, entirely marginalized Judaism, right up to the Final Solution and the death camps during World War II. The "thick palls" is a reference to the smoke produced by the chimneys of the crematoria at the camps. The clouds of dense smoke extend over the "cicatrix" [scar or wound], of Poland because "[t]he Nazis established six extermination camps on Polish soil. These were Chelmno (December 1941-January 1945), Belzec (March-December 1942), Sobibor (May-July 1942 and October 1942-October 1943), Treblinka (July 1942-August 1943), Majdanek (September 1941-July 1944) and Auschwitz-Birkenau (March 1942-January 1945)" ("The Holocaust Explained") and over "burnt-out Germany" because the fire-bombing of German cities at the end of the war left Germany in ruins.

When the speaker says of the various victims of Christian persecution, "They do not die," I believe she means that they live on in people's memories of them. Commentators often explain that the lines mean that those who go through the fire of purification are reborn, but I cannot derive that meaning from this line. The "grey birds," whose color recalls that of the smoke, represents the speaker's own obsessive guilt about the Holocaust: she literally feels as if she is walking through the smoke from the ovens getting the ash of burned humans in her mouth and in her eyes. In Elie Weisel's autobiographical account of the death camps, *Night*, the first thing he describes, as the train carrying him and his family nears Auschwitz, is the clouds of greasy, foul-smelling smoke from the crematoria.

"On the high / Precipice / That emptied one man into space / The ovens glowed…" I have read several interpretations of these lines, none of which made much sense of them for me. I believe that they describe a primitive act of human sacrifice (imagine Aztec prisoners climbing the steps of the temple pyramid at the top of which they will have their hearts cut out). The sacrificial victim is "emptied into heaven" at the moment he dies, and the industrialized killing of the Holocaust is simply the latest example of a long line of such sacrifice. The line "The ovens glowed like heavens, incandescent" is an oxymoron since it compares the ovens of the camps to "incandescent" "heavens." The word "incandescent" suggests not only the extreme heat, but also the passion that has generated the fire. The speaker now shifts to talk about her own personal "holocaust" – note the word is not capitalized here indicating that it does not refer to the historical Holocaust. She tells us that her holocaust is "a heart" and that she walks in it. This seems to mean that it is something that she carries around with her and that appears to surround her – in other words it is a state of being, an overwhelming guilt. Human sacrifice will do nothing to reduce the suffering. The "golden child" is the lamb in the oven being sacrificed which "the world will kill and eat." This is a reference to Holy Communion. At the Last Supper, *Matthew* 26:26-27 records,

> 26. And as they were eating, Jesus took bread, and blessed it, and brake it, and gave it to the disciples, and said, Take, eat; this is my body.
> 27. And he took the cup, and gave thanks, and gave it to them, saying, Drink ye all of it;
> 28. For this is my blood of the new testament, which is shed for many for the remission of sins.

Holy Communion is a sacrament in which the Eucharist (the consecrated bread and wine) is consumed as the body and blood of Christ or as symbols thereof. However, Christ's death will make no difference; none of the thousands and millions of deaths will ever make any difference. Commentators differ in their identification of the "golden child." Some suggest that it is Jesus, but it seems to make more sense that, at this moment, the speaker turns to her own son who will, like Jesus, be sacrificed by the world. This is "Mary's Song" and it is a lament for the future death of her child. This is where the opposition of male and female is implicit: the women are the life-givers, but it is the men who are the killers.

It is perfectly reasonable for critics to complain that comparing the suffering of an individual, possibly neurotic woman with death by fire for thousands of heretics and the extermination of millions of Jews in Poland is disproportionate. Plath is not saying that they are equivalent: she is showing us that her character regards them as equivalent – which is very different.

Selected Poems by Sylvia Plath

WINTER TREES

Dated 29th November. Bassnett writes:
> The poems from November 1962 onwards are full of complex patterns of references from Sylvia Plath's own life and previous writings, from classical mythology and Celtic mythology, from other literary sources, and from religion. Through this densely woven web of references the poems move outwards and take on a universality that makes them so extraordinary. The common critical appellage of Sylvia Plath as a 'confessional poet' breaks down here because these poems work on so many more levels than on the personal alone.
> (*Women Writers* 118)

This judgment seems to me to be entirely correct.

The poem is written in three unrhymed five-line stanzas with lines of varying length..

Stanza 1

1. What painting technique is used to describe the visual impression of the trees seen in fog?
2. "Memories growing, ring on ring" is a complex image, though not a particularly difficult one. What do you make of it?

Stanza 2

3. For what qualities does the speaker envy the trees?

Stanza 3

4. In what obvious sense are the trees "full of wings"? How does this lead naturally to the image of Leda and the swan?
5. Does the speaker mean that the trees are pietas? If so, why?
6. What is it that the "chanting" of the ringdoves fails to ease?

The trees emerge from the dawn mist and are first compared to an ink wash drawing of trees. (Ink wash is a technique similar to that used in watercolor: colors are lightened by thinning pigment with water which obviously softens the outlines.) In line two, they are compared to the impression of an ink drawing of trees left on a piece of blotting paper: the fog is the blotting paper on which the trees seem like "a botanical drawing"; that is, an illustration of a plant be printed with a botanical description in a book on plants.

159

A Study Guide

The trees rings mark the passage of time and for humans the accumulation of memories which grow "ring on ring," year on year. To the narrator, the rings represent, "A series of weddings." This seems to be an oxymoron since the whole idea of a wedding ring is to symbolize the "until death do you part" aspect of marriage. Presumably the speaker has given up on the idea of such a permanent relationship: life for her will be only a series of temporary relationships.

The second stanza expresses the speaker's envy of the trees because they are immune to the vagaries that make women's lives so difficult particularly when it comes to mating and reproduction: no abortions, not bitchy rivalries over the same man, no stealing another woman's man. The trees are entirely self-sufficient. Even the process of generation and giving birth is accomplished "effortlessly" without complication. The speaker's discontent with her womanhood is extreme. Then again, the narrator envies the trees because they experience the world in a way unattainable to her. They remain stationary, but the "footless" winds visit them, and because trees live for a long time they have experienced much more of history than has she.

The final stanza describes the trees as full of the wings of the birds that perch on their branches. The birds seem to embody "otherworldliness." Like Leda (who was raped by Zeus in the form of a swan), the trees are visited by the gods. For the first time the speaker directly addresses the trees. They are the speaker's "mother of leaves and sweetness," the source of all that is good and beautiful in the world. They are, however, "pietàs" (a pietà is a picture or sculpture of the Virgin Mary holding the dead body of Jesus Christ on her lap or in her arms) for like Mary (who was also visited by a God, through his angel, and made pregnant) they inevitably live to see the destruction of the good and the beauty to which they have given birth – it is their fate so to do. The "chanting" of ringdoves (symbols of peace and love) does nothing to ease the suffering. (The mention of rings echoes the earlier use of the word in the poem.)

SHEEP IN FOG

This poem was begun on December 2nd 1962 and revised on January 28th, 1963. Apparently Plath's revisions made the poem much more somber and dark, reflecting her own mood at this time. In December, Plath and her two children moved from her North Tawton home in Devon to London, a physical and psychological disruption that effectively interrupted Plath's writing of poetry for two months. This is the first of her final poems, of which Kendall writes, "these poems are cooler, and in one sense less urgent; the hope of rebirth has disappeared, to be replaced by resignation ... The element of fatalism, culminating in 'Edge', deprives Plath's speakers of options. There is no place for resourcefulness now: destiny has become inescapable ... Death ... has now become an ending associated with defeat, rather than a necessary route to glorious rebirth" (190, 207).

In a BBC interview, Plath said, "In this poem, the speaker's horse is proceeding at a slow, cold walk down a hill of macadam to the stable at the bottom. It is December. It is foggy. In the fog there are sheep." The foggy day leads to depressing thoughts of the emptiness of life. The difficulties of the poem spring from the juxtaposition of diverse, unconnected images in stream of consciousness writing which follows the (apparently) random thoughts and impressions of the speaker. In many ways, this poem seems to be the antithesis of the exhilarating transition described in "Ariel".

The poem is a first person monologue with five unrhymed stanzas of three lines. The language is simple and minimalistic. Frequent end-stopped lines slow the rhythm of the poem.

1. The only reference to sheep is in the title of the poem. Can you account for this?
2. Explain the image of the morning "blackening" and the speaker as being like "a flower left out."
3. Why do you think that the "far fields" seem to threaten?

The first line is a very precise description of the way fog abruptly cuts off the line of the hills which seem to disappear "into whiteness" as if consciously stepping off into oblivion. This thought prompts the speaker to make a damning judgment on her own failure expressed in a way that allows no contradiction, "People or stars / Regard me sadly, I disappoint them." The verb 'regard' implies cold evaluation, a judgmental not an empathetic looking. (Perhaps Plath was reflecting her own disappointment at the mixed reviews of her first novel *The Bell Jar* which had been recently published under a pseudonym.) If she disappoints both people and stars, then she feels alienated and rejected from both the worlds of society and of nature – there is not much else. The narrator describes a steam train in the near distance, its smoke trailing behind it like "a line of breath" which is reflected in the length of the alliteration of the 'l' sound

161

and of the vowels in the line. The wording is ominous: the train "leaves" its breath behind as though it is dying, giving up on life.

The line "O slow" is the shortest in the poem, but the long, rhyming 'O' sounds make it sound like a drawn-out lament. Only in the next line does it become evident that the protagonist is riding a horse the description of which is entirely negative: the horse is "slow"; it is the "colour of rust" suggesting age and decay; and its horseshoes striking the road sound like "dolorous [expressing great sorrow or distress] bells," perhaps the speaker has in mind funeral bells. This idea is continued by the pun in the next line "All morning [/mourning]." The simple description of her horse as "the colour of rust" has connotations beyond the literal. It perhaps suggests that the speaker has not ridden much recently. It also links the horse with the train both of which appear to be slow. (As an American Plath would have been familiar with the term 'iron horse'.)

It seems that the protagonist has been out riding all morning. Paradoxically (since morning is normally seen as a time the return of light and of rebirth) the speaker's perception is that the "Morning has been blackening" – another oxymoron. This probably refers to the fog condensing on everything and leaving black specks. (Although the Clean Air Act was passed in UK in 1956, the burning of coal still led to considerable pollution, particularly when the smoke was trapped in fog.) The mood is similar to that following the murder of Duncan by Macbeth when Ross remarks to the old man on the darkness:

> By th' clock 'tis day,
> And yet dark night strangles the travelling lamp.
> Is 't night's predominance or the day's shame
> That darkness does the face of Earth entomb
> When living light should kiss it? (*Macbeth* 2.4)

Evidently the speaker identifies herself as being "A flower left out"; it now seems that the morning has not been blackening everything, just her. The idea that the flower has been "left out" to suffer the effects of "blackening" implies that the protagonist feels herself to have been abandoned by people to whom she had some right to look for protection: she feels alone and vulnerable.

The speaker refers to her "bones" as though she were already dead. Looking across the fields frightens her because they disappear into the white nothingness of the fog and they seem to "threaten" her with the same fate. Notice the alliteration of the long 'f' sound and of the long vowels in the lines "the far / Fields melt my heart." The speaker makes it sound like a long and painful process. The poem ends with a vision of death which offers no promise of an afterlife. Such a "heaven / Starless and fatherless" is, of course, an oxymoron for a heaven without a God (God the father as in *First Corinthians* 8:6, "But to us [there is but] one God, the Father, of whom [are] all things, and we in him; and one Lord Jesus Christ, by whom [are] all things, and we by him" [KJV]) is a contradiction in terms. Of course, given the author's obsession with her biological father there is another level of meaning here as Rosenblatt explains, "The absent father is both the poet's dead father and the dead God of religion; and from their environment of blackness and starlessness, the poet can expect nothing at all" (101). Plath frequently uses water as a symbol of death but also of baptism and rebirth into another life and as a reunion with the father. There is no suggestion of that here.

An interesting aspect of the poem is that the only reference to sheep comes in the title. On one level, this makes perfect sense because the sheep are hidden by the fog, and though the speaker knows they are there, she cannot see them. There are, however, deeper levels of interpretation. The word 'sheep' is one of those nouns that can be either singular or plural: initially the reader assumes that it is plural (describing a flock of sheep), but if it is taken to be singular then the speaker *is* a sheep in fog, just as she *is* a flower left out in fog. Sheep are, of course, notoriously stupid animals. This gives us an image of the protagonist (and by implication everyman) as helplessly lost and confused in the 'white-out' of life with no hope of heaven. Any reference to sheep in such a context must inevitably call to mind the image of God as the shepherd and humans as his flock, as in *Isaiah* 56:3, "All we like sheep have gone astray; we have turned every one to his own way; and the LORD hath laid on him the iniquity of us all" (KJV). The most famous story reflective of this metaphor is Jesus' Parable of the Lost Sheep in *Luke* 15 which includes the lines, "What man of you, having an hundred sheep, if he lose one of them, doth not leave the ninety and nine in the wilderness, and go after that which is lost, until he find it? And when he hath found it, he layeth it on his shoulders, rejoicing" (verses 4 and 5, KJV). It is clear from this poem that no savior is out looking for the protagonist: for her there is no redemption.

It is informative to contrast this poem with "Ariel" which also describes the feelings engendered while riding a horse (presumably the same horse as in this poem). However, while "Ariel" explored rebirth, this poem presents death as the ultimate negation. The speaker is "threatened" to be "let through" to "a heaven / Starless and fatherless, a dark water." This is an oxymoron for the afterlife has none of the qualities of heaven: the dark water over which the two people row in "Crossing the Water" has become the destination not the point of access to a rebirth.

THE MUNICH MANNEQUINS

The poem is dated January 28th when Plath was living through a particularly cold winter in London, though she had visited Munich on a previous occasion. The setting could really be any modern city. It contains a chain of images of desolation, coldness, loneliness and silence. The poem shows the condensing of metaphors and similes that is characteristic of Plath's last poems. The shifts from image to image are not always easy to follow, nor is the reader always sure of how a particular image should be understood.

The theme is the sterility and bareness of a dehumanized society symbolized by both living German fashion models (impossibly beautiful and slim women who model the latest fashions for designers) and by inanimate mannequins (those perfect, human-like dolls used to display clothes in shop windows). The mannequins (both animate and inanimate) represent what women have been reduced to in a male-dominated society: out of their fear and disgust of women, men have objectified an idea of female perfection which reduces them to inhuman dolls (think Barbie here). The media publicizes this stereotype, with the result that women who fall short of it feel that they are failures. Bassnett explains, "The mannequins symbolize perfect women in that they represent the visual ideal image of what society declares to be beautiful but in the surreal straightness – "orange lollies on silver sticks" – they are the antithesis of productive, pregnant roundness. The spilt menstrual blood in the opening lines of the poem is symbolic of waste and unfulfilled femininity [because it marks a failure to conceive]" (*An Introduction* 74-75). The result is a sterile society the truth of which is hidden by a veneer of prettiness. The poem contrasts the sterility of death, symbolized by the color white, with the procreative urge represented by the woman's monthly flow of menstrual blood. Plath felt strongly that it was a woman's role to be a mother, something that some feminists would dispute.

The poem is written in thirteen unrhymed couplets and ends with a single one-line stanza.

Lines 1 - 15

1. In what sense is the "loveliness" of the mannequins a sort of "perfection"?
2. The line, "Orange lollies on silver sticks" is a description of the mannequins. (Mannequins are normally kept stable by a metal stand – the "stick.") What is the effect of this description?
3. Why is the monthly flow of menstrual blood "The absolute sacrifice"? Why is it "to no purpose"?
4. Give your ideas of the meaning of the lines, "It means: no more idols but me, / Me and you."

Lines 16 - 27

5. These lines broaden the description to the life of Munich. What points does the poem seem to be making about that life? How?
6. How is the second half of the poem a continuation of the theme and mood of the first half?

    The poem opens with a shocking oxymoron which goes against every assumption the reader brings to it: How can the perfect be "terrible"? The speaker immediately explains that neither the human nor the plaster mannequins can procreate: the messy process of pregnancy (the morning sickness, the bloated stomach, the pain of labor, etc.) would rob the human models of their "perfection" and the plaster dolls are infertile. Thus, "perfection" is compared to "snow breath" because it is cold and deadly; it "tamps [inhibits, literally pushes down with a series of light strokes] the womb" denying the woman her essential procreative function.
    As we have seen in "The Moon and the Yew Tree," yew trees traditionally symbolize rebirth and reincarnation (which is why they are so common in grave yards). So here, "the yew trees blow like hydras" in the womb: like the Hydra in Greek mythology where if you cut off one head two would grow in its place, so with the yew tree. Plath clearly has in mind the tree-like shape of a woman's fallopian tubes as they 'branch out' from the 'trunk' of the uterus, cervix and vagina, which she enthusiastically twice calls "the tree of life." The ovaries release their ovum or eggs ("moons") on a monthly cycle dictated by the moon, but they do so "to no purpose" since the woman's sense of the demands of her own perfection will never allow her to have unprotected sex, so the eggs will never be fertilized by a man's sperm. The woman's period, the "blood flood," is an act of love but, since it marks the failure to conceive, it is also, "The absolute sacrifice." There is a reference here to Christ's sacrifice on the cross. Recall that, at the Last Supper, Christ "took the cup, when he had supped, saying, this cup is the new testament in my blood: this do ye, as oft as ye drink it, in remembrance of me" (*Corinthians* 11:25, KJV). Christ gave his blood that man might gain eternal life, but the speaker insists that the woman's is, "The absolute sacrifice" giving of her own blood that a child might live – though in this case the woman's sacrifice is giving of her own blood even though a child will *not* result.
    The next two lines draw a conclusion, "It means: no more idols but me, / Me and you." The simple, monosyllabic words are startling, as is the abrupt colon causing the reader to pause before reading exactly what conclusion the speaker draws, yet for all the simplicity of vocabulary and structure these lines have puzzled commentators. I take the narrator to mean that, in the face of her own periods, she has been reduced to the same "perfection" as the mannequins: she, like them, has been robbed of her procreative function and reduced to a

perfect doll of a woman, an idol up to which men can gaze without having to acknowledge her essential womanliness.

The description of the "sulphur loveliness" of the mannequins is another oxymoron, for though sulfur (known in the Bible as brimstone) is an element essential to life, it carries connotations of burning, poison, and alchemy. It stresses the artificial beauty of the painted plaster mannequins. The cities of Paris and Rome were among the great centers of the European fashion industry and the location of the fashion shows at which the great designers presented their designs for the next season – designs which would dictate what women throughout Europe would wear for the next few months. Munich is an exception since it was never associated with high-end fashion. Presumably this is why the mannequins "lean tonight" in the shop windows of Munich (high-end fashion has become mass consumerism) which is called the "morgue between Paris and Rome." This is evidently a reference to the role of Munich leading up to and during World War II: Munich was the scene of Hitler's Beer Hall Putsch in 1923, was the venue for the disastrous Munich Agreement between Hitler and Chamberlain, and was heavily bombed (50% of the city and about 90% of the historic centre was destroyed). Thus, the city is identified with death.

The poem now turns to describe the mannequins in detail. The description begins with another oxymoron, "Naked and bald in their furs." The mannequins are wearing furs (it is winter), but since they *are* mannequins they have no clothes on under their fur coats and no hair under their fur hats. They are not human. The next metaphor compares them to a child's ice lolly. (The ubiquitous "orange" flavor recalls the color of sulfur; the "silver sticks" are the metal stands that support the mannequins; and the flat sides of the lolly reflect the slimness of the models.) The mannequins are "Intolerable, without mind."

The perspective of the description widens to include the whole city. The description begins with another oxymoron, "The snow drops its pieces of darkness." It is nighttime. The snow represents the negativity of society: the city is no more alive than the mannequins because there is nobody in the streets. In the hotels, people are reduced to body parts: "Hands" open doors, not people; "broad toes" (which suggest the massive contrast between the perfect mannequins and the rather unattractive reality of real people) are place in freshly cleaned shoes. It is all sterile and impersonal, automatic not emotional.

The narrator turns her attention back to the shop windows on the street. Her emphasis is not now the mannequins but the artificiality of "the domesticity" on display. Having established women's barrenness in modern society, she describes the delicate "baby lace" in one window. Even the concept of babies (no living baby is present, obviously) has been idealized and prettified in unrealistic ways. Similarly, in a bakery she notices "the green-leaved confectionery." She is describing delicate marzipan leaves which decorate

Selected Poems by Sylvia Plath

cakes or candies which are unreal, idealized imitations of real vegetation. There is no real life represented in the shop windows; there is only a sanitized version of life. In contrast with this vision, the narrator describes the unattractive reality of the Germans: they are "thick," a word that suggests both that they are heavily-built (compare the earlier reference to "broad toes") and slow-thinking. They are seen to be "slumbering" in their infinite "Stolz," that is in their arrogant pride and endless self-satisfaction.

The poem ends with an image of non-communication. The last four lines employ images that recur in Plath's poems. The "black phones on hooks" are as effectively silence as the black telephone in "Daddy' that is "off at the root," but the essential difference is that no one (certainly not the father who is absent in this poem) is any longer trying to get through to anyone – including the protagonist. Hooks in Plath's poems (see "Blackberrying", "Tulips" and Ariel") normally represent the restrictions of the poet's social roles which attempt to pull her back whenever she is tempted to seek release from those roles in death, but with the difference that here the hooks offer no such restraint. The black telephones are still on their hooks, their black Bakelite (an early form of plastic and therefore another example of the artificial) shining because no one has dirtied them by using them to talk to another human being. The repetition of the word "Glittering" (compare "Masturbating a glitter" in "Death & Co.) suggests deception, an apparently meaningful and/or attractive exterior concealing emptiness inside. The phones are "digesting / Voicelessness" which in a general way conveys the total failure of communication and empathy in society. I am reminded of Hamlet's response to Claudius' question about how he is faring, "Excellent, I' faith, of the chameleon's dish. I eat the air, promise-crammed. You cannot feed capons so" (*Hamlet* 3.2). What Hamlet means is that there is no real communications between Claudius and himself so that he too is left digesting voicelessness. Finally, the narrator returns to the snow, but that also "has no voice." Communion with nature offers no alternative to the failure of community: nature and society are equally dead.

WORDS

Dated February 1st, ten days before her suicide, the poem "meditates on the fate of poetry after the excitement of composition has terminated" (Axelrod in Gill Ed. *Companion* 87). The language is very simple with a high proportion of monosyllabic words. In many ways the poem is a development of the idea embodied in the final line of her earlier poem "Conversation Among the Ruins", "What ceremony of words can patch the havoc?" The 'I'-speaker of the poem appears only once. This is one of the few Plath poems where she is not evidently distancing herself from her poetic persona, if only because the speaker is not described in sufficient detail for the reader to form a picture of him/her

The poem is written in four short five-line stanzas with no rhyme scheme.

1. In stanzas one and two, how is the power of words established? (Look in particular at the images.)
2. In stanzas three and four, how is it made clear that words quickly lose their original power? What new power do they gain?
3. Susan Bassnett writes of this poem, "There is no sense at all of conscious crafting, of searching for effect. Instead there is a sense of spontaneity, of a poet using all the power she has stored up unconsciously, a sense of release" (*An Introduction* 66-67). Do you agree with this comment on the style of the poem?

On the literal level, the first stanza describes axes (the plural is important) chopping into trees and the echoes of their striking spreading out with the speed of horses. There is a simplicity to this description that is uncharacteristic of Plath, but the reader knows that landscapes in Plath are always symbolic. Symbolically, the axes represents the repeated actions of the poet to carve out of his/her own being (i.e.,, to create) words ("the echoes") which, as soon as they are written ("rings"), gain a life of their own independent of their creator ("echoes"). The tone appears to be positive: the verb "rings" suggests joy and vigor, as in the ringing of a bell in celebration, and the simile of sound as horses is similarly full of energy.

The realistic description lasts only into the first line of stanza two, and the positive tone evaporates immediately as the speaker turns the focus on the damage the axe strokes cause the tree. The axe cuts are filled with sap from the tree trunks which is compared to tears, a natural simile since cutting into a tree is wounding the tree: interpreted symbolically, "Words damage the organic wholeness of the body by bringing death into consciousness" (Rosenblatt 138).

Sap welling up suggests water, which leads to a second (parallel) image for the writing of poetry: it is like throwing a rock into water which then strives (as did the trees) to re-establish its surface ("its mirror"). The two similes have in common the attempt to heal a breach. Plath is symbolically describing the personal cost of artistic creation, and specifically of writing poetry: by this act of creating, the writer only injures him/herself triggering desperate, instinctive efforts by the psyche to heal the wounds. Disturbed by the act of writing, the water cannot settle to a stillness, in the mirror of which the speaker could see a clear reflection of herself. After the break before stanza three, the rock has morphed into, "A white skull," pure but lifeless, that falls into the water of a lake or stream to be, "Eaten by weedy greens." The long vowels convey the slow, inevitability of decomposition. This metaphor captures the self-destructive nature of writing poetry, the fatal cost of the creative act. The poet creates out of his/her own dying – out of his/her own agonies.

The poem has now become entirely symbolic. The description of encountering the echoes of her axe chops on the road in the form of riderless horses suggests the way in which a poet's words take on a life of their own over which she has no control (The pronoun "them" does not refer to the original ringing axe chops or to the skull in the water but to the sound made by the axe cutting into the wood, that is, to the words generated by the poet hacking into his/her own being.) Now the words resolutely and unstoppably make their own sound ("indefatigable hoof-taps") over which the writer has no control. Re-reading earlier poems, the words seem "dry" and unsatisfactory – no longer the author's. Poetry has failed; instead of healing the writer's wound, it has made it worse. Axlerod is certainly right when he states, "'Words' reveals a severe estrangement from the writing process ... [The persona] inhabits a linguistic world that is inchoate, uncontrollable, and ultimately foreign to her purposes" (74). Rosenblatt makes essentially the same point, "[T]he second half of the poem shows the hopelessness of revitalizing the self through poetry which is the most intense form of language" (138).

The last three lines of the poem return to the "bottom of the pool" where, of course, the speaker's "white skull" rests. The pool represents the poet's being/self/psyche as did the trees. Looking down on the water one sees the reflection of the stars as though the stars are actually in the pool. The image, taken from astrology, of stars governing a life is one that Plath has used before. It implies the helplessness of humans: there seems nothing that a person can do to avoid a fate already "fixed" in the stars. The reader might bring to mind Romeo's prophetic cry just after he has fallen hopelessly in love with Juliet:

> ... my mind misgives
> Some consequence yet hanging in the stars
> Shall bitterly begin his fearful date
> With this night's revels, and expire the term
> Of a despisèd life closed in my breast
> By some vile forfeit of untimely death. (*Romeo and Juliet* 1.4)

or perhaps Kent's conclusion, "It is the stars, / The stars above us govern our conditions" (*King Lear* 4.3). Rosenblatt writes that the final image of stars "defines Plath's fundamental sense of doom and fatality; the hand of the dead rules the living; language cannot overcome the primordial disturbance created in the self by the consciousness of the dead and death" (139). The poem is about the illusion of freedom that poetry gives to the writer and the fatal reality that lies beyond it.

Selected Poems by Sylvia Plath

BALLOONS

Dated February 5th, 1962, six days before her suicide.

The poem begins as a monologue by the mother of two children. Only at the end of stanza four does she turn to the elder of them (a girl), the younger (a boy) being too young to talk. I get the sense that the speaker is not just describing ordinary, round, colored balloons but those long, thin balloons that can be shaped into the form of animals; alternatively, perhaps the balloons have animal images printed or painted on them. Whatever the reason, in the eyes of the speaker they *appear* to be animals that have "lived with" her and her two children since Christmas, taking up lots of room, moving with the currents of the air, and occasionally bursting, "When attacked." When this happens, the helium rushes out of them and they scoot around for a second or so before coming to rest "barely trembling." This makes them, rather too obviously, symbols of the fragility of happiness.

In every sense, the description that the mother gives at the start of the poem is one of guileless innocence and pure joy. The balloons are like real pets; she calls them "Oval soul-animals." What she means is that she and her children can relate to the balloons/animals, innocence to innocence.

1. In the first four stanzas, the speaker describes the balloons that have survived in the apartment she shares with her two young children since Christmas. How does she feel about them?
2. In stanza five, the speaker describes to her daughter how her younger brother is playing with the balloons. How is his interaction with them different from her own?
3. The brother bursts the balloon he has been playing with. Look at the description of the boy in the final stanza. What does it tell you about the speaker's reaction to what he has done?

As Dyne writes, "The speaker ... takes a child-like delight herself in the balloons ... every new metaphor invests the balloons with breath, vitality, touchingly human innocence ('guileless and clear'), and vulnerability " (166). One balloon (or assemblage of balloons) is like a "Yellow cathead" and another like a "blue fish," at least in the imagination of the mother and her young children. When the mother calls the balloons "queer moons we live with / Instead of dead furniture!" she seems to be saying that these simple pleasures are more meaningful and influential in the lives of her and her children than "old furniture" which represents materialism. Plath's London flat was sparsely furnished and relatively Spartan (certainly by modern standards) which is reflected in the basic straw mats and bland white-painted walls. The one splash of color is provided by the balloons, "Globes of thin air, red, green" bouncing around the room. In a metaphor she compares them to "free / Peacocks blessing / Old ground with a feather." Peacocks are, of course, noted for their exotic and colorful plumage, particularly the long fan-like tail feathers. The metaphor, "Beaten in starry metals" describes the beautiful metallic design of the feather. The peacock feather is a symbol of immortality and renewal, in this case blessing "Old ground" which I take to refer to the speaker (who is by a long way the oldest of the three humans).

For the first time the speaker directly addresses her daughter drawing attention to her infant brother who is playing with his balloon and, by rubbing it, making it "squeak like a cat." The balloon is obviously red for looking through it he sees, "A funny pink world he might eat on the other side of it." He bites the balloon and it pops, so that he is left with, "A red / Shred in his little fist." Having burst his balloon, he sits back like a "fat jug" and contemplates "a world clear as water." The speaker's sensibility has given way to her male child's destructive appetite: he has destroyed the filter which made the world appear enticing and beautiful, and in doing so he has reduced everything to harsh reality. Dyne concludes that "The first vision bursts when the poet's metaphoric elaboration collides with the cruder hungers of her child. Interrupting her poetic free-flight, the child tugs the mother's attention back to himself" (167).

This poem does more than capture the innocent curiosity and happy play of a child. The balloons have transformed life in a dull apartment and made the lives of the three occupants happier, more colorful and less troubled. The balloons are, however, a diminishing resource – every so often, one of them gets burst. They are a filter through which the outside world looks better (the phrase 'rose-tinted spectacles' comes to mind), but ultimately the dream-like state of childhood must give way to harsh objective reality. That is what happens to the boy when, following an illusion, he destroys the "pink" filter that stands between himself and "a world clear as water." What happens to his mother is that her own artistic filter on the world (through which she has earlier described the balloons) is also shattered and she is brought back to the reality of lonely motherhood.

Selected Poems by Sylvia Plath

EDGE

Dated February 5th, this poem was written the same day Plath wrote "Balloons" though it is unclear which was completed first. These were the last poems she wrote before her death – she committed suicide on the morning of the 11th. Middlebrook writes that "when writing 'Edge', Plath was already experiencing the descent into breakdown that preceded her suicide" (Gill Ed. *Companion* 170). Perhaps as a result, the poem is ambiguous and difficult to interpret, but another reason might be that the poem was put together from parts of the drafts of several poems on which Plath had been working. In any event, we have no reason to suppose that the poem as we have it is anything other than complete and finished. The subject is a woman who has killed herself and her two infant children. The narrator describes the scene. The moon looks on impassively.

The poem has ten unrhymed two-line stanzas. It is expressed in simple language.

Stanzas 1 - 4

1. Explain the meaning of the first line.
2. What contribution do the words "illusion" and "seem" make to the meaning of these stanzas?

Stanzas 5 - 8

3. Stanzas 5 and 6 indicate that the woman has killed her children. How is this meaning made clear?
4. Explain the image of roses in stanzas 7 and 8.

Stanzas 9 - 10

5. Why does the moon look down on this suicide dispassionately?
6. The final line seems to refer to the black clouds which the moon is wearing like mourning. What do you make of the line, "Staring from her hood of bone"?
7. What parts of the poem do you still find difficult to understand? Why?

The third person narrator, a device which separates poet from protagonist, begins with a description of a woman as "perfected." Note that the present tense is used. The first line is end-stopped. Readers familiar with "The Munich Mannequins" will immediately suspect that the tone is ironic, for perfection cannot be achieved in life – life is messy and difficult. Only in the second line do we learn that the woman is dead, but "perfected ... dead" is an oxymoron. (Compare also the description of the dead snake in "Medallion" where, "The yardman's / Flung brick perfected his laugh.") Her entire body "wears the smile of accomplishment" as though she feels that she has performed a commendable act, though there is something artificial implied by the word "wears," as though the smile has been consciously 'put on' like clothing. This smile is the only suggestion of anything like happiness in the whole poem; however, the narrator, identifies the suicide (it will become clear later that the woman has committed suicide) as based on the "illusion of a Greek necessity" – the mistaken pursuit of perfection over life has led to a double murder-suicide. This refers to the Greek view of suicide that taking one's own life was not always blameworthy since there were situations in which suicide was the only honorable action a person could take. The woman wears a flowing toga, and her feet are bare. Only when we read these details, does the reader understand that the poem has a historical setting. Her bare feet "seem to be saying: / We have come so far, it is over," which suggests that the woman has perceived her life to be a long, harsh struggle and that she has finally given up, exhausted. The woman seems to think that she has made the right decision: her life has been a constant trial, she has finally stopped fighting an uneven battle, and now she is at peace.

Shockingly, the reader learns that beside the woman's body are her two children, also dead. (There may be an allusion here to the Greek myth of Medea, who, angry at being betrayed by her husband, Jason, killed their two children. However, Medea did *not* kill herself: she ascended into the heavens in a chariot. (The reverse is true of Plath, who *did* kill herself [whether she meant to do so or not is another issue] but did so in a way that ensured that her two small children would be safe.) Each infant is curled in the fetal position; the narrator describes them as coiled like "a white serpent [snake]," a pitcher of (presumably poisoned) milk placed beside each. This metaphor is ambiguous, but the "serpent" reference is not necessarily negative. These lines probably refer to the custom in some cultures of leaving out a saucer of milk for the house snake, a non-venomous snake which lives in and around houses catching vermin. In the United States the term 'milk snake' is often used to refer to a house snake. (It may also be significant that Plath put out milk for her children before killing herself.) The woman's body is described as a rose and the children as petals which have closed upon her as night comes on: she has metaphorically taken back possession of them and regained her wholeness so that all three (now one) can be "absorbed in the sweetness of the garden" (Rosenblatt 102). It is night in the garden, and everything is tranquil and sweet-scented.

The scene is observed by the moon which feels neither sorrow nor empathy, like the moon in "The Moon and the Yew Tree". The "hood of bone" suggests the white wimple of a nun, but if so she is a devotee of death rather than life (and certainly not of life after death). What has happened is all too common, which seems to imply that living is harder for women than it is for men. The final line hints at the malignant influence of the moon. The "blacks" are perhaps the marks on the moon out of which imagination can construct a face, but here it is the face of a witch that cackles in delight at her victories as she drags the oceans back and forth and controls the menstrual cycles of women (and through that their moods). It may be that the moon shares some responsibility for the harshness of the woman's life and for the despair that led to her suicide.

Obviously the mood is somber and dark. The poem is almost entirely bleached of color with the exception of white ("white serpents," "milk," and "hood of bone") with its connotations of cold and death. There is plenty of evidence in the poem to *explain* why the woman killed herself (though less to explain why she killed her children), but not one single indication of anything but disapproval from the narrator. The woman has evidently lived on the edge for some time and has finally, metaphorically, thrown herself over the edge. It is the moon that believes that such a suicide is of no great significance because it is a common occurrence, not the narrator. (Remember how uninvolved the moon was in "The Moon and the Yew Tree.")

The key question is whether the poem presents the suicide of the woman as an act of bravery and vision, or one of cowardice and defeat. It is virtually impossible to consider this question without referencing the fact that so many of the details in the poem prefigure Plath's own suicide days later. Some commentators have seen the poem as the equivalent of a suicide note. It has even been suggested that the death of the two Greek children is evidence that Plath intended to kill her own children – a conclusion for which there is no evidence whatsoever. However, there is good reason to believe that Plath did *not* identify herself with the woman in the poem – at least not to the extent of endorsing her actions. First, the statement that through suicide the woman "perfected" herself goes entirely against the theme of "The Munich Mannequins" and other poems – unless it is interpreted as being ironic. Second, the *differences* between the scenario in the poem and the tragic events in Plath's flat are much more significant than are the similarities. Third, the poem is third person narrative about an unnamed protagonist whom the narrator observes and judges. Fourth, the poem is set in Ancient Greece and the narrator explicitly states that the woman has acted on the basis of an "illusion of a Greek necessity" – that is, on the basis of a set of alien cultural beliefs. For these reasons, I believe that the poem should be read (like all of her poems) as Plath's attempt to understand her own psychological problems by making art out of them and that success in this involves distancing herself from her characters and narrators. Read this way, the poem is a firm *rejection* of the entire idea that a woman (moreover a woman with two children) should ever commit suicide. If anything, the poem is an anti-suicide note. (That Plath could so clearly reach this conclusion in her art but not be able to transfer it to her own life is part of her personal tragedy, but it is not relevant to a reading of this poem.)

Axelrod argues that "Plath's last poems attest to a new, positive association of creativity with the self," and in this poem he asserts that "the shadow of textual interdeterminacy darkens and subverts the quest for self-representation" (218). Since that may not be altogether clear, what he is saying is that through a series of images and verbal associations, the poet links the life of the dead woman to poetry. Thus, the "scrolls" of her toga suggest writing; the "coiled" children "folded" back into her represent her pages of writing, her manuscripts; and her "feet" is a pun on the meter (iambic foot, etc.) of her poems. If the reader accepts this associating of the protagonist with the creation of either literal texts (she was a poet) or figurative texts (she wrote her story in her own life and that of her children), Axelrod concludes, "The words 'illusion' and 'seem' imply the possibility that the unfortunate woman has fatally misread her own texts … The texts may actually be telling the woman to *live*, though she interprets them contrarily" (219). That seems to me to be a brilliant reading of the poem.

Works Cited

Axelrod, Steven. *Sylvia Plath: The Wound and the Cure of Wounds*. Baltimore: Johns Hopkins UP, 1992. Print.

Bassnett, Susan. *Sylvia Plath: An Introduction to Her Poetry*. 2nd ed. Basingstoke: Palgrave MacMillan, 2005. Print.

Bassnett, Susan. *Women Writers: Sylvia Plath*. Totowa: Barnes and Noble Books, 1987. Print.

Gill, Jo. Editor. *The Cambridge Companion to Sylvia Plath*. Cambridge: Cambridge University Press, 2006. Print.

Bloom, Harold. Editor. *Sylvia Plath: Bloom's Modern Critical Views*. New York: Infobase Publishing, 2007. Print.

Dyne, Susan. *Revising Life: Sylvia Plath's Ariel Poems*. Chapel Hill: University of North Carolina Press, 1993. Print,

Kendall, Tim. *Sylvia Plath: A Critical Study*. London: Faber and Faber, 2001. Print.

Lane, Gary. Editor. *Sylvia Plath: New Views on the Poetry*. Baltimore: Johns Hopkins University Press, 1979. Print.

Rose, Jacqueline. *The Haunting of Sylvia Plath*. Cambridge: Harvard University Press, 1991. Print.

Rosenblatt, Jon. *Sylvia Plath: The Poetry of Initiation*. Chapel Hill: University of North Carolina Press, 1979. Print.

Uroff, M. D., "Sylvia Plath and Confessional Poetry: A Reconsideration." Gale Literary Databases. The Gale Group. 1999. Web. 31 January 2017. [Article originally published in *Iowa Review*, Vol. 8, No. 1, 1977, pp. 104-15.]

Wagner, Linda. Ed. *Critical Essays on Sylvia Plath*. Boston: G. K. Hall and Co., 1984. Print.

Guide to Further Reading

The Plath literature is vast. All I can do is give some indication of the approach of the books I have read recently.

Steven Axelrod's *Sylvia Plath: The Wound and the Cure of Wounds* takes a biographical and psychoanalytical approach to Plath's writing. It is particularly strong on the Journals and Letters, but includes a useful chapter on the poetry.

Susan Bassnett's *Sylvia Plath: An Introduction to Her Poetry* actually covers Plath's prose and poetry helpfully linking both to the author's life without making the error of interpreting everything through biography. A good place to start, but relatively few poems are analyzed in detail. Bassnett's *Women Writers: Sylvia Plath* is an earlier edition of this text.

Harold Bloom's *Sylvia Plath: Bloom's Modern Critical Views* presents a number of well-written essays.

Susan Dyne's *Revising Life: Sylvia Plath's Ariel Poems* concentrates on the poems written in the last six months of Plath's life. The analysis combines Plath's own Journal, feminist criticism and analysis of the drafting process to provide a detailed and authoritative commentary.

Jo Gill's *The Cambridge Companion to Sylvia Plath* contains a range of thorough, authoritative essays on different aspects of Plath's life and work. The three essays at the start of Part II on Plath's poetry are recommended.

Tim Kendall's *Sylvia Plath: A Critical Study* takes a chronological approach to the poems often dividing them into groups on the basis of style and/or content. There are detailed readings of many poems, including use of Plath's drafts to trace the development of her ideas and style.

Jacqueline Rose's *The Haunting of Sylvia Plath* is a study of the reception of Plath's texts rather than of the texts themselves. The central thesis is that those who edited Plath's words and the critics who responded to them have tried to make her texts conform to their vision of what Plath was.

Gary Lane's *Sylvia Plath: New Views on the Poetry* is now almost forty years old and Plath studies have come a long way in the interim. Nevertheless, these essays stand up remarkably well. Most of the essays treat Plath as an important and original poet, but Kenner's "Sincerity kills" is an important contrary voice.

Jon Rosenblatt's *Sylvia Plath: The Poetry of Initiation* looks at Plath's poetry in terms of the ritual transformation of the self through symbolic death to rebirth. This seems to me to be a helpful perspective.

M. D. Uroff's essay "Sylvia Plath and Confessional Poetry: A Reconsideration" is highly recommended. (It is available online).

Linda Wagner's *Critical Essays on Sylvia Plath* has the virtue of publishing original reviews of Plath's poetry and prose.

Guide to Further Watching

Sylvia (2003), starring Gwyneth Paltrow as Sylvia Plath and Daniel Craig as Ted Hughes, is available in full on Youtube. It is certainly worth watching but bear in mind that it is only one of many versions of the events portrayed.

A Sample Essay: Sylvia Plath's Sense of Place

Those of Plath's poems which have a particular setting are typically located in places which represent or epitomize the extreme edge of existence: the meeting point of life and death, or the border line between civilization and wild nature. That Plath uses these landscapes as symbols is clear from an analysis of the poems "Wuthering Heights" and "Finisterre".

"Wuthering Heights" is set on the wild Yorkshire moors, and carries the inevitable literary associations of Emily Bronte's novel of the same name. One notices first the precise observation of the landscape with its horizons which:

> ... only dissolve and dissolve
> ... as I step forward.

Anyone familiar with walking in hilly moorland will recognize this description of the way in which one horizon is replaced by a further horizon as the walker advances. Plath also describes the effect of the dominant winds in such high moorland, "the wind ... bending / Everything in one direction." Plath's theme, however, is the age-old conflict between natural forces and human life. The speaker feels herself to be out of place and at the mercy of the elements:

> The sky leans on me, me, the one upright
> Among all horizontals.

This is a place where "there is no life higher than the grasstops," and so the sky presses down upon the speaker to reduce her to submission. As the sky presses her down, so the heather appears to tempt the speaker downwards:

> If I pay the roots of the heather
> Too close attention, they will invite me
> To whiten my bones among them.

There is deliberate irony in the word "invite," for behind its politeness is a destructive process which has won victories for centuries, for the process with threatens the speaker is the same as that which has destroyed the buildings whose ruins she finds:

> Hollow doorsteps go from grass to grass;
> Lintel and sill have unhinged themselves.

Here the word "hollow" implies a verdict on the human condition, and "unhinged" suggests a loss of sanity when faced with primal destructive forces. This landscape thus represents the brutal (and seductive) forces of death in opposition to the will to live which is represented by the speaker.

Only the sheep are at home in this landscape since they seem to be part of the weather rather than of life. Their dirty wool makes them look like clouds and they are, "Gray as the weather." They look on sardonically at the uneven battle between life and death which rages before them - a battle in which even the grass is battered by the wind so that it appears to be, "beating its head distractedly" because "Darkness terrifies it." The speaker's only retreat is into the valleys where human life does survive, though it is only "small change"

179

compared to the forces of death which rule Wuthering Heights.

"Finisterre" is one of several Plath poems set on the shores of the ocean. In reading these poems it is important to remember that for Plath the sea represents death and the land life - but ambiguously, since death often appears to be the more attractive alternative. "Finisterre" explores the contrast between the scene as it used to be when the sailors of the village had to dare the waters of "the Bay of the Dead" for a living, and the scene as it is now when everything has been adapted and falsified for the tourist. It is the former which interests Plath; the latter she merely despises. The life and death struggle was between "the land's end: the last fingers" and:

> ... the sea exploding
> With no bottom, or anything on the other side
> of it,

The power of the sea is suggested by the verb "exploding," whilst life seems to be hanging onto the cliffs weakly but desperately with "rheumatic" fingers. Those who lived there turned to their religion for protection, and a statue represents the devotion of the peasants to "Our Lady of the Shipwrecked," but ironically the statue which celebrates their faith shows its pointlessness, for:

> She does not hear what the sailor or the
> peasant is saying -
> She is in love with the beautiful formlessness
> of the sea.

The second line epitomizes the attitude of the speaker, but in the modern world, the power of the sea (its romance and its threat) appears to have been tamed. It is now simply exploited to provide:

> ... pretty trinkets ...
> Little shells made up into necklaces and toy
> ladies.

The "Black" sea has been replaced by:

> ... another place, tropical and blue,
> We have never been to.'

The speaker has no interest in this sea. It is as though once the threat of death has been removed, life itself becomes only trivial and silly, like the tourist trinkets. Symbolically, Finisterre was one place where the close proximity with death gave life the desperate energy to want to prolong itself.

Literary terms

NOTE: A selection of terms relevant to this text.

Allusion: a passing, brief or indirect reference to a well known person or place, or to something of historical, cultural, literary or political importance.

Ambiguous, ambiguity: when a statement is unclear in meaning – ambiguity may be deliberate or accidental: the former is usually considered a virtue and the latter a fault.

Analogy: a comparison which treats two things as identical in one or more specified ways (e.g., "What's in a name? That which we call a rose / By any other word would smell as sweet" [Juliet in *Romeo and Juliet*]).

Antithesis: the complete opposite of something (e.g., "Use every man after his *desert*, and who should 'scape *whipping*?" [Hamlet in *Hamlet*] – the two highlighted words are opposites).

Caricature: a written description or artistic representation of a person which exaggerates certain features for comic or satirical effect.

Connotation: the ideas, feelings and associations generated by a word or phrase or with an object or animal (e.g., roses carry connotations of love and romance – at least in Western cultures).

Dark or black comedy: comedy which has a serious implication – comedy that deals with subjects not usually treated humorously (e.g., death).

Euphemism: a polite word for an ugly truth (e.g., a person is said to be "sleeping' or to have "passed away" when they are actually dead).

First person: first person singular is "I" and plural is "we".

Foreshadowing: a statement or action which gives the reader a hint of what is likely to happen later in the narrative – sometimes the reader senses the foreshadowing immediately, and sometimes it is only evident in retrospect or on a second reading.

Genre: the type of literature into which a particular text falls (e.g., drama, poetry, novel).

Hyperbole: exaggeration designed to create a particular effect (e.g., I was like to have died of boredom).

Image, imagery: figurative language such as simile, metaphor, personification etc., or a description which conjures up a particularly vivid picture.

Imply, implication: when the text suggests to the reader a meaning which it does not actually state.

Infer, inference: the reader's act of going beyond what is stated in the text to draw conclusions.

A Study Guide

Irony, ironic: a form of humor which undercuts the apparent meaning of a statement:

Conscious irony: irony used deliberately by a writer or character;

Unconscious irony: a statement or action which has significance for the reader of which the character is unaware;

Dramatic irony: when an action has an important significance that is obvious to the reader but not to one or more of the characters;

Tragic irony: when a character says (or does) something which will have a serious, even fatal, consequence for him/ her. The audience is aware of the error, but the character is not;

Verbal irony: the conscious use of particular words which are appropriate to what is being said.

Juxtaposition: literally putting two things side by side for purposes of comparison and/ or contrast.

Literal: the surface level of meaning that a statement has.

Melodramatic: action and/or dialogue that is inflated or extravagant – frequently used for comic effect.

Metaphor / metaphorical: the description of one thing by direct comparison with another (e.g. the coal-black night).

Extended metaphor: a comparison which is developed at length.

Motif: a frequently repeated idea, image or situation in a text.

Oxymoron: the juxtaposition of two terms normally thought of as opposite (e.g., the silent scream, black gold).

Paradox / paradoxical: a statement or situation which appears self-contradictory and therefore absurd but which contains an important element of truth (e.g., "I must be cruel to be kind" [Hamlet in *Hamlet*]).

Parody: imitation which is exaggerated for comic effect.

Pathos: is pity, or rather the ability of a text to make the audience or reader feel pity.

Personified / personification: a simile or metaphor in which an inanimate object or abstract idea is described by comparison with a human (e.g., the door screamed shut).

Protagonist: the character who initiates the action and is most likely to have the sympathy of the audience.

Pun: a deliberate play on words where a particular word has two or more meanings both appropriate in some way to what is being said (e.g., "Now is winter of our discontent…made glorious *summer* by this *son* of York" [*Richard III*])

Selected Poems by Sylvia Plath

Realism: a text that describes the action in a way that appears to reflect life.

Rhetoric: any use of language designed to make the expression of ideas more effective (e.g. repetition, imagery, alliteration, etc.).

Sarcasm: stronger than irony – it involves a deliberate attack on a person or idea with the intention of mocking (e.g., "Thrift, thrift, Horatio! The funeral bak'd meats did coldly furnish forth the marriage tables" [*Hamlet*] – Hamlet explains that his mother remarried soon after his father's funeral to save money on the catering!).

Setting: the environment in which the narrative (or part of the narrative) takes place.

Simile: a description of one thing by explicit comparison with another (e.g., "My love is like a red, red rose" [Burns]).

Extended simile: a comparison which is developed at length.

Style: the way in which a writer chooses to express him/ herself – style is a vital aspect of meaning since how something is expressed can crucially affect what is being written or spoken.

Symbol, symbolic, symbolism, symbolize: a physical object which comes to represent an abstract idea (e.g. the sun may symbolize life).

Themes: important concepts, beliefs and ideas explored and presented in a text.

Third person: third person singular is "he/ she/ it" and plural is "they" – authors often write novels in the third person.

Tone: literally the sound of a text – how words sound (either in the mouth of an actor or the head of a reader) can crucially affect meaning.

A Study Guide

Literary terms activity

As you use each term in the study guide, fill in the definition of the term and include an example from the text to show how it is used. The first definition is supplied. Find an example in the text to complete it.

Term	Definition
	Example
ambiguous, ambiguity	*when a statement is unclear in meaning – ambiguity may be deliberate or accidental*
image, imagery	
irony, ironic, ironically	
metaphor, metaphorical	
paradox, paradoxical	

Selected Poems by Sylvia Plath

pun	
simile	
symbol, symbolic, symbolism, symbolize	
theme	

Appendix 1: How I Used the Study Guide Questions

Although there are both closed and open questions in the Study Guide, very few of them have simple, right or wrong answers. They are designed to encourage in-depth discussion, disagreement, and (eventually) consensus. Above all, they aim to encourage students to go to the text to support their conclusions and interpretations.

I am not so arrogant as to presume to tell teachers how they should use this resource. I used it in the following ways, each of which ensured that students were well prepared for class discussion and presentations.

1. Set a reading assignment for the class and tell everyone to be aware that the questions will be the focus of whole class discussion the next class.

2. Set a reading assignment for the class and allocate particular questions to sections of the class (e.g. if there are four questions, divide the class into four sections, etc.).

In class, form discussion groups containing one person who has prepared each question and allow time for feedback within the groups.

Have feedback to the whole class on each question by picking a group at random to present their answers and to follow up with class discussion.

3. Set a reading assignment for the class, but do not allocate questions.

In class, divide students into groups and allocate to each group one of the questions related to the reading assignment the answer to which they will have to present formally to the class.

Allow time for discussion and preparation.

4. Set a reading assignment for the class, but do not allocate questions.

In class, divide students into groups and allocate to each group one of the questions related to the reading assignment.

Allow time for discussion and preparation.

Now reconfigure the groups so that each group contains at least one person who has prepared each question and allow time for feedback within the groups.

5. Before starting to read the text, allocate specific questions to individuals or pairs. (It is best not to allocate all questions to allow for other approaches and variety. One in three questions or one in four seems about right.) Tell students that they will be leading the class discussion on their question. They will need to start with a brief presentation of the issues and then conduct a question and

Selected Poems by Sylvia Plath

answer session. After this, they will be expected to present a brief review of the discussion.

6. Having finished the text, arrange the class into groups of 3, 4 or 5. Tell each group to select as many questions from the Study Guide as there are members of the group.

Each individual is responsible for drafting out a written answer to one question, and each answer should be a substantial paragraph.

Each group as a whole is then responsible for discussing, editing and suggesting improvements to each answer, which is revised by the original writer and brought back to the group for a final proof reading followed by revision.

This seems to work best when the group knows that at least some of the points for the activity will be based on the quality of all of the answers.

Appendix 2: An Alternative Approach to Daddy

Sigmund Freud (1856-1939) the founder of psychoanalysis.

Freud's theories on the developing sexuality of young males and females help the reader to understand Sylvia Plath's poem "Daddy". Plath had certainly read and been influenced by Freud's theories.

It should be stressed that there is a difference between understanding Freud's theories and believing them. Indeed, Freud himself was continually changing his theories as his understanding of the human mind developed.

Freud argued that for all babies, regardless of their sex, the first human to excite feeling of love is the mother since it is the mother who provides food, warmth and physical comfort. As the baby becomes an infant, however, marked differences develop between the sexes. The boy infant typically deepens his attachment to the mother whilst increasingly coming to regard the father as a rival for the love and attention of the mother. The girl infant is typically attracted to the father and comes to see the mother as a rival.

As the boy-child enters adolescence, the attraction to the mother weakens. There may be many factors for this change: the boy is more aware of the mother's age in relation to his own youth; he becomes aware that certain kinds of feelings for his mother are not acceptable to society; the mother constantly fails to live up to his ideal of her; he finds a more appropriate object for his feelings of love in a girl of his own age.

In girls, the process is similar, although the girl's attraction to the father is often stronger and more enduring than is the boy's to the mother. The same factors, however, tend to weaken the tie.

It must be stressed that these phases (called by Freud the Oedipus Complex and the Electra Complex respectively) occur in all of us and are therefore quite normal and healthy. Problems occur only when an individual fails to progress satisfactorily through the stages and into adulthood. A mature man who has never developed out of the stage of being attracted to his mother, or a woman who retains her sexual attraction to her father, may repress this feeling (because they know how horrible society feel it to be) and this may result in serious psychological problems.

Keeping a Reading Diary of "Daddy" by Sylvia Plath.

A normal diary is used to record a person's thoughts, feelings and experiences each day in the context of important events in her/his life. A reading diary follows the same principle, but this time the context is provided by the person's experiences of a text.

In the case of a novel, a reading diary might include separate entries for each chapter, recording the reader's developing thoughts, feelings and experiences as the novel gradually unfolds. With a short text such as "Daddy",

Selected Poems by Sylvia Plath

this sort of approach is clearly not possible. "Daddy" is, however, a complex poem which is not to be understood fully at a first, second, or even a third reading. Your diary entries will be made at various stages in your reading and re-reading of the poem. In this way, the diary should form a record of your developing understanding (and, I hope, appreciation) of this remarkable piece of writing.

You should include any of the following in your diary entries: impressions and emotional responses (particularly in your early readings, the poem may produce strong feelings and these should be explored, even if you don't quite understand why or how they are produced); guesses at what the poem, or parts of it, may be saying (present your guesses as just that - hypotheses to be tested by later re-reading - and don't worry about offering alternative guesses particularly in the early entries); questions about parts that you don't understand (be honest and try to define exactly what it is that is causing you problems and how you might go about finding solutions); an account of any research or activity which you have done and how these have helped you to understand the poem (always come back to the poem, to the words on the page and your relationship to them); and your frustrations/anger/joy/excitement/ etc. (say what you really feel about this piece of writing). This list is intended to open up possibilities for you and not to restrict them. If you can think of other types of entry then please use them.

As your diary progresses, you will change your mind. Earlier statements will appear to be wrong, perhaps embarrassingly so! This does not matter at all! What does matter is that the diary shows you progressing towards a mature understanding of the poem, remembering always that in any work of literature there is some room for different interpretations and for widely different valuations of the quality of the text as a piece of writing.

It is important that you stick to the following structure:

****

ACTIVITY ONE: The poem will be read aloud by the teacher and you will be given some time to re-read it.

ENTRY ONE: Write a paragraph giving your initial reaction to the poem and your first impressions of its meaning.

****

ACTIVITY TWO: In a small group share your initial impressions and discuss them.

ENTRY TWO: Write a paragraph on what you have learned from this sharing.

****

A Study Guide

ACTIVITY THREE: There are a number of references in the poem to the role of Germany in World War II (e.g., Dachau, Luftwaffe, Aryan, Fascist, etc.), to Vampirism and the Occult ("Taroc ... a stake in your ... heart," etc). In a group, find as many of these types of references as you can and by discussion and research try to understand them.

ENTRY THREE: In a longer entry, give an account of how your efforts to understand the meaning of these references. What became clearer about the meaning of the poem and what remained obscure? What use does the writer appear to be making of these references?

****

ACTIVITY FOUR: Read and in groups discuss the sheet on Freud. What light does it shed on the poem? Construct two parallel timelines, one for the life of Sylvia Plath and the other for the person who is speaking in the poem. Mark off the significant events for each.

ENTRY FOUR: You should now be in a position to explain the ***theme*** of the poem and explore at least some of the ways in which this ***theme*** is developed (e.g., the significance of the references to World War II and to Vampirism and the Occult should be clear by now).

****

ACTIVITY FIVE: Much of the poem is devoted to expressing the speaker's feelings about her father. This is done in a series of ***images***, mainly ***metaphors*** (e.g., "black shoe ...a bag full of God," etc.). In groups, make a complete list of these ***images*** and discuss what feelings they suggest.

ENTRY FIVE: Write about the use of ***imagery*** in the poem to describe the father.

****

ACTIVITY SIX: Go through the poem and isolate any words, lines or sections which still do not make sense to you. Work in a group to sort out the meaning and as a last, desperate, measure, ask the teacher.

ENTRY SIX: You should now be able to give your considered understanding of the poem. Avoid repeating in detail points which you have already covered by referring back to them.

****

Keep in mind these three questions: What is the writer saying? How is she saying it? How effective is what she has written?

ACTIVITY SEVEN: Listen to Sylvia Plath reading this poem.

Selected Poems by Sylvia Plath

ENTRY SEVEN: What does her reading of the poem add to your understanding of it and your feelings about it?

****

ACTIVITY EIGHT: Read a critical essay on the poem.

ENTRY EIGHT: What did you agree with/disagree with?

To the Reader
Ray strives to make his texts the best that they can be. If you have any comments or question about this book *please* contact the author through his email: **moore.ray1@yahoo.com**

Visit his website http://www.raymooreauthor.com

Also by Ray Moore:
Most books are available from amazon.com and from barnesandnoble.com as paperbacks and also from online eBook retailers.

Fiction:
The Lyle Thorne Mysteries: each book features five tales from the Golden Age of Detection:
- *Investigations of The Reverend Lyle Thorne*
- *Further Investigations of The Reverend Lyle Thorne*
- *Early Investigations of Lyle Thorne*
- *Sanditon Investigations of The Reverend Lyle Thorne*
- *Final Investigations of The Reverend Lyle Thorne*
- *Lost Investigations of The Reverend Lyle Thorne*

Non-fiction:
The ***Critical Introduction series*** is written for high school teachers and students and for college undergraduates. Each volume gives an in-depth analysis of a key text:
- *"The Stranger" by Albert Camus: A Critical Introduction (Revised Second Edition)*
- *"The General Prologue" by Geoffrey Chaucer: A Critical Introduction*
- *"Pride and Prejudice" by Jane Austen: A Critical Introduction*
- *"The Great Gatsby" by F. Scott Fitzgerald: A Critical Introduction*

The ***Text and Critical Introduction series*** differs from the Critical introduction series as these books contain the original text and in the case of the medieval texts an interlinear translation to aid the understanding of the text. The commentary allows the reader to develop a deeper understanding of the text and themes within the text.
- *"Sir Gawain and the Green Knight": Text and Critical Introduction*
- *"The General Prologue" by Geoffrey Chaucer: Text and Critical Introduction*
- *"The Wife of Bath's Prologue and Tale" by Geoffrey Chaucer: Text and Critical Introduction*
- *"Heart of Darkness" by Joseph Conrad: Text and Critical Introduction*
- *"The Sign of Four" by Sir Arthur Conan Doyle Text and Critical Introduction*
- *"A Room with a View" By E.M. Forster: Text and Critical Introduction*

Selected Poems by Sylvia Plath

"Henry V" by William Shakespeare: Text and Critical Introduction
"Oedipus Rex" by Sophocles: Text and Critical Introduction

Study Guides - listed alphabetically by author
   * denotes also available as an eBook
NOTE Amazon has recently required Study Guides to reflect the nature of the book so eBooks are titled 'Study Guide on ...."

"ME and EARL and the Dying GIRL" by Jesse Andrews: A Study Guide*
"Pride and Prejudice" by Jane Austen: A Study Guide
"Moloka'i" by Alan Brennert: A Study Guide
"Wuthering Heights" by Emily Brontë: A Study Guide*
"Jane Eyre" by Charlotte Brontë: A Study Guide *
"The Myth of Sisyphus" by Albert Camus. A Study Guide*
"The Stranger" by Albert Camus: A Study Guides
"The Myth of Sisyphus" and "The Stranger" by Albert Camus: Two Study Guides *
"The Awakening" by Kate Chopin: A Study Guide
"The Meursault Investigation" by Kamel Daoud: A Study Guide
Study Guide on "Great Expectations" by Charles Dickens*
"The Sign of Four" by Sir Arthur Conan Doyle: A Study Guide *
"The Wasteland, Prufrock and Poems" by T.S. Eliot: A Study Guide
"The Great Gatsby" by F Scott Fitzgerald: A Study Guide
"A Room with a View" by E. M. Forster: A Study Guide*
"Looking for Alaska" by John Green: A Study Guide
"Paper Towns" by John Green: A Study Guide
"Catch-22" by Joseph Heller: A Study Guide *
"Unbroken" by Laura Hillenbrand: A Study Guide
"The Kite Runner" by Khaled Hosseini: A Study Guide
"A Thousand Splendid Suns" by Khaled Hosseini: A Study Guide
"Go Set a Watchman" by Harper Lee: A Study Guide*
"On the Road" by Jack Keruoac: A Study Guide
Study Guide on "The Invention of Wings" by Sue Monk Kidd*
"The Secret Life of Bees" by Sue Monk Kidd: A Study Guide
"Life of Pi" by Yann Martel: A Study Guide *
"Esperanza Rising" by Pam Munoz Ryan: A Study Guide
"Animal Farm" by George Orwell: A Study Guide
Study Guide on "Nineteen Eight-Four" by George Orwell*
"Selected Poems" by Sylvia Plath: A Study Guide *
"An Inspector Calls" by J.B. Priestley: A Study Guide
"The Catcher in the Rye" by J.D. Salinger: A Study Guide*
"Where'd You Go, Bernadette" by Maria Semple: A Study Guide
"Henry V" by William Shakespeare: A Study Guide

A Study Guide

Study Guide on "Macbeth" by William Shakespeare*
"Othello" by William Shakespeare: A Study Guide *
"Antigone" by Sophocles: A Study Guide *
"Oedipus Rex" by Sophocles: A Study Guide
"Cannery Row" by John Steinbeck: A Study Guide
"East of Eden" by John Steinbeck: A Study Guide*
"Of Mice and Men" by John Steinbeck: A Study Guide*
"The Grapes of Wrath" by John Steinbeck: A Study Guide
"The Goldfinch" by Donna Tartt: A Study Guide
"Walden; or, Life in the Woods" by Henry David Thoreau: A Study Guide
"The Bridge of San Luis Rey" by Thornton Wilder: A Study Guide *
A Study Guide on "The Book Thief" by Markus Zusak

Study Guides available as e-books:
Study Guide on "Heart of Darkness" by Joseph Conrad:
Study Guide on "The Mill on the Floss" by George Eliot
Study Guide on "Lord of the Flies" by William Golding
Study Guide on "Henry IV Part 2" by William Shakespeare
Study Guide on "Julius Caesar" by William Shakespeare
Study Guide on "The Pearl" by John Steinbeck
Study Guide on "Slaughterhouse-Five" by Kurt Vonnegut
New titles are added regularly.

Teacher resources:

Ray also publishes many more study guides and other resources for classroom use on the 'Teachers Pay Teachers' website:

http://www.teacherspayteachers.com/Store/Raymond-Moore

Printed in Great Britain
by Amazon